Studies in the History of Medieval Religion

VOLUME XLIV

THE CHURCH AND VALE OF EVESHAM, 700–1215

LORDSHIP, LANDSCAPE AND PRAYER

Studies in the History of Medieval Religion

ISSN 0955–2480

Founding Editor
Christopher Harper-Bill

Series Editor
Frances Andrews

Previously published titles in the series
are listed at the back of this volume

THE CHURCH AND VALE OF EVESHAM, 700–1215

LORDSHIP, LANDSCAPE AND PRAYER

David Cox

THE BOYDELL PRESS

First published 2015
The Boydell Press, Woodbridge

ISBN 978-1-78327-077-4

The Boydell Press is an imprint of Boydell & Brewer Ltd
PO Box 9, Woodbridge, Suffolk IP12 3DF, UK
and of Boydell & Brewer Inc.
668 Mount Hope Ave, Rochester, NY 14620-2731, USA
website: www.boydellandbrewer.com

A CIP catalogue record for this book is available
from the British Library

In memory of
Benjamin Gwynne Cox
antiquary

Contents

List of illustrations ix
Preface x
Timeline xii
List of abbreviations xiii

Part I. From minster to abbey (701–1078)

1 Æthelred and Ecgwine 3
2 A land of promise 14
3 A waiting people 24
4 Ecgwine and the first abbots 33
5 Decay and revival 42
6 On the defensive 50
7 Abbot Ælfweard and King Cnut 58
8 Abbot Manni, the town, and the Vale 68
9 Abbot Æthelwig under English and Norman rule 78

Part II. Abbot Walter (1078–1104)

10 A new regime 89
11 God's work 99
12 The estates under threat 109
13 Protecting the future 118

Part III. Twelfth-century themes (1104–1215)

14 Interested parties 129
15 Order and governance 140
16 Economic realities 149
17 Investment 158
18 Worship 167
19 Learning and writing 176

20 Religious buildings 184
21 Collapse and renewal 193

Afterword 205
Appendix: The abbots of Evesham to 1215 209
Select bibliography 210
Index 215

Illustrations

1 The *hamm* before 701: current archaeological evidence 8
2 The *hamm* before 701: the regional setting 11
3 Land-units around Evesham in 701 17
4 Murcot from the air © *English Heritage (Arnold Baker Collection)* 27
5 Boundary of the pre-Conquest minster precinct 73
6 Leaf from an antiphoner, possibly from Evesham *By kind permission of the Principal and Fellows of Jesus College, Oxford* 93
7 Seal matrix found near Evesham 97
8 The abbey church begun c.1079: ground plan 100
9 The conventual seal *By kind permission of the Chapter of Durham Cathedral* 155
10 The seal of Abbot Adam *Copyright: Dean and Chapter of Westminster* 156
11 Evesham: town plan elements 161
12 Bengeworth: plan of early features 163
13 Ampulla found near Penwortham *By courtesy of the Historic Society of Lancashire and Cheshire* 173
14 Stone lectern from the abbey © *Mrs Dorothy Cox* 186

Preface and Acknowledgements

THERE are few visible remains of the church of Evesham but there are many surviving records of its 800-year history, from its origin as a minster around the year 701 to its dissolution as a Benedictine abbey in 1540. For all those years it was a house of continual prayer while being at the same time an institution that governed the religious, economic, and social life of the Vale of Evesham. One could hardly find a more suitable part of England in which to observe the tense interplay of lordship and prayer over so many centuries. But the records are not straightfoward. Between the eleventh and the thirteenth centuries Evesham abbey used imagination and artifice to create documents that were meant to represent its early history. The procedure sought to give Evesham a foundation story that linked it to the Virgin Mary, to supply a set of title deeds to its estates, and to furnish an array of precedents and privileges to show that it had never been subject to the bishops of Worcester. To those ends, admirable in themselves, the monks felt justified in preparing a dossier of texts in which unfavourable facts were suppressed and favourable ones selected, and in which the meagre remnant was improved and augmented with myth and legend. So thoroughly were those elements blended that historians were long unable to get at the truth. It became customary for each to express a proper scepticism and then, for want of anything else, to relate exactly what the suspect records said. In 1904 the Benedictine scholar Dame Laurentia McLachlan found it to be the simplest course in her book *Saint Egwin and his Abbey of Evesham*, which is still the only full-length history of the house. But there have been such advances in the interpretation of documents and archaeological remains that the monks' difficult materials can now be probed more confidently.

Hence this book. I have tried to hold its themes in a chronological framework throughout, and that has not been difficult in the first two parts, which end in 1104. But coming to the twelfth century I have found so much information that I have separated it into thematic chapters. Even so, I have tried in Part III to keep some sense of movement through time. Any aspect of the early church of Evesham and its Vale might lend itself to more detailed treatment, and some topics have already received it, but few scholars would have the leisure to draw back and take in the whole; it is therefore for monographs such as this to show that monasticism and lordship have been lived out together and to the full — and in particular places. The book closes at the sudden intervention of three far-reaching changes. In 1214 the reforming Abbot Randal was the first abbot of Evesham to be consecrated after the final break with the bishop of Worcester; in the same year the king renounced royal participation in the choice of future abbots; and in 1215 an acceptable form of external control was devised when the pope established provincial general chapters to maintain uniformity of discipline and practice in the houses of 'black monks', the original Benedictines. The present work ends at that point, not because there is little more to say but because there is so much. The three centuries after 1215 are richly documented and the matter of Evesham abbey and its Vale becomes too intricate to be made a single story. There were impressive cultural achievements and acquisitions in the later period: one may instance the thirteenth-century Evesham Psalter, Walter of Oddington's works on science and musical theory, the Evesham *mappa mundi*, the letters of Robert Joseph and, at the very end, Abbot Lichfield's glorious tower. They are rightly celebrated but the local circumstances in which they were produced remain to be explored.

Everything that I know about Evesham and its Vale before the thirteenth century is to be found in the writings of other people, from Anglo-Saxon monks and scribes to scholars of today; if I may claim to have contributed something of my own it is only to have made connections between their works. It would be impossible to name all those writers here, but I should like to thank several scholars and friends who have gladly shared with me their long-standing interest in the church and Vale of Evesham. Among them I would mention Katherine Christensen, Howard Clarke, Michael Lapidge, and Jane Sayers, and, at Evesham, Gordon Alcock, Arthur Fryer, the late Bill Clarke, and the late Clifton Huddy. As usual my wife Janice has helped with advice on matters of written style. Impossible to estimate, however, is what I owe to my father Ben Cox, who introduced me when very young to the study of local antiquities and then encouraged me to write about them. It all began with him.

Timeline 675–1215

675–704	Æthelred king of the Mercians
c.680	Diocese of the Hwicce formed
708–15	Papacy of Constantine I
710	Death of Bishop Wilfrid
735	Death of Bede
778	Last record of under-kings of the Hwicce
793	First Viking raid on England
877	Vikings take eastern Mercia
c.880	Western Mercia subordinated to Wessex
899-924	Edward the Elder king of the Anglo-Saxons; ? the shires of western Mercia formed
927	England united by King Æthelstan of the Anglo-Saxons
957–75	Reign of Edgar; monastic revival in the south and Midlands; ? the Worcestershire hundreds formed
1016	Death of King Æthelred ('the Unready'); England taken by Cnut king of Denmark
1042	House of Wessex restored
1066	England taken by William duke of Normandy
1070–89	Lanfranc archbishop of Canterbury
1086	The Domesday inquest
1135–54	Civil war between King Stephen and the Empress Maud
1154–89	Reign of Henry II
1170	Murder of Archbishop Thomas Becket
1198–1216	Papacy of Innocent III
1208–13	The Interdict
1215	Magna Carta

Abbreviations

AB	*Analecta Bollandiana*
Abb. Wearmouth–Jarrow	C. Grocock and I. N. Wood, eds, *Abbots of Wearmouth and Jarrow*, OMT (Oxford, 2013)
Ann. mon.	H. R. Luard, ed., *Annales monastici*, 5 vols, Rolls Series (London, 1864–69)
Ant. Jnl	*Antiquaries Journal*
ASC	The Anglo-Saxon Chronicle [cited by MS (A–F) and date]
ASE	*Anglo-Saxon England*
Byrhtferth	Byrhtferth of Ramsey, *The Lives of St Oswald and St Ecgwine*, ed. M. Lapidge, OMT (Oxford, 2009)
Cal. Chart. R. 1226–57	[C. G. Crump and R. D. Trimmer, eds] *Calendar of the Charter Rolls preserved in the Public Record Office*, I (London, 1903)
CBA	Council for British Archaeology
Crowland Continuatio	'Petri Blesensis continuatio ad historiam Ingulphi', *Rerum Anglicarum scriptorum veterum*, I [ed. W. Fulman] (Oxford, 1684), pp. 108–31
Crowland Descriptio	'Descriptio compilata per dominum Ingulphum abbatem monasterii Croyland', *Rerum Anglicarum scriptorum veterum*, I [ed. W. Fulman] (Oxford, 1684), pp. 1–107
DB	'Great' Domesday Book [cited by folio]
DB Worcs. (Thorn)	F. Thorn and C. Thorn, eds, *Worcestershire*, Domesday Book 16 (Chichester, 1982)
DB Worcs. (Williams)	[A. Williams and R. W. H. Erskine, eds] *The Worcestershire Domesday* [introduction and translation] (London, 1988)
Dominic, *V. Ecgwini*	Dominic of Evesham, 'Vita s. Ecgwini episcopi et confessoris', ed. M. Lapidge, *AB* 96 (1978), 65–104
Dugdale, *Mon.* II	W. Dugdale, *Monasticon Anglicanum*, ed. J. Caley, H. Ellis, and B. Bandinel, II (London, 1819)

Durham Liber vitae	D. Rollason and L. Rollason, eds, *The Durham Liber vitae*, 3 vols (London, 2007)
EHD c.500–1042	D. Whitelock, ed., *English Historical Documents c.500–1042*, English Historical Documents 1, 2nd edn (London, 1979)
EHR	*English Historical Review*
EPNS	English Place-Name Society
Evesham Chron.	W. D. Macray, ed., *Chronicon abbatiae de Evesham, ad annum 1418*, Rolls Series (London, 1863)
Evesham Officium	H. A. Wilson, ed., *Officium ecclesiasticum abbatum secundum usum Eveshamensis monasterii*, HBS 6 (London, 1893)
G. Foliot, *Lett.*	Z. N. Brooke, A. Morey, and C. N. L. Brooke, eds, *The Letters and Charters of Gilbert Foliot* (Cambridge, 1967)
Geol. Surv.	Institute of Geological Sciences, Geological Survey of Great Britain (England and Wales)
Haddan and Stubbs, III	A. W. Haddan and W. Stubbs, eds, *Councils and Ecclesiastical Documents relating to Great Britain and Ireland*, III (Oxford, 1871)
Harley 3763	British Library, Harley MS 3763 [an Evesham cartulary]
HBS	Henry Bradshaw Society
HE	Bede, 'Historia ecclesiastica' [cited by book and chapter]
Hemming	T. Hearne, ed., *Hemingi chartularium ecclesiae Wigorniensis*, 2 vols (Oxford, 1723)
Izod, 'Plan'	N. Izod, 'Plan of the Parishes of All Saints and Saint Lawrence in the Borough of Evesham' (1827): Worcester, Worcestershire Archives, ref. r899:251, BA 5044/15
J. Worc.	R. R. Darlington and P. McGurk, eds, *The Chronicle of John of Worcester*, II–III, OMT (Oxford, 1995–98)
JBAA	*Journal of the British Archaeological Association*
Lanfranc, *Const.*	D. Knowles and C. N. L. Brooke, eds, *The Monastic Constitutions of Lanfranc*, OMT (Oxford, 2002)
Lincoln Acta 1067–1185	D. M. Smith, ed., *Lincoln 1067–1185*, English Episcopal Acta 1 (London, 1980)
O. Clare, *V. Edw.*	M. Bloch, ed., 'La Vie de S. Édouard le Confesseur par Osbert de Clare', *AB* 41 (1923), 5–131
ODNB	H. C. G. Matthew and B. Harrison, eds, *Oxford*

	Dictionary of National Biography, 61 vols (Oxford, 2004; and online)
OMT	Oxford Medieval Texts
OS	Ordnance Survey
PASE	'The Prosopography of Anglo-Saxon England' (online)
Penwortham Docs	W. A. Hulton, ed., *Documents relating to the Priory of Penwortham and Other Possessions in Lancashire of the Abbey of Evesham*, Chetham Soc. 30 (Manchester, 1853)
Peterborough Chron.	J. A. Giles, ed., *Chronicon Angliae Petriburgense*, Caxton Soc. 2 (London, 1845)
PL	J.-P. Migne, ed., *Patrologiae cursus completus ... series Latina*, 222 vols (Paris, 1841–64) [cited by volume and column]
Ramsey Chron.	W. D. Macray, ed., *Chronicon abbatiae Rameseiensis, a saec. X. usque ad an. circiter 1200*, Rolls Series (London, 1886)
Red Bk Exch.	H. Hall, ed., *The Red Book of the Exchequer*, 3 vols, Rolls Series (London, 1896)
Regesta Hen. I	C. Johnson and H. A. Cronne, eds, *Regesta Henrici primi 1100–1135*, Regesta regum Anglo-Normannorum 2 (Oxford, 1956)
Regesta Steph.	H. A. Cronne and R. H. C. Davis, eds, *Regesta regis Stephani ac Mathildis imperatricis ac Gaufridi et Henrici ducum Normannorum 1135-1154*, Regesta regum Anglo-Normannorum 3 (Oxford, 1968)
Regesta Wm I	D. Bates, ed., *The Acta of William I (1066–1087)*, Regesta regum Anglo-Normannorum (Oxford, 1998)
Regesta Wm I and II	H. W. C. Davis, ed., *Regesta Willelmi conquestoris et Willelmi rufi 1066-1100*, Regesta regum Anglo-Normannorum 1 (Oxford, 1913)
Regula Benedicti	The 'Rule of St Benedict' [cited by chapter]
Regularis concordia	T. Symons, ed., *Regularis concordia Anglicae nationis monachorum sanctimonialiumque: The Monastic Agreement of the Monks and Nuns of the English Nation*, Medieval Classics (London, 1953)
Rolls Series	*Rerum Britannicarum medii aevi scriptores, or Chronicles and Memorials of Great Britain and Ireland during the Middle Ages*, 255 vols (London, 1858–99)

S	P. H. Sawyer, *Anglo-Saxon Charters: An Annotated List and Bibliography*, Royal Historical Soc. Guides and Handbooks 8 (London, 1968; and online as 'Electronic Sawyer') [cited by entry number]
Stephen, *V. Wilf.*	Eddius Stephanus, *The Life of Bishop Wilfrid*, ed. B. Colgrave (Cambridge, 1927)
Stow, *Survey*	John Stow, *A Survey of London*, ed. C. L. Kingsford, 2 vols (Oxford, 1908)
T. Marlb.	Thomas of Marlborough, *History of the Abbey of Evesham*, ed. J. Sayers and L. Watkiss, OMT (Oxford, 2003)
TNA	London, The National Archives
TWAS	*Transactions of the Worcestershire Archaeological Society*
VCH	*The Victoria History of the Counties of England* [cited by county volume]
VEHS Res. Pap.	*Vale of Evesham Historical Society Research Papers*
Vesp. B.XXIV	British Library, Cotton MS Vespasian B.XXIV [an Evesham cartulary]
W. Malmesb. *GP* I	William of Malmesbury, *Gesta pontificum Anglorum*, I, ed. M. Winterbottom, OMT (Oxford, 2007)
W. Midl. Arch.	*West Midlands Archaeology*
Winchcombe Landboc	D. Royce, ed., *Landboc sive registrum monasterii beatae Mariae virginis et sancti Cenhelmi de Winchelcumba*, 2 vols (Exeter, 1892–1903)
WHS	Worcestershire Historical Society
Worc. Acta 1062–1185	M. Cheney, D. Smith, C. Brooke, and P. M. Hoskin, eds, *Worcester 1062–1185*, English Episcopal Acta 33 (Oxford, 2007)
Worc. Acta 1186–1218	M. G. Cheney, D. Smith, C. Brooke, and P. Hoskin, eds, *Worcester 1186–1218*, English Episcopal Acta 34 (Oxford, 2008)

Secondary works frequently cited are given in an abbreviated form in the footnotes; full details may be found in the bibliography.

PART I

From minster to abbey (701–1078)

CHAPTER 1

Æthelred and Ecgwine

In the last decades of the seventh century Æthelred son of Penda was king of the Mercians, having succeeded his father in the year 675. By armed force King Æthelred had gained control over the south-east of England and the kingdom of Lindsey (part of modern Lincolnshire), and Mercia itself comprised all the Midlands after annexing weaker territories that had once been independent. Politics and war were inseparable. The rapid expansion of Mercian rule had created a realm that in Æthelred's day was culturally and racially diverse. In its western parts British Christians and the followers of other Romano-British cults were continuing to practise, centuries after the end of Roman rule; they had hardly been touched by the intrusive Germanic culture of eastern Britain or by the continental form of Christianity that rulers such as Æthelred were adopting in response to St Augustine's mission of 597 and to the decisions of the Synod of Whitby in 664. And none of the west Mercian territories that Æthelred controlled presented a broader cultural diversity than the former kingdom of the Hwicce. It embraced the lower valleys of two long rivers, the Severn from Wales and its tributary the Avon from the east Midlands, which met and flowed as one to the Severn Estuary. Like the two rivers, the British and the Germanic cultural traditions met within the Hwiccian boundary. The name of the people called Hwicce may in fact have been British[1] but by the 690s their territory was governed for Æthelred by a dynasty of under-kings with names that were English, from which it is a fair assumption that the upper layer of Hwiccian society was culturally Germanic while the racial origin of the people was probably for the most part British.

For Æthelred it was a time of spiritual renewal. Penda had believed in the old-established pagan gods that inhabited the Germanic world of his forefathers but Æthelred was a Christian and one of the generation of rulers in England that was experiencing the faith for the first time and encouraging its spread among their peoples. He faced a personal dilemma, however, for he was a Christian by choice but as a king he could not choose also to be a pacifist. In those days it was only by means of warfare that a kingdom could be defended against its neighbours or

[1] Coates 2013.

enlarged at their expense, and only success in war would enable a king to secure the loyalty of his people. Æthelred knew and regretted that his Christianity sat uncomfortably with his need to preserve the ancestral habit of armed aggression but he was at least able to assuage an unquiet conscience and seek divine forgiveness by founding and endowing churches and by appointing bishops to enact at second hand his full duty as a Christian. Thus in 698 or 699 Æthelred appointed a certain Ecgwine to be bishop over the sub-kingdom of the Hwicce.[2] We know nothing directly about Ecgwine's earlier life but we can entertain some guesses. Two of Ecgwine's predecessors as bishops of the Hwicce had been among the notable men that the Venerable Bede listed as having been trained under Abbess Hild (d.680) in her Northumbrian minster at what is now Whitby. But Ecgwine does not appear in Bede's list of Hild's distinguished pupils[3] and his absence indeed from any of Bede's writings suggests that Ecgwine did not come from Northumbria but from somewhere that Bede knew less well. It is therefore possible to imagine that Ecgwine was a Mercian. At a further level of speculation one might suggest that King Æthelred's decision to make him bishop of the Hwicce would have been especially easy if Ecgwine not only had the personal qualities that were needed for the role but was already known to Æthelred as a kinsman. The early history of the see appears to have been bound up with the rulers of Mercia more than with the under-kings of the Hwicce;[4] if Ecgwine was of royal blood, as his first biographer dutifully alleged,[5] it was probably of the Mercian line.

Whatever the basis of their collaboration it was understood by both Æthelred and Ecgwine that a bishop's duty was to extend a knowledge and love of Christ beyond the pagan ruling circles that had already embraced them and out into the general population of the diocese. The bishop was limited as to how far he could do that just by moving about the diocese and meeting people but he had recourse to a policy that promised more lasting results, and that was to encourage Christian landholders to build and endow permanent local churches on their estates. Such early churches are sometimes called minsters and they were manned by small resident groups headed by an abbot or abbess, which suggests that they were somehow meant to bring the inward-looking culture of monasteries to their outward-reaching function as mission stations, and thus to act as beacons of holiness in a benighted country. So it was that most of the minsters in the diocese of the Hwicce were founded, in the seventh and eighth centuries, by members of

2 T. Marlb. pp. 128–9 n. 2. See also Sims-Williams 1990, p. 142 n. 124.

3 HE IV, 23.

4 A. S. McKinley, 'Understanding the Earliest Bishops of Worcester', *Leaders of the Anglo-Saxon Church from Bede to Stigand*, ed. A. R. Rumble (Woodbridge, 2012), pp. 77–95 (at pp. 83–9).

5 Byrhtferth, pp. 218–19.

landed families, with the groups of men and women who served in them being ruled by abbots and abbesses who, typically, were related to the founders.[6] An early minster set up in that way was in some respects a family possession more than a public institution; and that was its weakness, for it might easily become a small hereditary commune in which idleness and other sins could take hold and which would then have no spiritual benefit for its members or for their neighbours.[7]

Bishop Ecgwine's actions were to show that he intended, with King Æthelred's support, to avoid the evident limitations of family minsters by establishing a well-ordered minster under his own control. Although no previous bishop of the Hwicce had tried to do that, Ecgwine could look to precedents in other dioceses. The most obvious models were the Mercian minster foundations of the energetic, cosmopolitan, and already celebrated Bishop Wilfrid, and it may be no coincidence that Wilfrid had been King Æthelred's protégé in the 690s when Ecgwine was appointed.[8] Ecgwine soon found an opportunity to establish such a church when he was called upon to revive a defunct private minster that stood near the right bank of the Avon at Fladbury. The origin of the Fladbury minster is not recorded but we know that there had been a church there at some period before 697. The name Fladbury means 'Flæde's *burh*'; Flæde was a woman's name and it has been argued that the element *burh* ('defended place') when prefixed by a woman's name may in some instances denote a minster that she had headed or founded.[9] In the case of Fladbury minster the name Flæde may therefore refer to an aristocratic founder or abbess. She may have been a member of the Mercian royal family, for 'Flæde' is a diminutive and the Flæde at the old Fladbury minster may thus have been the Ælfflæd, whose sister Osthryth was King Æthelred's wife.[10] That suggestion would accord with the fact that by 697 Queen Osthryth was in possession of the lands of the defunct minster; Osthryth's title to the estate may have come from her sister Ælfflæd, if Ælfflæd had been the Flæde who had given her name to Fladbury. After the death of Queen Osthryth[11] her husband the king had granted Fladbury minster and its lands to Oftfor, who was Ecgwine's predecessor as bishop of the Hwicce. In doing so Æthelred apparently intended that Oftfor should restore the place to a proper religious life under a

6 Sims-Williams 1990, pp. 92–6.

7 Bede, 'Epistola ad Ecgbertum', *Abb. Wearmouth-Jarrow*, pp. 124–61 (at pp. 146–9).

8 On Wilfrid see: *ODNB*; Higham 2013.

9 F. M. Stenton, 'The Historical Bearing of Place-Name Studies: The Place of Women in Anglo-Saxon Society', Stenton 1970, pp. 314–24 (at pp. 318, 320–21); Sims-Williams 1990, pp. 92–3.

10 Hooke 1985, p. 11; Sims-Williams 1990, pp. 92–3.

11 HE V, 24.

worthy abbot,[12] but Oftfor died soon afterwards[13] and the task of recreating the minster at Fladbury as a well-managed institution fell to the newly-appointed Bishop Ecgwine.[14] That project would not, however, be the complete fulfilment of Ecgwine's idea, which was that of a model minster to be founded by him on a new site and to be kept under his personal direction.

The first church

The opportunity that Ecgwine was hoping for came soon afterwards, when King Æthelred granted him a vacant riverside site a few miles upstream from Fladbury at a place called the *hamm*.[15]

No writing produced for the church of Evesham between the eighth century and the middle of the tenth has survived in its original form; we only have versions that were created between the tenth century and the thirteenth. They were crafted to meet current needs, so each must be searched for signs of deliberate falsity. They include a 'Testament of St Ecgwine', supposedly written by the founder,[16] a royal charter of confirmation dated 709,[17] two papal privileges bearing the dates 709 and 713,[18] other purported charters,[19] and a list of abbots from the eighth century to the tenth.[20] The earliest known *vita* (life story) of Ecgwine was written by Byrhtferth of Ramsey in the early eleventh century,[21] and the only extant history of the church of Evesham before the thirteenth century is that completed by Thomas of Marlborough between 1218 and 1230.[22] Since Byrhtferth and Thomas were as much propagandists as historians their tales need close scrutiny.

If Ecgwine's acquisition of the *hamm* was marked at the time by a written deed there is no surviving copy of it, not even a forged one, but we have no reason to doubt the essence of the story, which has come down from the early eleventh century, that Æthelred gave the *hamm* to Ecgwine; Ecgwine's title to it seems never to have been challenged, even by the envious powers that afterwards threatened the Evesham minster and its property. We cannot determine the date when Æthelred made the gift except to say that it was presumably between 698

12 S76.
13 T. Marlb. pp. 128–9 n. 2.
14 S62.
15 Byrhtferth, pp. 244–5.
16 Byrhtferth, pp. 240–67. See below, this chapter.
17 S80. See below, ch. 13.
18 Dominic, *V. Ecgwini*, pp. 88–90; T. Marlb. pp. 318–21. See below, ch. 13.
19 See below, ch. 12.
20 T. Marlb. pp. 139–41. See below, chs 4, 6.
21 Byrhtferth, pp. 206–303. See below, ch. 7.
22 T. Marlb. pp. 2–480. See ibid. pp. xv–lxxii.

(or 699), when Ecgwine became bishop, and 704, when King Æthelred abdicated and retreated from secular life. In the twelfth century Ecgwine was said to have received his grant of the *hamm* in 701[23] and the date is plausible; it cannot be far wrong even if the authority for it is late.

There are some indications that it was Ecgwine more than King Æthelred who first wanted to build a minster at the *hamm*. Although both were active supporters of new churches, Evesham minster was the only church of which Ecgwine was directly involved in the foundation, and he was afterwards attached to it above all other places, for his body was eventually taken there to be buried.[24] Successive bishops shared his regard for Evesham. Although many of the minsters that had originated as private foundations were to be annexed or reformed by the bishops of the Hwicce before the tenth century, Evesham was recognized at the time as being different and special because it had been founded by a bishop, and it was allowed to continue untouched. Æthelred, meanwhile, had had many ecclesiastical interests and his particular devotion had not been to Evesham but to the church of Bardney, far away in the fenlands of Lindsey.[25] That was where he chose to retire in 704 in order to become a monk,[26] having been able to withdraw at last from the secular duties of a king.

The *hamm* was virtually an unoccupied piece of land when Ecgwine acquired it. For that reason its name was a topographical one; that is to say, it alluded to the nature of the land and was not 'habitative', the kind of name that would have referred to the presence of a settlement. From the air one would have seen that the river Avon performed a long sequence of great bends and loops as it passed westwards through the broad Vale of Evesham towards its final dissolution in the Severn. One such loop of the river embraced the south-facing promontory that would become the site of Ecgwine's minster (Fig. 1). Along the inner edge of the loop lay a narrow flood plain and from that rose the end of the promontory itself, which took its form from two broad gravel terraces deposited one upon the other that made a plateau of dry land some thirty-five feet (about eleven metres) above the Avon.[27] Thus the river loop encompassed what was called in Old English a *hamm*, a word that is also found written as *homm*. On the lower reaches of the Avon it meant in particular 'land *hem*med in by water'. Examples of its use in that sense are found a few miles upstream of the Evesham promontory in the names

23 Dugdale, *Mon.* II, p. 14; T. Marlb. pp. 130–31.

24 Byrhtferth, pp. 280–81.

25 HE III, 11.

26 HE V, 24; ASC (E); William of Malmesbury, *Gesta regum Anglorum: The History of the English Kings*, ed. R. A. B. Mynors, R. M. Thomson, and M. Winterbottom, I, OMT (Oxford, 1998), pp. 112–13.

27 Geol. Surv. Map 1/50,000, sheet 200, solid and drift (1974 edn).

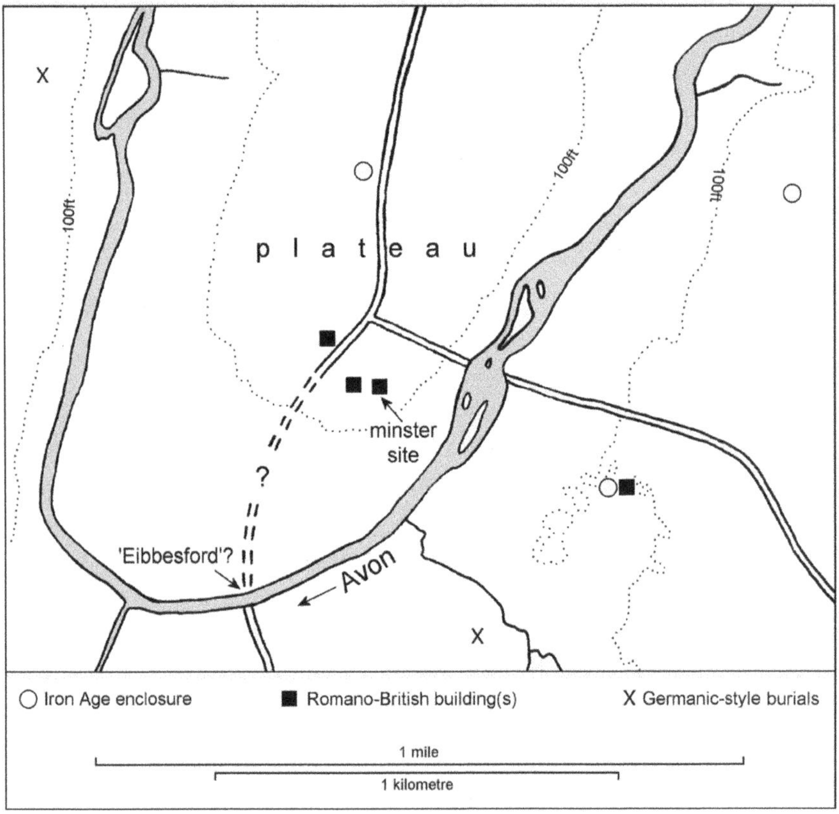

Fig. 1. The *hamm*: current evidence for human activity before 701.

of Offen*ham* and Pickers*om* and a little downstream in those of Pens*ham* and Birling*ham*; the last two places are surrounded by exceptionally tight loops of the river.[28] In the seventh century the flood plain around the edge of the particular *hamm* that Ecgwine acquired was frequented by cranes, which are large and gregarious wading birds with a loud call. The crane was called *cronuc* in Old English[29] and one of the early names used for Ecgwine's promontory or *hamm* was therefore 'Cronuchamm', also written 'Cronuchomm' and 'Cronochomm',[30] a name that distinguished the *hamm* 'where the cranes are' from other *hamms* up and down the Avon. In early medieval England as a whole the crane was so conspicuous in the places where it lived that its name was often used as the first element

[28] Mawer and Stenton 1927, pp. 188, 221–2, 266. See M. Gelling and A. Cole, *The Landscape of Place-Names* (Stamford, 2000), p. 49.

[29] Smith 1956, I, p. 111.

[30] S54, S78, S80, S97, S226, S1175, S1599. All are forged or suspect, but S54 (dated 706) and S97 (datable 716×717) may include some authentic material.

of the place-name, and the places where that happened occurred especially near water.[31] The crane eventually became extinct in Britain but in Europe it still breeds in reed beds along rivers in forested areas.[32]

Concerning the creation of a minster at the *hamm* the principal source of explicit information is a first-person narrative that purports to have been written by Ecgwine himself. It has not come down to us in an authentic form, but a version of it is embedded within the first *vita* to have been composed about Ecgwine, which was written by Byrhtferth of Ramsey in the early eleventh century.[33] Byrhtferth's version of Ecgwine's narrative begins with the bishop's decision to build a church and ends with its consecration at Evesham. The idea that Ecgwine should have left a written record, and that a credible version of it should have survived to the eleventh century, may invite scepticism, but it is not without parallel, for there exists another first-person narrative known as 'St Mildburg's Testament'.[34] It is ostensibly the work of Ecgwine's contemporary the abbess of Wenlock, whose minster lay in what is now Shropshire. There have been questions about the authenticity of 'St Mildburg's Testament' in its present form.[35] Moreover, the similarity of that document to Byrhtferth's version of 'St Ecgwine's Testament' is distant; Mildburg's 'Testament' is much shorter than Ecgwine's and treats only of the estates that she gained. If 'St Ecgwine's Testament' in the form presented by Byrhtferth has no close parallel in pre-Conquest hagiography, therefore, its singularity argues that it is not to be cursorily dismissed as a late literary invention that was modelled on others of its kind, for there are no others. Instead it could be a version that Byrhtferth constructed out of some earlier and simpler document that was known at Evesham in the early eleventh century. In the earliest surviving version of 'St Ecgwine's Testament' the imaginative hand of Byrhtferth cannot be doubted but if the supernatural parts of it be set aside and the incredible elements of the rest be taken out, there remains a small but irreducible body of information that deserves to be evaluated. Incidentally we may ignore the three versions of the 'Testament' that came after Byrhtferth's; one of them was produced by the monk Dominic before 1100[36] and two others present

31 S. Boisseau and D. W. Yalden, 'The Former Status of the Crane *Grus grus* in Britain', *Ibis* 140 (1998), 482–500.

32 L. Svensson and P. J. Grant, *Collins Bird Guide* (London, 1999), p. 118.

33 Byrhtferth, pp. 240–67.

34 Finberg 1972, pp. 201–4.

35 See P. A. Hayward, 'The *Miracula inventionis beate Mylburge virginis* attributed to "the Lord Ato, Cardinal Bishop of Ostia"', *EHR* 114 (1999), 543–73 (at 544), and assessments cited there.

36 Dominic, *V. Ecgwini*, pp. 86–7.

the 'Testament' in the form of a charter bearing the date 714[37] (by the thirteenth century that was reputedly the year in which Ecgwine had retired to Evesham).[38] None of those adds anything of substance to Byrhtferth's text.

Presumably Ecgwine began building soon after he acquired the *hamm*, and the church was later said to have been standing by 703.[39] If that was no more than a guess, it was a fair one if one assumes that construction had begun at the *hamm* about two years earlier. The church was probably built of stone, for in the later tenth century the minster church at Evesham suffered some kind of collapse and it was certainly stone-built then because some squared blocks lay amidst the fallen rubble; Byrhtferth does not suggest that it could have been any other than the original church built by Ecgwine, and Dominic expressly states that it was.[40] There was no suitable stone to be dug at or close by the building site but Ecgwine's workmen may have found some of their materials, including stone blocks, among the ruins of the Romano-British buildings that may once have been there.[41] When Ecgwine's church was finished it was consecrated, according to Byrhtferth's version of 'St Ecgwine's Testament', by the great Bishop Wilfrid following a synod (a church council) that had been convened at Alcester,[42] ten miles from Evesham but in the land of the Hwicce (Fig. 2). It is not at all improbable that Wilfrid did consecrate Ecgwine's new church. Wilfrid, an exile from Northumbria, had been in Mercia since the early 690s under the protection of King Æthelred and there had consecrated Ecgwine's predecessor Oftfor as bishop of the Hwicce, and therefore perhaps Ecgwine too. If Wilfrid did consecrate Ecgwine's finished church it was probably in or shortly before 703; by 704 Wilfrid had left Mercia for Rome, and after that he did not return to live in Mercia but went back to Northumbria and died in 710.[43]

It is also quite possible that there had been a solemn assembly at Alcester shortly before the consecration, because there are indications that Alcester was then the nearest regional capital, its region being that of the Arosætna. Some years earlier the kingdom of the Hwicce had absorbed the territory of the Arosætna, a people that had taken its name from the river Arrow, which flowed southwards through

37 S1250, S1251.

38 T. Marlb. pp. 128–9.

39 T. Marlb. pp. 130–31.

40 Byrhtferth, pp. 300–301; *Evesham Chron.* p. 40.

41 Below, ch. 2.

42 Byrhtferth, pp. 264–5. Byrhtferth's version of the alleged events that were incidental to the synod and consecration need not be taken seriously.

43 C. Cubitt, 'The Chronology of Stephen's Life of Wilfrid', in Higham 2013, pp. 334–47 (at p. 347).

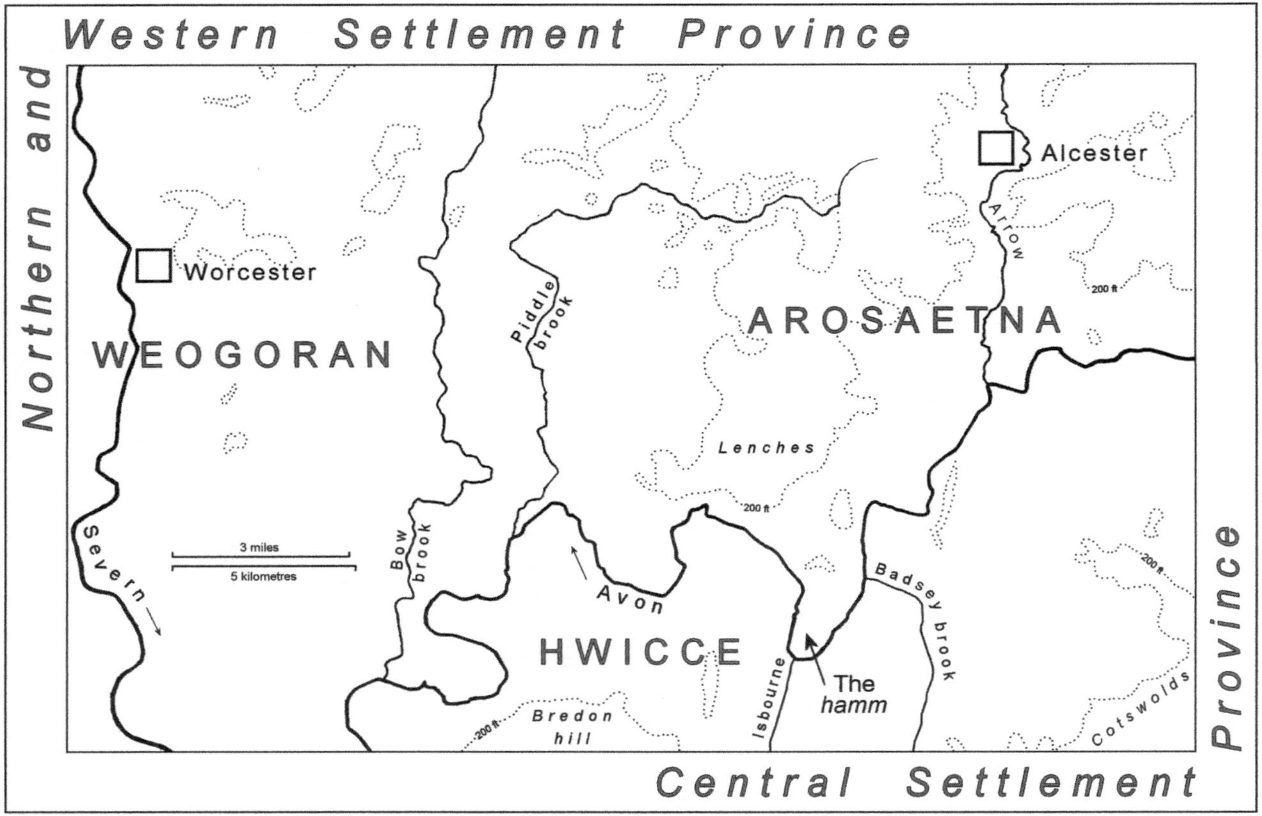

Fig. 2. The *hamm* before 701 in relation to the English settlement provinces, to Romano-British towns (Alcester and Worcester), and to early-Anglo-Saxon territories (the Weogoran and Arosætna were annexed to the Hwicce before 701).

their land.[44] The Arrow was a tributary of the Avon and entered it a few miles upstream of the *hamm*. Although historians have never established the western boundary of the Arosætna it probably lay some miles downstream of the *hamm* and perhaps on another tributary of the Avon, either the Bow brook or the Piddle brook; for on one of them may have lain the eastern boundary of a separate territory that was based on the former Roman town of Worcester and which probably belonged to a people called the Weogoran.[45] If the Arosætna met the Weogoran downstream of the *hamm*, which in turn lay downstream of the river Arrow, the *hamm* must once have lain, like Alcester, in the territory of the Arosætna. In Ecgwine's day the Arosætna had only one place that was formerly a Roman town, and that was Alcester. In the Roman period its buildings had included some that were of a quality unusual in small towns, which permits the suggestion that Alcester had then been important as a local centre; it may even have been the capital of an administrative district in the later fourth century.[46] Archaeological evidence for post-Roman activity at Alcester is slender by comparison but it supports the idea that the site may have included a small trading settlement.[47] Unlike anywhere else in the territory of the Arosætna, Alcester may have had vestiges of Roman prestige and authority when Ecgwine's minster was founded at the *hamm* and thus, though under-populated and economically weak, it could still have been acknowleged as the local administrative capital. Byrhtferth's version of Ecgwine's 'Testament' deems that Alcester was a 'famous place' at the time of the synod,[48] and in relation to the *hamm* it does seem to have been by default the nearest place that would have been suitable for an important assembly. Be that as it may, the story of the Alcester synod should not be dismissed merely on the ground that the synod and an associated consecration by Wilfrid could not have taken place in 709, the year implied by Byrhtferth's version of the 'Testament'. Wilfrid had left Mercia long before 709 and is unlikely to have performed the consecration then, but Byrhtferth at that point was simply trying to manufacture a spurious link between, on the one hand, a reputed synod and consecration and, on the other,

44 M. Gelling, *The West Midlands in the Early Middle Ages* (Leicester, 1992), p. 85.

45 Hooke 1985, pp. 80–83; S. Bassett, 'Churches in Worcester before and after the Conversion of the Anglo-Saxons', *Ant. Jnl* 69 (1989), 225–56 (at 238–43, 246–7).

46 B. C. Burnham and J. Wacher, *The 'Small Towns' of Roman Britain* (London, 1990), pp. 92–7; Cracknell 1996, pp. 127–40.

47 M. A. Stokes and R. Brownsword, 'An Anglo-Saxon Belt Fitting from Alcester, Warwickshire', *W. Midl. Arch.* 27 (1984), 97–100; W. A. Seaby, 'Alcester, Field opposite Cherry Trees Motel', *W. Midl. Arch.* 29 (1986), 47; Cracknell 1996, pp. 97–8, 139; C. Coutts, 'Alcester, adj. Lloyds Bank, Bleachfield Street', *W. Midl. Arch.* 40 (1997), 70–71 (at 70); P. Booth and J. Evans, eds, *Roman Alcester: Northern Extramural Area*, CBA Research Report 127 (London, 2001), pp. 111, 114–15, 120–21, 305–6.

48 Byrhtferth, pp. 258–9.

an event datable from the undisputed writings of Bede, which was the journey by King Coenred of the Mercians and Offa of the East Saxons to Rome in 709.[49] In fact the date of the alleged Alcester synod was shortly before the date of the alleged consecration, which would probably have taken place before the end of 703, and Wilfrid was certainly still in Mercia in that year.

The story of the Alcester synod and of the consecration of Ecgwine's church by Wilfrid, as told in Byrhtferth's version of the 'Testament', seems less convincing when one compares Byrhtferth's prolix treatment of it with an unconnected passage in an earlier part of the 'Testament'. In that place Byrhtferth reports Ecgwine as saying merely that 'After some small time I built there and consecrated a church. Subsequently I erected in the same place larger monastic buildings.' Those two sentences, which contain no mention of Wilfrid or a synod, may represent more closely the bare simplicity of an original 'Testament', or of a version of it that was earlier and more reliable than Byrhtferth's. Nevertheless, whatever the true circumstances of the consecration of Ecgwine's church and after every due doubt has been conceded, it seems certain that Bishop Wilfrid, during his years in Mercia, would have known Ecgwine and, being a vigorous founder of minsters, would have approved of Ecgwine's new foundation. Nor is there any reason to doubt that Ecgwine's acquisition of the *hamm* and the building and consecration there of his church and associated buildings were achieved in the space of a few years beginning in or about 701. The extent to which Æthelred and Ecgwine had been guided throughout by Bishop Wilfrid remains, of course, a matter of speculation.

[49] HE V, 19.

CHAPTER 2

A land of promise

The minster site

No remains of Ecgwine's church have been identified but one begins with the assumption that it was built on the same spot as the later abbey church of Evesham, on the higher ground that overlooked the flood plain at the *hamm*. To some extent the character of the site can be reconstructed as it was immediately before building began, and that makes possible some suggestions as to why that particular position was chosen for the new minster. Ecgwine was not the first to find it an attractive place. The high ground provided a fertile plateau that had supported Bronze Age and Iron Age farmers,[1] and in Roman times there had been some buildings on it, though their nature and distribution are yet to be properly understood (Fig. 1). Finds of Roman roof tiles indicate that there were some robust structures within the area occupied by the medieval town, but no trace of important Romano-British buildings has been seen there in spite of much disturbance of the ground in modern times. That may simply be because the best Roman buildings were on the site later occupied by the abbey, an area that has hardly been explored below the level of the post-Conquest monastic remains; the distribution of finds of Romano-British material is certainly consistent with a possible concentration in the area of the first church.[2] Indeed, traces of a superior Romano-British building seem to have been found on the very site of Ecgwine's minster in the twelfth century. In 1125 the historian William of Malmesbury is the first to mention the matter, having been told locally that the remains could have been those of a small 'British' church,[3] which meant presumably one that was Romano-British. It was evidently a recent discovery when William heard about it because Ecgwine's eleventh-century biographers, Byrhtferth and Dominic, say nothing about so interesting a find; surely they would have been pleased to acknowledge an early

[1] Edwards and Hurst 2000; 'Evesham, Abbey Road', *W. Midl. Arch.* 51 (2008), 117–18.

[2] Hughes 1990, pp. 150, 168–71, 174, 180–81, 196–7; M. Napthan, J. D. Hurst, and E. A. Pearson, 'Evesham, Cotswold House, High Street', *W. Midl. Arch.* 37 (1994), 31–2 (at 31); 'Evesham, Outfall Sewer', *W. Midl. Arch.* 45 (2002), 137–8 (at 138); 'Evesham, Abbey Gate', *W. Midl. Arch.* 46 (2003), 186–7 (at 186); Locket and Griffin 2006, p. 67.

[3] W. Malmesb. *GP* I, p. 452.

Christian presence at the minster site, had they known of it. Dominic's *vita* was completed in the years just before 1100,[4] which implies that the foundations of the small church-like structure were uncovered after Dominic finished the *vita* and probably during the great building works that were in progress at the abbey before William of Malmesbury wrote his book.[5] Had the remains of an ancient religious building been visible there in Ecgwine's time they might have influenced his choice of that site for his minster but the silence of Byrhtferth and Dominic suggests that no-one in 701 knew of a former Romano-British church at the *hamm*.

The preference of cranes for unfrequented and wooded areas provides a useful clue to the natural environment of Ecgwine's *hamm*. Whatever signs of human activity may have been visible at the *hamm* in Roman times, we are told in 'St Ecgwine's Testament' that by the end of the seventh century the land on which the minster would be built was full of trees and bushes among which pigs were herded.[6] It was a literary commonplace to portray a religious site as formerly a wilderness[7] but at Evesham reality and literary convention seem to have converged in the 'Testament', for there are indications that the 'Testament' does convey some correct information about the overgrown character of the place in 701; archaeology and early topographical references tend to confirm it. In particular, the excavation in 2001 of evidence for Romano-British buildings near the medieval abbey precinct found that the site excavated seemed to have been abandoned in the third century and to have been buried until the twelfth under a deep accumulation of soil.[8] Moreover, there seem to have been no finds of any early post-Roman material on the plateau. Together those observations are consistent with the supposition that any buildings there had been abandoned by the end of the Roman period and that by 701 the place had reverted to nature and thus to woodland.

There is some independent evidence of that process. An area of the town was called 'Ruinhill' c.1190[9] and 'Runhulle' c.1230[10] and lay on the slightly rising ground on the north-east side of the plateau;[11] it gives its name to the present Rynal Street. There are several possible meanings of 'Ruinhill', but the first element could be

4 Byrhtferth, p. xc. The dating evidence is questioned (but not discredited) in S. O'Rourke, 'Hagiography and Exemption at Medieval Evesham, 1000–1250: The Evidence of the *Vitae Ecgwini*', *Mediaeval Studies* 75 (2013), 271–305 (at 286).

5 T. Marlb. pp. 178–81.

6 Byrhtferth, pp. 244–5.

7 Blair 2005, pp. 191–4; H. Gittos, *Liturgy, Architecture, and Sacred Places in Anglo-Saxon England* (Oxford, 2013), pp. 31–8.

8 Locket and Griffin 2006.

9 Vesp. B.XXIV, fol. 43v.

10 T. Marlb. pp. 544–5.

11 Rudge 1820, p. 106; Izod, 'Plan', parcel nos 92 ('Rynell'), 100 ('Rynell Orchard').

Old English **hruna* ('a tree trunk, a fallen tree, a log').[12] Before the Conquest 'Ruinhill', just beyond the northern edge of the town, may thus have been a place where woodland had been felled. That interpretation of the name may be mistaken, but if one considers the landscape a little northwards of the Evesham plateau there was certainly much woodland over that in the eleventh century. The north-western boundary of what would become the manor of Lenchwick (Fig. 3) was marked in one place by a 'grove' and in another by an 'old swine enclosure', which was a feature to be found in the kind of wood-pasture where pigs could be fattened. Significantly, the northern part of the Lenchwick manorial boundary did not touch upon any arable fields.[13] In fact the manor was at the southern edge of a heavily wooded landscape that covered much of central Worcestershire in the eleventh century. The Evesham plateau, which lay to the south of Lenchwick, was relatively clear of tree cover by then,[14] but if one assumes that Evesham's emergence as a town in the later-Anglo-Saxon period had caused a northward clearance of woodland by the eleventh century there is no difficulty about accepting the word of 'St Ecgwine's Testament' that in the seventh century the plateau itself had been covered with trees and bushes.

The very name of Evesham may have emerged from an association of the place with seventh-century woodland. One of the early names for the *hamm* was 'Eofeshamm'[15] (or 'Eoveshamm' by the eleventh century)[16] and its most obvious interpretation is that a man called Eof had once been associated with the place. Byrhtferth, writing in the early eleventh century, evidently knew a little about the same Eof but he thought his name was Eoves, which is a mistaken back-formation from 'Eoveshamm'. Byrhtferth's version of Ecgwine's 'Testament' portrays 'Eoves' as a swineherd, which may not be far from the truth; the real Eof could have been connected with pig-rearing if the plateau was then wooded. The fact that the Old English for a wild boar was *eofor* is suggestive. Some individuals may have been given the name Eofor,[17] perhaps as a by-name because of their boar-like characteristics or because their principal occupation involved pigs. 'Eof', a name also recorded in Kent in 844,[18] may perhaps have been a shortened form of Eofor and

[12] Smith 1956, I, p. 266. The asterisk denotes a conjectural form.

[13] S80, S1591a, S1599.

[14] Monkhouse 1971, pp. 245, 247–9; H. C. Darby, 'The Midland Counties', *The Domesday Geography of Midland England*, ed. H. C. Darby and I. B. Terrett, The Domesday Geography of England, 2nd edn (Cambridge, 1971), pp. 421–49 (at pp. 438, 441).

[15] ASC (CD) 1037, (D) 1045, (CD) 1054.

[16] S1423.

[17] A. H. Smith, *The Place-Names of the East Riding of Yorkshire and York*, EPNS 14 (Cambridge, 1937), p. 233 ('Everingham'). But *Eofor* is not recorded in PASE.

[18] S1439.

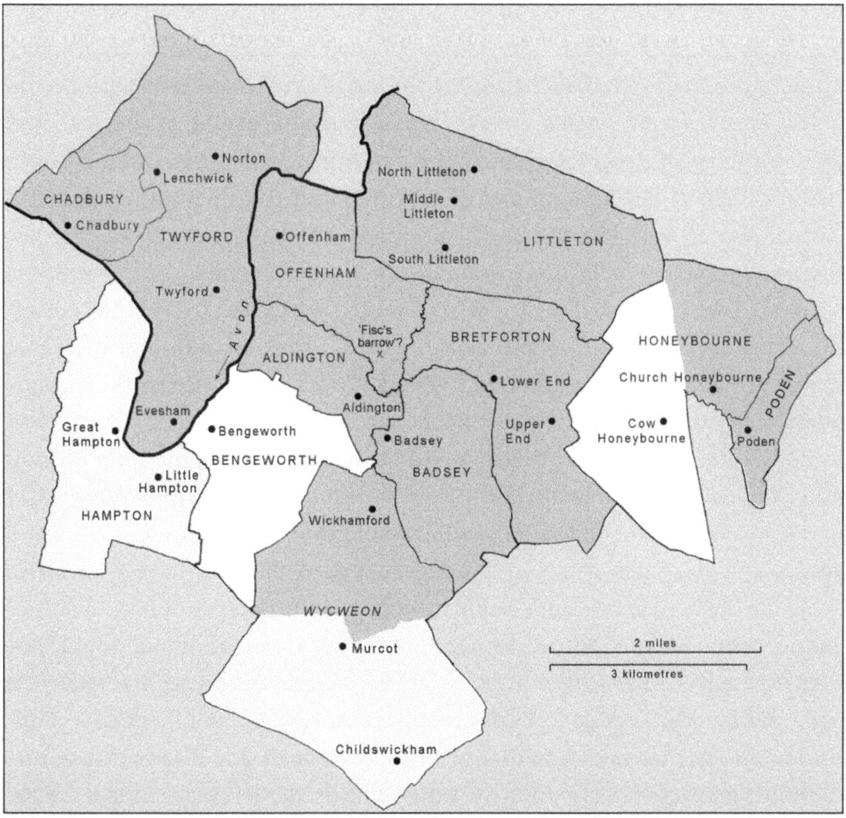

Fig. 3. Land-units around Evesham in 701. The boundaries shown are based on those of earlier-nineteenth-century parishes. The chief settlements are marked at their later-medieval locations. Shading denotes Evesham abbey estates that were in 'Fissesberg' hundred in 1086.

thus a particularly apt name at the *hamm* for someone whose life revolved around pig-keeping.

Having followed the evidence as far as it will go, one may be inclined to picture the seventh-century plateau as an unfrequented spot hemmed in by the river, the timeless rustlings and murmurs of its trees interrupted only by the grunting of pigs, the distant calling of cranes from the river bank, and, from time to time, the muffled blows of a woodsman's axe. In short, the plateau's apparently deserted state in 701 would have conformed pleasingly enough to the literary ideal of a fresh site uncorrupted by mankind and ready to be claimed for Christ. But what Ecgwine's church actually needed was accessible isolation, and that is what he found. Though there could be no true desert in the Avon valley, the illusion that Evesham was a retreat from the busy world would have appealed to someone seeking a site for a minster, and Ecgwine may have embraced the notion of a desert monastery such as those of Roman Egypt and Syria. But he would also have been glad that Evesham was not really cut off: that his minster could be sustained by the goods and produce of the outside world and could interact with the people.

The river was a thoroughfare of sorts but in the late Middle Ages it was shallower than it is today and was interrupted by fords, bridges, and mills. In the fifteenth century Richard Beauchamp, earl of Warwick, had the ambition to make the Avon navigable from Warwick to its confluence with the Severn at Tewkesbury so that small vessels could bring up wine and other goods from Bristol. He wanted to bypass the shallower reaches by means of 'gutters' (artificial channels), to enlarge the arches of bridges, and to have mills removed.[19] Nothing came of that scheme, however, and according to Thomas Habington (1560–1647) the river 'never bore a boat of any burden' until improvements were made in the 1630s.[20] Nevertheless, in the seventh century sizeable ships could sometimes negotiate quite shallow waterways; an unladen boat half the size of the Sutton Hoo ship of c.625 would have had a draught of only twelve inches (about thirty centimetres).[21] With such vessels light high-value goods and small groups of people could have been carried along the Avon in the seventh century, subject to the number of boats available and to seasonal variations in the depth of water. Water transport would have been especially convenient in winter when the stream was deeper and faster, the highways muddy, and the fords dangerous to use. Boats could then moor at the *hamm* to supply the nearby minster with goods, visitors, and ideas, not just from the immediate area but also from the east Midlands, the Severn basin, and the rest of the world.

Heavy loads, however, could come to Evesham only by road. Thus in 1086, when building stone for the abbey was being quarried at Cleeve hill, which was very near the Avon and only a few miles upstream, it still had to be hauled to Evesham by oxen.[22] But Evesham was at no particular disadvantage, because a convenient network of long-distance and local roads had been established well before the seventh century. As for the *hamm*, it seems to have been accessible by road from the north along a line represented by the medieval High Street, which

19 John Rows [John Rous], [*The Rows Rol*] ed. W. Pickering and W. Courthope (London, 1845 [1859]), ch. 50 (unpaginated).

20 T. Habington, *A Survey of Worcestershire*, ed. J. Amphlett, II, WHS (Oxford, 1899), p. 468.

21 R. L. Bruce-Mitford, *The Sutton Hoo Ship Burial: A Handbook*, 3rd edn (London, 1979), p. 76; E. Gifford and J. Gifford, 'The Sailing Performance of Anglo-Saxon Ships as derived from the Building and Trials of Half-Scale Models of the Sutton Hoo and Graveney Ship Finds', *The Mariner's Mirror* 82 (1996), 131–53 (at 132, 152).

22 DB, fol. 175v. For the quarries see B. J. Williams and A. Whittaker, *Geology of the Country around Stratford-upon-Avon and Evesham*, Memoirs of the Geol. Surv. (London, 1974), p. 35.

included what is now Vine Street (Fig. 1).[23] That seems to have been a very early route, for the enclosure ditches of an Iron Age settlement near the High Street were aligned with the highway.[24] The course of the medieval High Street keeps to the middle of the plateau, at the end of which a line can be imagined continuing down to the flood plain and leading across that to the river bank; on the opposite bank the line is continued by the road (now Cheltenham Road) that starts at the river and leads southwards towards Winchcombe.[25] The presumed route along that line seems to have crossed the river at Evesham by an early ford, now long abandoned. In a plan of 1827 the meadow on the Evesham side at the supposed crossing comprised 17.8 acres[26] and in 1540 the abbey had a meadow at Evesham that was said to be of 17.5 acres and called 'Eibbesford'.[27] The record does not specify the location of 'Eibbesford' but it presumably lay on the flood plain, like the meadow of 1827. Thus we have reason to believe that an early ford called 'Eibbesford' had once connected the *hamm* to the Winchcombe road, as part of an ancient north–south route. Meanwhile, a particularly broad and shallow stretch of the river lay on the south-east side of the *hamm*, and that was also a suitable site for a ford; if there was an ancient ford there, it would account for the presence of the medieval bridge that was later built at the same point.[28] An early crossing there would also prove the antiquity of a long-distance route to the *hamm* from the south-east, which still ascends the plateau on the line of what is now Bridge Street.[29] In the early eighth century the roads to the *hamm* were probably already ancient and, if so, Evesham minster could have been visited from any direction by river or by road and the people living within it could have travelled to any other place.

The first endowments

From the very beginning there was no intention that the minster should be a self-sufficient commune. No doubt its members could have kept themselves in food and clothing by cultivating the *hamm* and rearing animals on it, but no-one

[23] A house stood c.1230 '[in] magno uico iuxta murum cimiterii uersus portam abbacie': T. Marlb. pp. 546–7. The abbey gateway was in the present Vine Street and the graveyard gateway was in the Market Place: Cox 1990, pp. 133–5. A processional route from the Merstow to the graveyard gateway c.1300 passed 'per magnam stratam' (*Evesham Officium*, col. 70), by which Vine Street must be meant.

[24] Edwards and Hurst 2000, pp. 75, 81, 83, 85.

[25] Ogilby 1675, pl. 44; Izod, 'Plan'.

[26] Izod, 'Plan', parcel nos 7, 15, 16.

[27] Dugdale, *Mon.* II, p. 43.

[28] See Rudge 1820, plan facing p. iii.

[29] Ogilby 1675, pl. 44.

expected them to do that. On the contrary, it was soon taken for granted that they would always live off the labour and produce of a multitude of tenants, the occupiers of estates that came quickly to the minster from the hands of eager benefactors. Byrhtferth's version of 'St Ecgwine's Testament' is vague as to the first landed endowments of the minster outside Evesham but it does say that Coenred king of the Mercians (704–9) granted eighty hides of land on both sides of the Avon;[30] a hide was a unit of rateable value and in Byrhtferth's day eighty hides would have represented an area of perhaps twenty-five square miles or thereabouts.[31] Other sources suggest that Coenred was merely confirming several grants already made to the minster by other people. In either case the king's support for the minster was essential to its early growth. King Æthelred had appointed his nephew Coenred to succeed him, and Coenred seems to have been an earnest Christian, like his uncle. Like Æthelred, Coenred eventually abdicated to become a monk and he went into retirement at Rome in 709 with Offa of the East Saxons.[32] By then both Coenred and Offa had followed Æthelred's example as benefactors to Ecgwine's minster, and its community could count itself among the great landholders of the Hwicce.

There are three early lists of the minster's benefactors, documents that were begun at some unknown time and completed in the twelfth century. One of the lists appears in an Evesham abbey cartulary,[33] another is incorporated in Thomas of Marlborough's thirteenth-century history of the abbey,[34] and another was transcribed by the Elizabethan herald Robert Glover from an Evesham register that is now lost.[35] It is difficult to determine how reliable or mutually independent the lists might be, for we have no wholly genuine charters to compare with them, especially for the very earliest endowments; but where the lists seem credible they need to be cited. There can be doubts and debates about the details given by the three lists but the extent of the alleged land grants and the quality of the land that was said to have been granted suffice to show that the donors were wholehearted supporters of Ecgwine's new minster. Their motives, however, need not have been exclusively religious; while they can have expected no economic gain from making large sacrifices of their property, they did perhaps perceive a social advantage in being known to follow the royal example.

King Æthelred had given the Evesham site, and in 703 he allegedly granted an estate that lay upstream of it at Stratford and another that was downstream

30 Byrhtferth, pp. 254–5.

31 An approximate figure for the average number of hides per square mile on Evesham's core estates in the eleventh century can be calculated from their Domesday hidations.

32 HE V, 13, 19.

33 'De principalibus Eoveshamensis coenobii benefactoribus', Dugdale, *Mon.* II, p. 14.

34 T. Marlb. pp. 130–39.

35 Dugdale, *Mon.* II, p. 14.

at Chadbury. Stratford, like Fladbury, was said to have been the site of an old minster,[36] while Chadbury (Fig. 3) was named after a hilltop fortification '(on) Ceadweallan byrig' ('Ceadwealla's fortification');[37] the name Ceadwealla is a Celtic one and was presumably that of a British man who had ruled in the Chadbury area. It was also in 703 that Offa 'king' of the East Saxons is said to have given Evesham minster the estate of Twyford,[38] which adjoined Chadbury. Although Twyford lay far from Offa's homeland, the story is not incredible, for Offa son of King Sighere of the East Saxons seems to have had estates elsewhere in the sub-kingdom of the Hwicce[39] and to have been related to one or other of the ruling families of the Mercians and the Hwicce, and possibly to both. Offa's mother may have been Osgyth, who was said to have been King Æthelred's niece.[40] That Offa was thereby a kinsman of Æthelred's nephew and successor Coenred is suggested by the fact that Offa accompanied Coenred into retirement at Rome in 709.[41] Offa was also reputed to be a kinsman of Æthelheard the under-king of the Hwicce, and eventually it was Æthelheard's brother Osweard who claimed to be the heir to Offa's Mercian lands.[42]

Twyford, which included Lenchwick and Norton, took its name, a topographical one, from a ford where an ancient salt way from Roman *Salinae* (now Droitwich) crossed the Avon.[43] Much of the Twyford land unit was high ground at the southern end of an upland area that was known before the Conquest as 'lencdune' and today is called the Lenches (Fig. 2). The edge of the Lenches slopes steeply and is cut by narrow valleys that were described by the Old English (and formerly British) word *cumb*, for example at Craycombe[44] and '(æt) wænnacumbe'.[45] In the Roman period the land at Twyford may have been managed from a settlement, carefully sited, that lay astride the salt way and overlooked the ford from an

36 Byrhtferth, pp. 252–5; Dugdale, *Mon.* II, p. 14; T. Marlb. pp. 32–3, 130–31.

37 S1591a (interpreted by Hooke 1990, pp. 378, 380).

38 T. Marlb. pp. 130–31, where 'eandem terram uiginti mansarum in Thuiforde' refers to an item, now missing, in the immediately preceding list of Offa's benefactions; that Offa was the donor is affirmed on pp. 132–3.

39 S64 (possibly containing elements of a genuine charter).

40 D. Bethell, 'The Lives of St Osyth of Essex and St Osyth of Aylesbury', *AB* 88 (1970), 75–127 (at 107–9); J. Blair, 'Frithuwold's Kingdom and the Origins of Surrey', *The Origins of Anglo-Saxon Kingdoms*, ed. S. Bassett (London, 1989), pp. 97–107 (at pp. 105–7); *ODNB* ('Osgyth').

41 HE V, 19.

42 T. Marlb. pp. 130–33.

43 S1591a (interpreted by Hooke 1990, pp. 380–81).

44 Mawer and Stenton 1927, p. 126.

45 S80, S1599 (interpreted by Hooke 1990, pp. 48, 50, 409–10).

elongated area of gravel.[46] The settlement site was represented in 1794 by an orchard,[47] and in 1827 a field opposite the orchard and on the other side of the salt way was called 'Old House Ground'.[48] It was in the orchard that signs of Romano-British occupation into the fourth century (pottery, a seal box, and coins) were found when an electricity sub-station was built; the immediate surroundings of the sub-station have since yielded Romano-British tiles, more pottery, and a fourth-century coin; and within the Old House Ground much Romano-British pottery has been reported on the surface next to an electricity pylon.[49] The Romano-British inhabitants were apparently buried nearby, for 'innumerable bones' were reported near the river in the late eighteenth century, with no mention of grave goods.[50]

It was probably in Ecgwine's time that the minster received a somewhat larger body of land that lay on the other side of the river from Evesham. It certainly belonged to the minster in the early tenth century[51] and late Evesham sources say that it was given in 703 by Offa 'king' of the East Saxons.[52] That is quite possible because new minsters were still being generously endowed at the beginning of the eighth century — that is to say, before the Church's hold on so much property had come to be seen as harmful to lay society.[53] Those lands, which the minster acquired at an early date on the opposite (left) bank of the Avon, approximated to the drainage basin of a tributary of the Avon called the Badsey, Blackminster, or Broadway brook.[54] They offered a terrain that was quite different from the *hamm* and its hinterland, being a wide and fertile tract that was gently undulating and well watered. The basin extended from the Avon south-eastwards for six miles or more to the foot of the Cotswolds, while lesser hills defined it on the north-east and south-west. The Badsey brook, with its many small tributaries, ran throughout the basin and into the Avon. The land was not only well drained but also

46 Geol. Surv. Map 1/50,000, sheet 200, solid and drift (1974 edn).

47 At OS Nat. Grid SP 046457: Tindal 1794, pp. 326–7. For Tindal's topographical reference points see Cox 1988, pp. 12, 30–31. The orchard is shown on C. and J. Greenwood, *Map of the County of Worcester* (London, 1822).

48 Izod, 'Plan', parcel no. 136.

49 Cox 1967, p. 16 no. 24; R. Taylor, 'Chance Finds reported to Birmingham Museum and Art Gallery', *Worcs. Archaeology and Local History Newsletter* 18 (1976), 7–8 (at 8); D. C. Cox, 'A Medieval Bridge on the Avon at Twyford, near Evesham', *VEHS Res. Pap.* 7 (1979), 57–62 (at 61 n. 7).

50 Tindal 1794, pp. 235–6.

51 Below, ch. 5.

52 Dugdale, *Mon.* II, p. 14; T. Marlb. pp. 130–31.

53 Bede, 'Epistola ad Ecgbertum', *Abb. Wearmouth–Jarrow*, pp. 124–61 (at pp. 142–7). See Blair 2005, pp. 121–34; Foot 2006, pp. 127–34.

54 Cox 1975, pp. 31, 41.

had an exceptional natural fertility that was founded on favourable soils and a benign microclimate,[55] assets that had been recognized early and then enhanced by centuries of husbandry. In the Roman period the area was already intensively cultivated and farmsteads were evenly scattered over it. They were served by several minor Roman roads that supplemented an established network of earlier ways.[56] In so well-developed an environment some Romano-British farmers are known to have produced such ample surpluses that they could afford to buy the luxuries of central heating, painted wall plaster, and mosaic floors.[57]

55 K. M. Buchanan, *Worcestershire*, The Land of Britain 6, pt 68 (London, 1944), pp. 628–31.

56 Hooke 1985, pp. 215–16; R. A. Jackson, J. D. Hurst, and E. A. Pearson, 'A Romano-British Settlement at Leylandii House Farm, Norton and Lenchwick', *TWAS* 3rd series 15 (1996), 63–72 (map at 70); Cox 2006, pp. 77–80.

57 OS Map 6", SP 04 SE (1955 edn); Cox 1967, pp. 15–16; Reynolds 1971, p. 12; P. Price, 'The Use of SWAG', *W. Midl. Arch.* 30 (1987), 78–80 (at 79); B. Watson, 'Blake's Hill: A Romano-British Settlement in North Littleton', *Worcs. Archaeology and Local History Newsletter* 40 (1988), 4–7 (at 4); C. J. Evans and others, 'Unlocking the Past (South Worcestershire Collections): Stage 3 Report and HER Enhancement', Worcs. County Council Historic Environment and Archaeological Service Report no. 1591 (Worcester, 2008), pp. 65–6 (in the 'Online Archaeology Library' of Worcs. Archive and Archaeology Service); Hurst and Patrick 2012, p. 41.

CHAPTER 3

A waiting people

It is clear from archaeological finds that Anglo-Saxon cultural influences had arrived in the left-bank area by the early sixth century,[1] and by the end of the seventh century there were several burial grounds in which the graves were furnished in Germanic style with such items as beads, brooches, spears, and shields.[2] Before the Norman Conquest other places nearby were reputed to be the sites of pagan burials.[3] The richest of the Germanic-style graves known to us were discovered when a railway cutting was made at Great Hampton near Evesham in 1862. The remains of at least two people were found there and two spearheads and a large knife blade were recovered.[4] Also in the graves at Great Hampton was a delicately made seventh-century gold and garnet pin suite, a dress or hair fastening made up of two pins linked by an ornamental chain and pendant.[5] So costly an item shows that in the seventh century the local population included not only subsistence farmers but also men and women with money and prestige. Such privileged people may have had high standing within an orderly and stratified society; order is certainly implied by the existence of an early place of public assembly at a burial mound called 'Fissesberg' ('Fisc's barrow'), which has been plausibly identified at Blackminster near Offenham (Fig. 3).[6] From some unknown period matters affecting the whole area were discussed there and decisions approved and

1 Dalwood and Ratkai 1998, p. 13; D. Kendrick, 'News from the County Museum', *Worcs. Recorder* 76 (2007), 6–8 (at 7).

2 T. J. S. Baylis, 'Anglo-Saxon Burial Site', *TWAS* new series 31 (1954), 39–42; Dalwood and Ratkai 1998; Cox 2006, p. 79.

3 S1590, S1591a, S1599, S1664. See Gelling 1997, pp. 157–8.

4 The spearheads and blade are in the museum of the Society of Antiquaries of London, object no. LDSAL 442. The society's 'Catalogue of Drawings and Museum Objects' (online) says that they were found 'in a railway cutting at Evesham'.

5 'Thursday, 4th December, 1862', *Proceedings of the Soc. of Antiquaries* 2nd series 2 (1861–64), 162–6 (at 163–4), where the site is wrongly described as on the 'right' bank of the Avon near 'Little' Hampton. On the pin-suite (British Museum, Dept. of Prehistory and Europe, registration no. 1864,1220.1) see *VCH Worcs.* I, pp. 229–30 and pl. facing p. 228; G. Baldwin Brown, *The Arts in Early England*, III (London, 1915), p. 372 and pl. LXXXI.1; IV (London, 1915), p. 428; British Museum, 'Collection Online' (online catalogue).

6 Cox 2006.

promulgated. Much remains uncertain but it seems reasonable to believe that Evesham minster's lands on the left bank of the Avon were not marginal in 703 but were populous and productive, just as they had been in Roman times. There is even some evidence that in 703 the farmers, though Anglo-Saxon in culture, were of the same Celtic blood as their Romano-British predecessors and were occupying settlements that had evolved directly from theirs.

The Britons

Anglo-Saxon culture pervaded the Vale of Evesham by the end of the seventh century but most of the inhabitants of the minster's land on both sides of the river were probably descended from Iron Age or Romano-British people.[7] Local evidence of that comes from the former land unit known as 'Wycweon',[8] which lay about two miles south-east of Evesham and has long been divided into the conjoined parishes of Childs*wickham* and *Wickham*ford (Fig. 3). The name 'Wycweon' may have descended from a combination of two Celtic elements to convey the meaning 'inhabited site near the marsh or moor'.[9] If so, the marsh can only have been the place known by 972 as '(on) egsan mor' ('Egsa's marsh'), which lay at the centre of the original 'Wycweon' land unit[10] and near the present low-lying hamlet of Murcot, where the Badsey brook is joined by a tributary. The English name Murcot comes from *mor* ('marsh') and *cot* ('cottage, hut, shelter') and thus appears to be a direct translation of Celtic 'Wycweon'; 'Murcot' is less likely to have been a new coinage applied by coincidence to the same landscape features. The place-name element *cot* is not attested anywhere before the mid-eighth century, but that is not decisive, for there are few documents of an earlier date that would mention the names of such small settlements in any case; the element *cot* could therefore have been in use before the eighth century,[11] and Margaret Gelling raised the possibility that *cot* names (such as Murcot) were 'sometimes

[7] D. J. Tyler, 'Early Mercia and the Britons', *Britons in Anglo-Saxon England*, ed. N. Higham (Woodbridge, 2007), pp. 91–101 (at pp. 93, 96–8); Coates 2013.

[8] S1591a.

[9] R. Coates and A. Breeze, *Celtic Voices, English Places: Studies in the Celtic Impact on Place-Names in England* (Stamford, 2000), pp. 176, 232–3, 298, 342, 356; R. Coates, 'The Place-Name "Childswickham"', in C. Patrick and D. Hurst, 'Archaeological Survey and Excavation along the Cotswold Supply Trunk Main: Archive Report', Worcs. County Council Historic Environment and Archaeology Service Report no. 1140 (Worcester, 2004), pp. 120–21 (in the 'Online Archaeology Library' of Worcs. Archive and Archaeology Service).

[10] S786 (interpreted by Hooke 1990, pp. 227, 415).

[11] Cox 1976, p. 66.

applied to farmsteads originally built and inhabited by Celtic-speaking people'.[12] Surface finds suggestive of a Romano-British farmstead have indeed occurred at Murcot, and they include such luxury materials as imported Samian pottery and a flue tile from a central-heating system;[13] and the finds coincide with a dense wider pattern of undated linear and circular features that has been recorded from the air (Fig. 4).[14] It is therefore quite possible that by 700 a former Romano-British settlement with a Celtic name, 'Wycweon', had been continuously occupied since Roman times and was inhabited by the descendants of Romano-British people, who were now ready to adopt English speech and had translated the name of their settlement, or would soon do so, from 'Wycweon' to Murcot.

By the mid-eighth century, at the latest, British speech was clearly dying out in the Evesham area, with English place-names generally replacing British ones.[15] People who were still culturally Celtic then became a conspicuous minority. For example, just downstream of Evesham minster the English place-names Comberton and Walcot denoted settlements that were remarkable for being inhabited by or named after 'Welsh' people.[16] The names may have been coined in or after the early eighth century, because that is when the earliest records of names in *tun* and *cot* are usually found; but *tun* and *cot* names could be older than that, since earlier documents are unlikely to mention the small places to which those elements were applicable.[17] Whatever may be the date of the names Comberton and Walcot, they imply that English culture was then considered the norm in that part of Mercia.

Old settlements with new names

In 703 'Wycweon'/Murcot was probably the kind of settlement that typified the whole area acquired on the left bank of the river by the new minster at Evesham: a landscape of dispersed farms and hamlets, perhaps a few of them still with British names, and each shifting about on a small site that had been occupied since the Roman period, if not earlier. For continuity of occupation at such places we may look to the evidence from Bengeworth, which lay immediately over the

12 Gelling 1974, p. 68.

13 OS Map 6", SP 04 SE (1955 edn); Cox 1967, p. 16 no. 19.

14 English Heritage Archives, National Monuments Record, oblique aerial photos, NMR SP 0640/1–17; English Heritage, 'PastScape' (online), Monument No. 328389.

15 M. Gelling, 'Why aren't we speaking Welsh?', *Anglo-Saxon Studies in Archaeology and History* 6 (1993), 51–6 (at 54–5).

16 Gelling 1997, pp. 93–6, 251.

17 On the chronology of the elements *tun* and *cot* see Gelling 1974, pp. 68–9; Cox 1976, pp. 63, 65–6; Gelling 1997, p. 254.

Fig. 4. The hamlet of Murcot (left) from the south. The boundary between Childswickham (Gloucestershire) and Wickhamford (Worcestershire) follows the lane from the right of the frame to the centre, then makes a northward right-angle to follow the hedge line; Wickhamford is on the north-east side of the boundary. Photo by W. A. Baker 1967. English Heritage Archives, ref. NMR SP 0640/10 (WAB 48/23).

river from Evesham. Provisional results of an excavation south of the medieval churchyard at Bengeworth include indications of an Iron Age ditched settlement enclosure that was also occupied in the Roman period and from the early part of the Anglo-Saxon period up to the twelfth century (Fig. 12).[18] It is therefore permissible to suggest that by the time Ecgwine's minster was founded the ditched enclosure had been in continuous use since the Iron Age, and had therefore once had a British name. That name was probably replaced by an English one before c.700. The place-name Bengeworth is English and seems to be early. It refers to a *worð* ('enclosure') at '*Benning' (or '*Benninge'), which was a place named after someone called Benna or Beonna. On philological grounds it would seem that the place '*Benning(e)' was already so called in Primitive Old English and thus before c.700;[19] the place-name survived as 'Bench' in the thirteenth century[20] and as 'Benge' in the fifteenth,[21] and the present names Bengehill ('Benches hill' in 1541)[22] and Bengeworth ('Bengesworth' in 1329)[23] refer to it. Whether the ditched enclosure was the principal *worð* of 'Benge' in the early eighth century, having by then lost its British name, is another matter. It may have been, but in the early nineteenth century there was a Moat Orchard about sixty yards south-west of the church;[24] the name suggests an ancient ditched enclosure there, and that too could have been the *worð* from which Bengeworth was named.

Beliefs and unbelief

The relationship beween paganism and Christianity in the lands that the minster acquired around the time of its foundation can to some extent be suggested, but one suspects that there were hidden complexities, even in the soul of the

18 J. Wainwright, 'Durcot Lodge, Church Street, Evesham: Archive Summary of a Programme of Archaeological Works', unpublished TS (Clun, 2001). I am indebted to Jo Wainwright for a copy of this report.

19 J. McN. Dodgson, 'The *-ing-* in English Place-Names like *Birmingham* and *Altrincham*', *Beiträge zur Namenforschung* Neue Folge 2 (1967), 221–45; for the name Bengeworth specifically see Dodgson's 'Various Forms of Old English *-ing* in English Place-Names', ibid. 325–96 (at 363).

20 J. O. Halliwell, ed., *The Chronicle of William de Rishanger, of the Barons' Wars. The Miracles of Simon de Montfort*, Camden Soc. (London, 1840), p. 94.

21 *Evesham Chron.* p. 304.

22 Public Record Office, *List of Lands of Dissolved Religious Houses*, Lists and Indexes Supplementary Series 3, reprint (New York, 1964), pt 4, p. 108.

23 R. M. Haines, ed., *Calendar of the Register of Adam de Orleton Bishop of Worcester 1327–1333*, WHS new series 10 (London, 1979), p. 15.

24 G. May, *The History of Evesham* (Evesham, 1834), p. 138; J. P. Shawcross, *Bengeworth: Being some Account of the History of the Church and Parish* (Evesham, 1927), p. 124.

individual believer. Nor should it be taken for granted that all who took care to observe the outward forms of their religion, whether pagan or Christian, were wholeheartedly convinced by it.

The evidence for paganism in the territory that passed to the minster is stronger than that for early Christianity. At Harrow hill, about a mile to the north of Blackminster, there seems to have been in the seventh century a pagan religious site that dated back at least to the Iron Age and incorporated a holy well. It had evidently been a centre of Celtic religion, but we cannot tell precisely what form of belief the site was supporting c.700. Such wells often lost their pagan associations in the course of time and became nominally Christian; in modern times the one at Harrow hill was sometimes called St Anne's well, and local Christians were still taking water from it as a cure for sore eyes.[25] It is assumed, however, that the people represented by the area's many seventh-century furnished burials were of Germanic culture and regarded themselves as adherents of the Germanic gods. Moreover, if one takes a view of the whole of Britain in the middle of the seventh century, the land across the river from Evesham was on the western fringe of the Germanic cultural zone that comprised most of eastern and south-eastern England. Conversely, Evesham itself lay on the south-eastern fringe of those lands in which British culture, including the practice of Christianity, had predominated since Roman times.[26] In other words, Evesham minster was planted in a transitional zone between two cultures, one to the south-east that had become mainly pagan and the other to the north-west that was residually Christian. The invisible cultural and religious boundary had not settled there by chance; it was determined by a deep and ancient divide in the pattern of human activity in Britain. Brian Roberts and Stuart Wrathmell have taken the whole of England and defined and mapped three 'settlement provinces'; and Evesham lay near the boundary of two of those, which they have named the 'central province' and the 'northern and western province' (Fig. 2). Differences between those two provinces have been apparent throughout history, whether manifested in the distribution of Roman villas, of Anglo-Saxon pagan burials, of medieval villages, or of parliamentary inclosures, all of which were especially characteristic of the 'central province', or in the extent of pre-Conquest woodland, which was much more abundant in the 'northern and western province'.[27] It was in the

25 D. C. Cox, 'A Currency Bar Hoard from Harrow Hill, Middle Littleton', *VEHS Res. Pap.* 7 (1979), 31–8 (at 33–6).

26 Sims-Williams 1990, pp. 63, 74–5, 85–6; Blair 2005, pp. 13–15; Celtic place-names mapped in Higham and Ryan 2013, p. 98.

27 B. K. Roberts and S. Wrathmell, *An Atlas of Rural Settlement in England* (London, 2000); B. K. Roberts and S. Wrathmell, *Region and Place: A Study of English Rural Settlement* (London, 2002).

geographical frontier zone to which Evesham belonged that Anglo-Saxon paganism had virtually halted in the sixth century in its advance towards northern and western Britain,[28] and by 700 Christianity was actively reclaiming the paganized area. Thus when Evesham minster was founded the religious boundary on which it stood was already dissolving.

While the immediate surroundings of the new minster were appropriate to a monastic retreat, its wider setting offered a promising field for missionary work, and King Æthelred and Bishop Ecgwine may have had that in mind when they sited the minster at a vestigial religious frontier. In the land of the Hwicce the boundary between the 'central' and 'northern and western' settlement provinces broadly coincided with the river Avon[29] and Evesham was therefore a good place on which to build an outpost of Christian mission to the paganized 'central province' on the opposite bank. There was much to do, for the leaders of the British Church based in the 'northern and western province' had previously failed to take up the challenge of missionary work[30] and were even said to have rejected calls to do so.[31] Ecgwine's predecessor Bishop Oftfor was remembered, however, as 'preaching the word of faith' in the land of the Hwicce[32] and Byrhtferth's eleventh-century *vita* of Ecgwine assumes that Ecgwine too embarked on a mission among King Æthelred's subjects there: 'He used to preach to all peoples the severe and gentle things which are to come, requesting silence with his hand from those who scarcely wished to believe him or to come to the mysteries of the Mass'.[33] Presumably they included not only the unconverted but also the isolated, the lapsed, the inconsistent, the confused, and, of course, the indifferent.

The burden of lordship

Evesham on its own was a suitable setting for a life of monastic seclusion, and the land that the new minster acquired across the river created an opportunity to bring the inhabitants there to a better understanding of Christianity through preaching and the sacraments. Within a regime designed for contemplation and missionary work, however, it was hard to accommodate the secular obligations common to every institutional holder of land: to maintain favourable relations

28 Inhumation cemeteries mapped in S. Lucy, *The Anglo-Saxon Way of Death* (Stroud, 2000), p. 142; place-names relating to possible pre-Christian temples mapped in Higham and Ryan 2013, p. 150.

29 D. Hooke, *England's Landscape: The West Midlands* (London, 2006), p. 10, fig. 1.1.

30 Sims-Williams 1990, p. 78.

31 HE II, 2.

32 HE IV, 23.

33 Byrhtferth, pp. 224–5.

with political leaders, to manage and defend the estates, to regulate the conduct of the people who lived on them, and to dispose of the surplus revenues that the estates brought in. Even if the minster could fulfil all of those tasks, there would remain the most difficult of all challenges: the temptations to pride, physical comfort, and earthly pleasure that lay in the possession of corporate wealth and power. It was inevitable from the outset that the minster's secular concerns would tend to induce worldly pragmatism—a distraction from its purposes as a religious community—and would do so increasingly when its involvements with the world grew more numerous and complex.

Events were to show that the minster estate had become less secure even before the departure of Coenred and Offa to Rome in 709 and the accession of Æthelred's son Ceolred as king of the Mercians; and the missionary Boniface (d.754) alleges that Ceolred, who died in 716, was a violator of nuns and a despoiler of minsters.[34] Such an extreme view is not consistent with reports that Ceolred asked the dying Bishop Wilfrid to be his spiritual director[35] and gave land to the minster at Evesham,[36] but the accusations do suggest that churches felt unable to rely on Ceolred for protection. Ceolred's long-lived successor King Æthelbald (716–57) also had a mixed reputation in religious circles[37] and certainly, in the centuries that followed, the accession of a weak or unsupportive king always left the minster and its estates exposed to outside threats.

Soon after Evesham minster was founded disappointed family members might challenge or forcibly retract the early gifts of land made by their kinsmen. Thus after King Æthelred's retirement in 704 Bishop Ecgwine was unable to resist claims to Fladbury and Stratford by Æthelheard under-king of the Hwicce, the kinsman and heir of Æthelred's late queen Osthryth. Æthelheard took Stratford from Ecgwine and held it until Ecgwine leased Fladbury to him for life. It is not clear whether Ecgwine's predecessor Bishop Oftfor had earlier managed to revive the Fladbury minster but Ecgwine's lease of Fladbury to Æthelheard seems to have contained a condition that regular religious life was to be maintained there,[38] and a minster was certainly in being at Fladbury c.780.[39] The corresponding return of Stratford to Ecgwine, however, was short-lived. Later Evesham sources say that after Offa of the East Saxons and King Coenred retired in 709 the heir to Offa's Mercian lands, Osweard brother of Æthelheard, took back Twyford, which Offa had granted to Evesham minster. Osweard is said to have then used Twyford as

34 *EHD c.500–1042*, p. 820 no. 177.
35 Stephen, *V. Wilf.* pp. 138–9.
36 S81 (spurious); Dugdale, *Mon.* II, p. 14; T. Marlb. pp. 130–33.
37 Sims-Williams 1990, pp. 146–7.
38 S1252; Byrhtferth, pp. 254–5; T. Marlb. pp. 32–5, 130–33.
39 S62.

a bargaining token to make Bishop Ecgwine return to him the Stratford estate which, according to Osweard, his late brother Æthelheard had had no right to give away.[40] During those disputes there is no record that King Æthelred's successors Coenred and Ceolred tried to intervene on Ecgwine's behalf. Ultimately then, Ecgwine and the bishops after him lost control of Fladbury for an indefinite period and Evesham minster had to give up Stratford altogether in order to keep Twyford. Nevertheless, the exchange of a more distant estate, Stratford, for a nearer one, Twyford, was not entirely regrettable, for it enabled Ecgwine's minster to gain lasting possession of a consolidated area on the right bank of the Avon that comprised the *hamm* on which the minster stood, Twyford to the north of that, and Chadbury to the north-west (Fig. 3).

40 Byrhtferth, pp. 254–5; T. Marlb. pp. 34–5, 130–33.

CHAPTER 4

Ecgwine and the first abbots

As bishop of the Hwicce Ecgwine had responsibility for an area that would later constitute the counties of Gloucester and Worcester and part of Warwickshire. The territory was so large that he would have been unable to devote more than a fraction of his attention to any particular part of it, and he could not have seen to the daily administration of his new minster at Evesham. According to Byrhtferth Ecgwine was the first abbot there,[1] but that would have been in the sense that he had strategic control over the minster's affairs, not that he lived at Evesham with the community. As soon as the minster began to function Ecgwine would have needed to delegate the day-to-day management of it to a resident superior, just as Benedict Biscop had done some twenty years before in his foundations at Jarrow and Wearmouth; Benedict was abbot of both but each had its own abbot subordinate to him.[2] At Evesham the first resident head was probably Æthelwald. He is the first man named in a tenth-century chronological list of the abbots.[3] He also seems to be mentioned in a papal privilege in favour of Evesham; it purports to have been granted in 713 by Pope Constantine I at the request of Æthelwald, who is there described as the minster's envoy to Rome.[4]

Some elements of the 713 privilege, in its received form, are clearly anachronistic,[5] but at least one of the clauses may be authentic because there seem to be contemporary parallels for it: the Evesham privilege stipulates that the community should be allowed to elect its own abbot after the death of the previous head. A clause to that effect can be found in other alleged papal privileges of the period such as that which Pope Constantine is said to have granted for the minsters at Bermondsey and Woking,[6] a document that may have an authentic basis,[7] and the privilege that Pope Agatho (678–81) issued for the minster of St

1 Byrhtferth, pp. 208–9.
2 Bede, 'Historia Abbatum', *Abb. Wearmouth–Jarrow*, pp. 22–75 (at pp. 38, 40).
3 T. Marlb. pp. 139–41.
4 Ibid. pp. 318–19.
5 Below, ch. 13.
6 Haddan and Stubbs, III, pp. 276–8.
7 F. M. Stenton, 'Medeshamstede and its Colonies', Stenton 1970, pp. 179–92 (at pp. 185–8).

Peter and St Paul (later St Augustine's abbey) at Canterbury,[8] where the surviving text is certainly based on a genuine original.[9] It is also recorded that Benedict Biscop obtained a papal privilege for Wearmouth in 679 and that Wilfrid did the same for Ripon and Hexham between 679 and 680.[10] The skill of medieval forgers is not to be underestimated and the man who redacted the Evesham privilege to create the version that we now have could have introduced Æthelwald's name into the document to make it look more authentic. On the other hand it is not clear why, in that case, the obscure Æthelwald should have been named instead of the illustrious Ecgwine, who was still alive in 713. The evidence can be debated but it allows one to suggest that in 713 Pope Constantine did grant a privilege of papal protection for Evesham minster through its representative Æthelwald. The forged or enhanced text that emerges in the twelfth century could have been intended not so much to deceive a later generation as to restore imaginatively what was known of a genuine privilege that had decayed or been lost.[11]

There is every indication that Ecgwine remained bishop of the Hwicce until he died and that he held the upper abbacy of Evesham concurrently. He was still a bishop in 716[12] and as such was assumed also to have been a witness to proceedings at a great church council held at 'Clofesho' (a notable but unidentified place) in July of that year; the record of the council seems to be spurious but the appended list of witnesses may be sound.[13] It was said that his successor as bishop, Wilfrith, was chosen in Ecgwine's lifetime and took office as bishop as soon as Ecgwine had died, which was on 30 December in 716 or 717.[14] Everything suggests that Ecgwine never resigned as bishop but in his later years had been able to leave a portion of the episcopal work to Wilfrith before at last being taken to Evesham for burial.[15] It seems quite possible that Ecgwine had always wanted to retire to Evesham and end his days in seclusion there and that finally he did so.

8 Haddan and Stubbs, III, pp. 124–5.

9 W. Levison, *England and the Continent in the Eighth Century*, The Ford Lectures (Oxford, 1946), pp. 25–6, 187–90.

10 Ibid. p. 24.

11 Below, ch. 13.

12 S102.

13 S22; S. D. Keynes, *The Councils of* Clofesho, Vaughan Papers in Adult Education 38 (Leicester, 1994), pp. 10–11.

14 J. Worc. II, pp. 174–5.

15 Byrhtferth, pp. 280–81.

Abbots, bishops, and kings

In the eighth and ninth centuries many of the private minsters in the diocese of the Hwicce were taken into the bishop's estate and in that way lost their lands and probably any monastic character that they may once have had.[16] That Evesham, in contrast to them, enjoyed independence and continuity during that period is suggested by three observations. First, there is a continuous list of the abbots of Evesham for the eighth and ninth centuries; secondly, there is a record that fundamental changes did not take place at Evesham until c.941; and, thirdly, Evesham was among the few old minsters in the diocese that survived to receive new life as Benedictine monasteries in the reign of Edgar (957–75). The last two observations will be discussed in their proper chronological place but the list of early abbots can be explored now. A numbered list of the abbots from the foundation of the minster was completed at Evesham in the mid-tenth century[17] and it seems to be reliable because several of the names are the same as those of abbots that occur in genuine and datable documents relating to the land of the Hwicce. Thus the Evesham list seems to have the abbots in correct chronological order, although it does not mention any dates. It is reassuring to find that some of the abbots in the Evesham list do not appear in any other known document, for that allows one to suggest that Evesham minster did not search extraneous sources for random names that it could use to construct or complete the list; that may have happened but we have no particular reason to think that it did.

Abbot Æthelwald, the first on the list, had probably been Ecgwine's resident local deputy as abbot and seems to have remained in office for some time after Ecgwine's death. An abbot called Æthelwald was the third among the four abbots that witnessed a charter granted between the later 720s and 737 by King Æthelbald of the Mercians for his *comes* ('nobleman') Æthelric. Æthelric was a son of the former King Oshere of the Hwicce and the grant concerned an estate at Wootton Wawen (now in Warwickshire), which was in the diocese of the Hwicce.[18] It is the date and the Hwiccian context of the charter that suggest that Abbot Æthelwald, one of the witnesses, was the Evesham abbot of the same name. A Hwiccian connection also helps one to identify some of the abbots who came after Æthelwald in the Evesham list. It is possible that 'Tildbrith', the fifth name listed, represents the Abbot Tilberht who in 759 was the first among the three abbots that witnessed

[16] C. Dyer, *Lords and Peasants in a Changing Society: The Estates of the Bishopric of Worcester, 680–1540* (Cambridge, 1980), pp. 13–15; Sims-Williams 1990, pp. 144–6, 169–72.

[17] T. Marlb. pp. 138–41.

[18] S94. On the date see Scharer 1982, p. 178.

a grant by the joint under-kings of the Hwicce of an estate at Andoversford (now in Gloucestershire).[19] The eighth abbot of Evesham in the numbered list, Credan, was in office by 777, when he was the third among seven abbots that witnessed the grant of an estate at Sedgeberrow near Evesham that King Offa of the Mercians made to his *subregulus* ('subordinate ruler') Ealdred ealdorman of the Hwicce;[20] and at some time between 777 and 780 Credan was the first of two abbots to subscribe when Ealdred granted a lease of Fladbury minster.[21] In due course Credan was buried next to the minster church at Evesham, in a grave that was identifiable as his in the eleventh century.[22]

If Evesham minster had some of the attributes of a monastic retreat in Ecgwine's day, it seems possible that within 100 years of its foundation the place had acquired an elegant copy of the 'Rule St Benedict', which is preserved as MS Hatton 48 in the Bodleian Library.[23] The manuscript appears to have been produced in the Midlands or the south of England between c.700 and the mid-eighth century and for an important minster in the diocese of the Hwicce, possibly, therefore, for Evesham. The volume is a handsome one measuring about 31cm by 22cm; the text is written in two columns in the Uncial script and with decorated initials. By c.1100 it was at Worcester cathedral priory but its ownership history before that is not recorded and Evesham could have been the first place in the diocese to have owned it. Bishop Wilfrid, a strong advocate of the Benedictine 'Rule', is presumed to have known Ecgwine and if Wilfrid kindled Ecgwine's interest in the 'Rule' Ecgwine or one of the eighth-century abbots could have acquired the Hatton copy for Evesham. It could easily have passed later to Worcester, in one of the several periods before c.1100 during which the bishop had direct control of Evesham; the last of them was from the 990s to c.1014[24] and thus soon after Worcester itself had adopted the 'Rule'. The Hatton manuscript, whether or not Evesham was the first owner of it, proves that in the eighth century the 'Rule' was understood in the diocese of the Hwicce and therefore at Evesham. Various other monastic rules were known in England at the time, however, and one should not assume that Evesham could only have been influenced by that of Benedict. We ought probably

19 S56.

20 S113 (the relevant part is apparently genuine). On the date see Scharer 1982, p. 241.

21 S62. Credan also appears in the suspect charters S54 and (as 'Tredan') S57.

22 *Evesham Chron.* p. 324.

23 This paragraph is based on D. H. Farmer, ed., *The Rule of St Benedict: Oxford, Bodleian Library, Hatton 48*, Early English Manuscripts in Facsimile 15 (Copenhagen, 1968), pp. 21–6.

24 Below, ch. 6. Cf. Sims-Williams 1990, p. 205, where an Evesham provenance is dismissed on the incorrect assumption that Evesham 'never came under the control of the see'.

to think of the Hatton copy as an inspirational treasure for whichever minster first had it, but not necessarily as the place's governing text.

As an episcopal foundation Evesham minster had always been accepted as resting in the special care of the bishops and, if the enhanced version of the alleged papal privilege of 713 is to be believed, the minster was also under the protection of the archbishop of Canterbury and the pope. The ninth-century bishops of the Hwicce certainly had influence at Evesham and that may have extended at times to actual control. In Ecgwine's time the abbot had been nominated, supervised, and protected by the bishop and there had been no cause since then for the arrangement to be abandoned. Thus some of the ninth-century abbots can be cautiously identified as former members of the bishop's *familia* ('clerical household') and they may have come to Evesham as his nominees. In October 803 Abbot Credan's successor Thingcferth was apparently one of four named abbots from the diocese of the Hwicce who accompanied their bishop, Deneberht, to a church council held at 'Clofesho'. While there, Thingcferth was the second among the Hwiccian abbots who inserted their names in a long list of witnesses to a decree forbidding the lay control of minsters;[25] it was a matter about which the contemporary bishops of the Hwicce had a well-attested unease.[26] In 824 an Abbot Ecgberht was the third among three abbots that were included in a list of the many priests who witnessed an agreement between Bishop Heahberht of the Hwicce and the minster community of Berkeley concerning land at Westbury on Trym in that diocese.[27] The witness Ecgberht was perhaps the same as the 'Ecbrith' who appears in the Evesham list as the eleventh abbot. If that is so, his occurrence among a list of priests in 824 confirms that at least one member of the church of Evesham had been ordained priest. The minster community needed to include priests because only they were entitled to celebrate Mass in the minster church. Moreover, the minster had to have men in priest's orders if it was to undertake the pastoral work of offering the sacraments to local people. 'Elferd', the twelfth abbot on the Evesham list, was one who may have come to Evesham from the bishop's *familia*; that assumes that he can be identified as 'Eueferth', the second among three deacons who witnessed in 855 a lease by Alhhun bishop of

25 S1431b.

26 N. Brooks, *The Early History of the Church of Canterbury: Christ Church from 597 to 1066* (Leicester, 1984), pp. 179–80; C. Cubitt, *Anglo-Saxon Church Councils, 650-850* (London, 1995), pp. 229–30; Blair 2005, pp. 115–17; M. Ryan, '"Ad sedem episcopalem reddantur": Bishops, Monks, and Monasteries in the Diocese of Worcester in the Eighth Century', *Discipline and Diversity: Papers read at the 2005 Summer Meeting and the 2006 Winter Meeting of the Ecclesiastical History Soc.* ed. K. Cooper and J. Gregory, Studies in Church History 43 (Woodbrige, 2007), pp. 114–29.

27 S1433.

the Hwicce concerning land at Cutsdean (now in Gloucestershire) and 'Sture'.[28] Abbot 'Elferd' was succeeded at Evesham by Abbot 'Wlfard'. He was possibly the priest Wulfheard, who had been one of the *familia* and had thus witnessed leases of Bishop Alhhun in 849 and 855.[29]

An abbot of Evesham who does not appear on the minster's own list is Wulfsige, who, a late source alleges, became the bishop of London of that name.[30] If that is correct Wulfsige was appointed to London some time between 897, when London's Bishop Heahstan died,[31] and 899, when Wulfsige was no longer abbot of Evesham. Wulfsige, 'abbot of Evesham', is also the first among three abbots to witness a charter of King Burgred of the Mercians for Crowland minster (now in Lincolnshire); it is dated 868 but was forged some time after the Conquest.[32] The alleged date is clearly wrong for Abbot Wulfsige but the document does attest to a later belief in his existence. If Evesham really had an Abbot Wulfsige his omission from Evesham's own list suggests that the list was not being maintained continuously at the end of the ninth century, when his name should have appeared, but was extended later.

'Kinelm', the fourteenth abbot in the Evesham list, is presumed to have been Cynehelm, an abbot who witnessed all those deeds of Wærferth, bishop of the Hwicce, that are known to have been issued between 899 and 904 and that have survived as genuine and complete texts. On each occasion Cynehelm signed immediately after the bishop.[33] Abbot Cynehelm and Bishop Wærferth also both occur as witnesses to a deed issued in 903 by Edward the Elder king of the Anglo-Saxons, his sister Æthelflæd, and her husband Æthelred 'lord of the Mercians' relating to an estate at Monks Risborough (now in Buckinghamshire); Cynehelm was the second of only two abbots to sign.[34] That document is the first known instance of an abbot of Evesham witnessing a royal charter that did not relate to some place in the territory of the Hwicce; Cynehelm, therefore, seems to have appeared as Bishop Wærferth's personal associate on that occasion instead of as a representative of the Hwiccian clergy. Before he became an abbot Cynehelm seems to have been a deacon in the bishop's *familia*; he appears in that position in

28 S1273.

29 S1272, S1273.

30 J. Harrison, 'The English Reception of Hugh of Saint-Victor's Chronicle', in 'Electronic British Library Jnl 2002' (online), article 1 (33 pp.), p. 22 n. 87.

31 ASC (A).

32 S213.

33 S1279, S1280, S1281, S1283.

34 S367.

897,[35] and in 899 he signs as 'abbot and deacon'.[36] In both of those deeds he signs immediately after the bishop. It does seem probable that in the ninth century, and perhaps before, most of Evesham's abbots had been recruited from the bishop's *familia*, and it is clear that Abbot Cynehelm was in some sense the bishop's assistant. A forged charter of 907 even alleges that he was Wærferth's kinsman,[37] and that, if true, would go some way to explaining his special status.

Cynehelm's successors as abbots of Evesham seem likewise to have been prominent among the bishop's associates. According to the Evesham list Cynehelm was succeeded as abbot by 'Kinath'. He was probably the Cynath that had been a member of the *familia* of Bishop Wærferth and in that role had been among the witnesses of the bishop's leases between 899 and 904; in 904 he signs as a deacon. In the leases it appears, however, that Cynath was not then so prominent a witness as Cynehelm;[38] he was probably younger. Cynath may have become abbot of Evesham by 915 or 916, for an Abbot Cynath was then third among the three abbots who witnessed a grant by Æthelflæd lady of the Mercians, possibly relating to Farnborough in the diocese of the Hwicce and issued at the unidentified Mercian *burh* called 'Weardburh'. Abbot Cynath may have witnessed this quasi-royal charter as an associate of Bishop Æthelhun of the Hwicce, who was another witness.[39] In 925 Abbot Cynath and Bishop Wilfrith of the Hwicce witnessed a grant by Æthelstan king of the Anglo-Saxons, which may have concerned land in Derbyshire. This time Cynath is the only abbot named in the witness-list[40] and again it is presumably only the presence of the bishop of the Hwicce that accounts for Cynath being there; since the deed did not concern any place in the Hwiccian diocese, Cynath seems to have witnessed as the bishop's personal associate, a role that Abbot Cynehelm had apparently fulfilled in Bishop Wærferth's time.

Abbot Cynath remained close to Bishop Wilfrith's successor Koenwald (or Cenwald), who became bishop of the Hwicce in 928.[41] In 929 Koenwald was chosen by Æthelstan, by then king of the English, to head a diplomatic mission to Germany, and the bishop called upon Cynath to be part of the group that went

35 S1442.

36 S1279.

37 S1282.

38 S1279, S1280, S1281, S1283.

39 S225.

40 S395. Cynath also appears in the suspect S394, dated 925.

41 For this paragraph see J. A. Robinson, *The Times of St Dunstan* (Oxford, 1923), p. 39; S. Keynes, 'King Athelstan's Books', *Learning and Literature in Anglo-Saxon England: Studies presented to Peter Clemoes on the Occasion of his Sixty-Fifth Birthday*, ed. M. Lapidge and H. Gneuss (Cambridge, 1985), pp. 143–201 (at pp. 198–200 and pls XIII–XV).

with him on the journey. In Cynath's absence from Evesham his duties there seem to have been performed by an Abbot Eaba ('Ebba'); a temporary interruption of Cynath's abbacy would explain why Cynath's name appears immediately before and immediately after that of Eaba in the Evesham list. One purpose of Bishop Koenwald's journey was to present two of King Æthelstan's half-sisters before Henry I, the king of Germany, as possible brides for his young son Otto. Of the two girls Henry had suggested Eadgyth as the better match, but Otto was allowed to choose between her and her sister (or half-sister) Ælfgifu. Both girls presumably travelled to Germany in Koenwald's party, for it was not until they got there that Otto saw and chose Eadgyth. The couple were soon married and Eadgyth became queen when her husband succeeded to the throne in 936; in 2008 her bones were discovered in Magdeburg cathedral.[42]

The other object of Bishop Koenwald's mission was to visit German monasteries and to present them with expensive gifts from King Æthelstan, and it is in connection with that part of the mission that Abbot Cynath is expressly named. The full itinerary of the bishop's party has not been recorded but the group is known to have travelled as far as the abbey of Sankt-Gallen (now in Switzerland), which is about 800 miles from Evesham by land and sea. Koenwald and his companions arrived there on 15 October 929 and stayed for four days. On 16 October, which was the feast of the Deposition of St Gall, they were present in the great abbey church and there Koenwald placed a large sum of money on the altar and gave another sum to the abbey's brethren for their use. In return the monks of St Gall entered the names of King Æthelstan and other English notables in their book of remembrance together with those of Bishop Koenwald and his companions, to be prayed for every year for ever. Among the names was written that of 'Kenod abba', the *d* presumably representing the Old English character ð (eth); and that is the direct evidence for Abbot Cynath's presence in the bishop's entourage in Germany. The English party seems to have returned home by the following year, for in 930 King Æthelstan is said to have granted an estate at Dumbleton and Aston Somerville, both near Evesham, to Abbot Cynath and his successors.[43]

By 931 Cynath had been succeeded at Evesham by Abbot Eadwine and between then and 934 Eadwine travelled with Bishop Koenwald to meetings of King Æthelstan's *witenagemot* ('council') in various parts of Wessex, and there he and the bishop witnessed the king's charters. Eadwine regularly witnessed them in those years and he usually signed second among the four to six abbots who were present at the meetings.[44] Eadwine's association with Bishop Koenwald in the

[42] *The Times*, 23 Oct. 2010, p. 64.

[43] S404 (spurious but probably based on genuine material).

[44] S413, S416, S417, S418, S418a, S422, S425.

conduct of King Æthelstan's business in places that lay far from Evesham and from the diocese of the Hwicce is consistent with the supposition that the abbots of Evesham remained personally attached to their bishop after they had been recruited from his *familia*. To him, it seems, they owed their status at Evesham and at the king's council.

CHAPTER 5

Decay and revival

A profitable estate

In the early tenth century the cares of the abbot of Evesham were considerable. He was playing a necessary part in the bishop's business and indirectly in the king's, and at the same time he and his minster community were lords of an enviable landed estate that was indeed envied. By the 930s the minster had nearly 10,000 acres (about 4,000 hectares) of productive land on the south side of the Avon and nearly 5,000 acres on its own side of the river, where much of the landscape was wooded.[1] The woodland too was productive; it was a source of timber, fuel, game, and honey, and of grazing for pigs. By then the church of Evesham may also have had some outlying estates, probably in the nearby wooded Arden district, and twenty miles south of Evesham in the Cotswolds,[2] all within the territory of the Hwicce.

Not only were the minster's estates extensive but parts of them were also economically vigorous and increasingly valuable. It seems likely that a phase of warmer and dryer weather[3] had for some time been causing the population on the south side of the river to grow and the land to be farmed more intensively. It is by postulating the growth of population and the higher productivity of the land that one may perhaps account for a pre-Conquest process that has left evidence of itself in local documents and on the modern map; that is to say, the division of early land units into smaller but still viable estates (Fig. 3). It was a process in which 'Wycweon' was divided to make Childswickham and Wickhamford, Bretforton was split into an Upper End and a Lower End (which were so named by c.1300),[4] Hampton into Great and Little Hampton, Honeybourne into Church Honeybourne and Cow Honeybourne, and Littleton into North, Middle, and South Littleton. North of the river the same process seems to have taken place. The Twyford land unit was divided up before 1086 and Lenchwick, Norton, and Chadbury were then put together as

1 Cox 1975. The acreages are calculated from *VCH Worcs.* IV, pp. 466, 472.

2 Clarke 2012a, pp. 129–30.

3 P. Dark, *The Environment of Britain in the First Millennium AD* (London, 2000), pp. 27–8.

4 Dugdale, *Mon.* II, p. 32 (for the date see *VCH Worcs.* II, p. 362).

the manor of Lenchwick; the Twyford stretch of the salt way became the boundary between the township of Evesham on the one hand and those of Lenchwick and Norton on the other.[5] Bretforton and Littleton were probably subdivided by the early tenth century, because their divisions were separately assessed for the hidation that seems to have taken place at that time.[6] Although the subdivision of early land units in the Vale of Evesham cannot be dated exactly, it would have taken place before the divisions acquired their separate common-field systems.[7]

When an estate was divided each part could devolve to a different holder, and instances of separate tenure can be found in the documents. Thus at Childswickham the place-name may allow its tenure to be traced back to the early eighth century if not earlier, for in the divided 'Wycweon' Childswickham took its distinctive name from a *cild*. In Old English *cild* meant a 'youth', 'younger son', or 'young nobleman',[8] and a man who would have fitted the description was Æthelric, a son of Oshere king of the Hwicce.[9] Æthelric (fl.736)[10] was said to have held Childswickham and in 706 to have given Evesham minster eight hides (*mansae* or *manentes*) there.[11] The documents relating to the transaction are late and some of them were evidently concocted to support Evesham's title to a lost estate;[12] the details of the grant are therefore uncertain. But even if Æthelric did not give Childswickham to Evesham, or did not do so in 706, he may nevertheless have been the *cild* who held it. If he was, that would be evidence for the early existence of Childswickham as a separate estate and thus for the early division of the former 'Wycweon' land unit. There can be reasonable doubts about the period at which Childswickham became distinct. Nevertheless, the separate tenure of such estates, as divisions of earlier land units, was well advanced by the early tenth century when the Worcestershire–Gloucestershire boundary was drawn. The boundary placed Wickhamford and Church Honeybourne in Worcestershire because their lord, Evesham minster, was based in that shire; but the counterparts of those estates — that is to say, Childswickham and Cow Honeybourne — then had other lords and were assigned to Gloucestershire.[13]

5 S1591a, S1599 (interpreted by Hooke 1990, pp. 377–82, 408–17); DB, fol. 175v.

6 Cox 1975, pp. 26–32.

7 Below, ch. 8.

8 A. H. Smith, *The Place-Names of Gloucestershire*, II, EPNS 39 (Cambridge, 1964), p. 6.

9 S53.

10 S89.

11 Byrhtferth, pp. 256–7; Dugdale, *Mon.* II, p. 14; T. Marlb. pp. 34–5, 130–31; S1174 (spurious).

12 Darlington 1933, p. 190 (from 'Evesham N'). The titles 'Evesham A' to 'Evesham Q' (omitting 'I') for the sixteen estate surveys in Harley 3763 and Vesp. B.XXIV are now in general use: see *DB Worcs.* (Thorn), app. IV.

13 Cox 1975, pp. 26–32.

The process of estate division wrought changes in the chief settlements from which the original land units had been managed, because each new subdivision needed a chief settlement of its own. In some cases, when an old land unit was divided two new centres were established, one for each of the new divisions, and the old central settlement was then allowed to shrink. That seems to be what happened at Wickhamford and Childswickham, where new central villages were established near the sites of prosperous Romano-British houses,[14] while the original nucleus of the old 'Wycweon', which was apparently at Murcot, was allowed to decline. Likewise the settlement at Twyford, which had a Romano-British origin, was allowed to shrink after a boundary was drawn through it. In other cases, however, an old estate centre kept its site and status but was divided into two parts by the boundary that was set between the new divisions. Each part of the nucleus was then to be found near the edge of the division to which it belonged. For instance, the medieval villages of Church and Cow Honeybourne were adjacent to each other but were probably once a single settlement at the centre of the early Honeybourne estate; division of Honeybourne into two estates seems to have caused its chief settlement to split into adjoining but independent villages, with the estate boundary (later a county boundary) drawn between them.

After c.701 fundamental changes in the geography of administration and settlement on the minster's estates would not have unfolded spontaneously, or solely by agreement among the tenants. They could only have taken place with the abbot's authority or under his direction. Thus by the middle of the tenth century the strategic management of the minster's estates demanded an investment of careful thought, and from time to time a removal of the abbot's attention from religious matters. It was an unavoidable distraction.

A failing monastery

After 934 Abbot Eadwine's name disappears from the lists of witnesses to King Æthelstan's charters. That does not necessarily mean that Eadwine had died, for the abbots who had been accustomed to sign with him also disappear from the witness-lists at the same time; in fact, Eadwine is likely to have survived the 930s, because the Evesham list of abbots continues to the reign of King Edmund (939–46) and no successor to Eadwine appears on it. After Eadwine, however, there would be no more abbots for thirty years. When King Æthelstan died in 939 Edmund his half-brother succeeded to a kingdom that had latterly come to embrace the whole of England, but he was only eighteen years old, and in the north and in the east Midlands the country was under immediate threat from

14 Reynolds 1971; Hurst and Patrick 2012, pp. 39–48.

the Viking rulers of Dublin. For practical purposes Edmund urgently needed to delegate some of his powers to regional leaders, as ealdormen, and for that reason in 940 he appointed Ealhhelm, a thegn (a rich and influential holder of land), as ealdorman over an area that probably corresponded to the former sub-kingdom of the Hwicce.[15] Since Evesham lay within that area the minster then became subject to Ealhhelm instead of directly to the king, and, soon afterwards, possibly in 941,[16] King Edmund gave the minster and its estates wholly to Ealhhelm, Abbot Eadwine having died.[17] The precise moment at which control of the minster would pass from the king to an ealdorman could not have been foreseen in the 930s but some such event may already have been inevitable; it just happened to be precipitated around 941 by a national emergency.

When Ealhhelm acquired the minster it was already failing as a monastery — that is to say, as a place of spiritual seclusion — but it was still able to provide priests to attend to the pastoral care of the local people. The readiness with which secular clergy had been drawn from the bishop's *familia* during the previous 100 years to become abbots of Evesham shows plainly how secular was the minster's personnel in the early tenth century. Moreover, the abbots' long involvement in the episcopal and royal administration, though it had contributed to the minster's prestige, had required the abbots to take increasingly frequent and lengthy absences from the minster community. Meanwhile, management of the estates was taking up valuable time for those left at Evesham. In the circumstances it is probable that the abbot's role as the ultimate spiritual director at Evesham was not being adequately fulfilled; he would have been too busy to guide the minster community towards a contemplative life even if his secular background had equipped him to do so. Whatever the particular situation at Evesham, the monastic ideal had already been widely abandoned by then in other English churches even while some individuals still cherished a respect for it. No direct evidence for the presence of monks has been found in any of the minster communities of the Hwiccian diocese in the late ninth and early tenth century, and none even in those minsters that were headed by men that used the title 'abbot'.[18] Asser, King Alfred's biographer, was claiming by 893 that for some time in Wessex and elsewhere 'the desire for the monastic life had been totally lacking'. He suggested that one cause might have been 'the people's enormous abundance of riches of every kind',[19] and one

15 S470; Hart 1975, p. 328; Williams 1982, p. 145.

16 'De abbatibus Eveshamiae, &c.', Dugdale, *Mon.* II, p. 26.

17 T. Marlb. pp. 140–41.

18 Tinti 2010, pp. 15, 17–18, 228–43.

19 S. Keynes and M. Lapidge, trans., *Alfred the Great: Asser's* Life of King Alfred *and Other Contemporary Sources* (Harmondsworth, 1983), p. 103, from W. H. Stevenson, ed., *Asser's Life of King Alfred* (Oxford, 1904), pp. 80–81.

may add that such abundance in the hands of Evesham minster can hardly have been helpful to any seeker after personal poverty there. Certainly England had few truly monastic communities by 930, if there were any at all. That was so not only in regions whose minsters had suffered directly from Viking attacks; it seems also to have been true in the diocese of the Hwicce, where the impact of Viking raids was not great and where the continued existence of old minsters was more evident.[20]

Even so, the Evesham minster community of the 930s seems to have consisted of men who were called 'monks', however tenuous their right to the name, for Ealdorman Ealhhelm is said to have dismissed the 'monks' after he acquired the minster, and to have reconstituted it as a house of secular priests (*canones*). He is further said to have assigned some of the minster estates to the priests and to have kept the rest for his own use.[21] It meant the abandonment of any remaining aspirations to monastic life at Evesham and involved a significant seizure of church land. But Bishop Koenwald of the Hwicce, who had been close to the last two abbots of Evesham, Cynath and Eadwine, is not known to have voiced any opposition to the new arrangements. Koenwald may even have accepted that the changes could be justified; Ealdorman Ealhhelm needed estates to maintain his household, to finance his regional administration on behalf of the king, and to reward his subordinates and supporters, while the old minster had owned far more land than it needed for the sustenance of its members, for the maintenance of its buildings, and for the provision of pastoral care in the neighbourhood. What is more, the church of Evesham was over 200 years old and had probably become as tired and inactive as any unreformed institution that had existed so long. Its renewal as a community of secular priests may therefore have been as much in the public interest as in that of Ealhhelm personally. Nor, in the context of England as a whole, was there anything exceptional or catastrophic about the changes that took place at Evesham c.941. Although the formal secularization of the minster probably seemed sudden at the time, it had been delayed for longer at Evesham than elsewhere; since the ninth century many minsters, having failed to sustain a way of life that was monastic in the ordinary sense of the word, had been deprived of some or all of their lands but had continued thereafter as useful secular churches.[22]

Some of Evesham minster's former estates, after they had been annexed by Ealdorman Ealhhelm, were dispersed over the next thirty years among various landholders. Thus in 949 King Eadred granted lands at Bourton on the Water,

[20] Knowles 1963a, pp. 31–6; Blair 2005, pp. 306–8, 342–6; Foot 2006, pp. 339–47.

[21] T. Marlb. pp. 140–41.

[22] Blair 2005, pp. 323–9.

Maugersbury, and Daylesford, all in the Gloucestershire Cotswolds, to Wulfric 'ripa' a thegn;[23] according to later Evesham sources those lands had once belonged to the minster.[24] King Edmund's son Edgar, who became king of the Mercians and Northumbrians in 957 and king of the English in 959, allegedly confirmed to Oswulf bishop of Ramsbury (c.950–970) the Dumbleton estate that had been given to Abbot Cynath.[25] A later Evesham chronicler alleged that Oswulf was among a succession of people who 'possessed' the minster after its secularization;[26] on that point the narrative is vague and possibly confused but the community of minster priests must have included a resident head and it is therefore possible that Oswulf became an absentee superior over him.[27] Meanwhile, the Evesham priests presumably lived off the estates that Ealhhelm had assigned to them, and they probably continued, with the head of their house, to respect the authority of the bishop of the Hwicce.

The Benedictine revival

Ealdorman Ealhhelm is last mentioned in 951.[28] Those former estates of Evesham minster that were then in his hands probably passed within a few years to his son Ælfhere, and in 956 Ælfhere became ealdorman over the same part of Mercia as his father had ruled.[29] By then, however, continental ideas of a purified monasticism based on the 'Rule of St Benedict' were slowly making their way to England, and in some thoughtful minds they mingled there with nostalgia for the golden days of English monasticism, powerfully evoked in the narratives of Bede and his contemporaries and perceived to have been in the seventh century. At Evesham Abbot Cynath (fl. 916–30) must have become aware of continental monasticism, for he had taken part in Bishop Koenwald's tour of German monasteries in 929. Cynath would have seen at first hand how the monks of St Gall continued to observe the 'Rule' when in many other places it had lapsed, and Koenwald made a personal decision to take monastic vows.[30] Koenwald remained bishop of the Hwicce until c.958, but the individual inclinations of such as himself and Cynath could not be translated into a Benedictine reform of their churches as long as the support of the king and his ealdormen for such a course was lacking. Some progress may have

23 S550.
24 S935, S1238 (both spurious); T. Marlb. pp. 144–9; DB, fol. 165r.
25 S404 (spurious but probably based on genuine material).
26 T. Marlb. pp. 140–41.
27 Barrow 2008, p. 221.
28 S558.
29 Williams 1982, pp. 155, 169.
30 Tinti 2010, pp. 16–17.

been expected when Koenwald was succeeded briefly as bishop of the Hwicce by Dunstan, an abbot who had reformed Glastonbury abbey on Benedictine lines and had since spent two years on the continent observing monastic life there. But it was only when the young King Edgar promoted Dunstan to the archbishopric of Canterbury in 959 that the emerging monastic reform movement acquired the status of national policy.

The reforms were to be led by three bishops chosen and backed by Edgar. One of them was Archbishop Dunstan. Another was Æthelwold, Dunstan's protégé and another student of continental monasticism. He had been tutor to the young Edgar, and Edgar as king appointed him bishop of Winchester in 963. The third was Oswald, who had also studied on the continent and whom Edgar appointed to succeed Dunstan at Worcester in 961. Early in his reign the king had thus placed Benedictine reformers in three of the greatest English sees, and during the lives of the three bishops a number of ancient minsters in southern England were deliberately transformed into Benedictine monasteries on the continental model. It was Bishop Oswald, supported by King Edgar, who carried out the reform at Evesham,[31] where the priests were replaced with monks who were subject to the 'Rule of St Benedict' and were governed by an abbot called Osweard. At about the same time the church of Evesham regained some of its lost estates, particularly those that Ealhhelm had not granted away[32] and which had therefore passed into the hands of his son Ealdorman Ælfhere.[33] The precise chronology of the reform has not been established but Abbot Osweard was in post at Evesham by 970 when he witnessed some of the king's charters.[34] The date may imply that Osweard's appointment as abbot had been delayed until the death in 970 of Oswulf bishop of Ramsbury, who may have remained until then as a non-resident superior over the minster priests.[35]

In order to strengthen the new monasteries in Worcestershire that were created out of old minsters by the Benedictine reform, King Edgar reorganized and redefined the shire's ancient hundreds, which were its subdivisions for secular administration. The purpose of the changes was to prevent the Worcestershire lands and tenants of individual Benedictine houses being inconveniently split between different hundreds. Thus were formed the triple hundred of Oswaldslow (containing the lands of Worcester cathedral priory) and the triple hundred of Pershore (for those of Pershore abbey); the boundaries of 'Fissesberg' hundred were allowed

31 Cox 2002.

32 T. Marlb. pp. 142–3.

33 Williams 1982, pp. 159, 169.

34 S777, S781.

35 Barrow 2008, pp. 221–2.

to remain unchanged, however, because they already enclosed all the Evesham abbey estates that lay in Worcestershire.[36] The formal secular powers that Edgar allowed to the heads of the Worcestershire monasteries in the assemblies or courts of their respective hundreds were not as great as their successors in office would afterwards allege. Nevertheless, it is not difficult to imagine the weight of influence that sole landlords such as Bishop Oswald in Oswaldslow or Abbot Osweard in 'Fissesberg' would have had over the daily life and conduct of the people.[37]

[36] Cox 1975, pp. 35–40; *DB Worcs.* (Williams), pp. 13–17, 32–7.

[37] P. Wormald, 'Lordship and Justice in the Early English Kingdom: Oswaldslow revisited', *Property and Power in the Early Middle Ages*, ed. W. Davies and P. Fouracre (Cambridge, 1995), pp. 114–36; P. Wormald, 'Oswaldslow: An "Immunity"?', Brooks and Cubitt 1996, pp. 117–28.

CHAPTER 6

On the defensive

Fortified by history

DURING Osweard's short abbacy Ecgwine's original church building suffered a sudden collapse. In other places the minster churches of Ecgwine's time, if built of stone, were solid structures; at Evesham the fall may therefore have been far from catastrophic. After it happened, however, the event was invested with great significance because the container that had held Ecgwine's remains had been unharmed by the crash, a circumstance that would be represented some forty years later as a miracle. The relics that were rescued were in a receptacle that was later described by the imprecise terms *locellus* and *vasculum*. All that one can say about its appearance is that the container was rectangular, for it was alleged to have survived without a mark 'either on the front or the back' ('nec ante nec retro'); and that it was portable because the monks were said to have picked it up from the rubble. A possible interpretation of those small observations is that before the crash Ecgwine's bones had been translated from their original resting place to a box-like reliquary, which was kept inside the church.[1] If so, the cult of Ecgwine may be said to have started at Evesham before the sudden structural accident took place, whether or not he had yet been accorded the title of saint. There is no evidence, however, as to precisely how old or how mature the cult may have been by the 970s; perhaps it had assumed significance only with the Benedictine reform. Be that as it may, it seems that the Benedictine abbey's new sense of purpose in the 970s was being sustained not only by the wholehearted monasticism that had recently been introduced but also by a culture of reverence for the house's remote origins in the great monastic age immortalized by Bede. The retrieval of Ecgwine's remains from the rubble of his church may have seemed to Osweard and his monks an obvious analogy for the revival of Ecgwine's monastic ideals after the demise of the old minster. It was a parallel so striking as to account for the exaggerated terms in which the rescue was later reported. The monastic revival at Evesham under Osweard may thus have caused the cult of St Ecgwine to be established or

1 Byrhtferth, pp. 300–303.

enhanced[2] and it is perhaps no coincidence that in the forty years after the reform some alleged miracles effected by Ecgwine and his relics began to be noted.[3]

It was probably also in Osweard's time, and thus during the Benedictine revival at Evesham, that the monks chose to preserve a numbered list of the abbots who had governed the minster from its foundation to its secularization c.941. The list survives only in a thirteenth-century copy[4] and its completeness and accuracy may never be fully confirmed. Nevertheless, we have gathered from external sources that certain names on the list correspond to those of men that really existed at the right dates and appeared in the right contexts to be identified as abbots of Evesham. The Evesham list is not unlike a list of Glastonbury abbots that was completed in the tenth century. The Glastonbury list may be datable to the year 969[5] and if that is so it is virtually contemporary with the Benedictine reform at Evesham. Glastonbury and Evesham may therefore have preserved their lists at one time and in the same spirit, that of fresh pride in their past. In the late tenth century the Evesham list would have reflected and nourished the nostalgia that animated the Benedictine reform. It would also have provided documentary support to an argument: that the reconstituted abbey was not a novel creation but was the heir to a continuous monastic tradition, one upheld by a succession of abbots that had only recently and wrongfully been broken. Together the Evesham list and the cult of the founder are signs that by the late tenth century Evesham abbey had come to take sustenance from what it could preserve of its past. Indeed, the plausible materials that were used to furnish the new abbey with historical roots proved so helpful that for centuries thereafter Evesham would invoke a version of its own history whenever it needed to advance and defend its interests.

Setbacks under King Edgar's sons

Abbot Osweard remained in post in 974[6] but everything at Evesham rested precariously on the support of the king, and the following year came news that King Edgar had died, apparently of natural causes and in his early thirties. With Edgar gone the abbot's position weakened rapidly, for Edgar's elder son Edward had succeeded to the throne as a boy of about thirteen and was in no position to

2 A. Thacker, 'Saint Making and Relic Collecting by Oswald and his Communities', Brooks and Cubitt 1996, pp. 244–68 (at p. 261).

3 Byrhtferth, pp. 280–303. On the datable miracles see ibid. pp. 291 n. 81, 300 n. 112.

4 T. Marlb. pp. 138–41.

5 S. Foot, 'Glastonbury's Early Abbots', *The Archaeology and History of Glastonbury Abbey: Essays in Honour of the Ninetieth Birthday of C. A. Ralegh Radford*, ed. L. Abrams and J. P. Carley (Woodbridge, 1991), pp. 163–89 (at pp. 165–6, 168, 187–9).

6 S795.

offer the personal protection and active support that his father had bestowed on the reformed abbeys. Abbot Osweard soon faced claims from the dispossessed recipients of lands that had belonged to the old Evesham minster; under the late King Edgar they had been made to surrender them to the new abbey. At first the abbey was successful in contesting some of the claims in local courts,[7] but without the essential element of royal intervention Evesham could not resist the most powerful among the claimants, Ælfhere son of Ealhhelm, who was by then ealdorman of the whole of Mercia, including the Hwicce.[8] Ælfhere had a quite natural desire to retrieve estates that had belonged to his late father Ealhhelm and to himself, but he was driven also by personal animosity towards Bishop Oswald of Worcester, who had refounded Evesham abbey in Edgar's reign.

The reasons for Ealdorman Ælfhere's dislike of the bishop were not religious but political and local. After the death of King Edgar the succession to the crown had been disputed and it was only a section of the nobility that had favoured the elder son Edward, who in fact became king, and Oswald was of that party. Ælfhere had belonged to the unsuccessful opposing party, which had wanted Edgar's younger son Æthelred to succeed. It also rankled with Ælfhere that Oswald's power and prestige rivalled his own in the land of the Hwicce, not least in the triple hundred of Oswaldslow and in the hundreds attached to the monasteries that Oswald had reformed at Evesham and Pershore. It was allegedly with the backing of Queen Ælfthryth, Æthelred's mother,[9] that Ealdorman Ælfhere proceeded to close down the reformed monasteries of Oswald's diocese, not only at Evesham but also at Pershore, Winchcombe, and Deerhurst.[10] At Evesham Ælfhere acquired the abbey and all the remaining monastic estates, possibly in 977,[11] and he installed a few priests there in place of the monks. The precise date of this reversal of the Benedictine reform cannot be confirmed and it may in fact have taken place in the early years of King Æthelred, who had succeeded in 978 at the age of no more than twelve following the murder of his half-brother King Edward.

The priests were to remain at Evesham for another twenty years while Ælfhere assigned to himself the abbey's estates at Evesham and Offenham and the rest of the estates that lay contiguous to them, which together comprised what had been the early-tenth-century core of the minster's lands and of 'Fissesberg' hundred. He granted one of the abbey's more distant estates, at Ombersley in north Worcestershire, to one of his brothers and gave another detached abbey estate at

7 T. Marlb. pp. 80–83.

8 Williams 1982, p. 157.

9 *Crowland Descriptio*, p. 54.

10 Williams 1982, pp. 160, 166–8.

11 'De abbatibus Eveshamiae, &c.', Dugdale, *Mon.* II, p. 26.

Binton in Warwickshire to some of his thegns. For the maintenance of the priests at Evesham Ælfhere assigned other abbey lands, which seem likewise to have lain at a distance from Evesham. Afterwards the priests granted some of them, such as Wixford and Mappleborough in Warwickshire, to local men of importance in order, it was said, to ensure their support against any future attempt to restore the monks to Evesham;[12] evidently the reversal of the Benedictine reform at Evesham was itself insecure.

Before his death in 983, Ealdorman Ælfhere gave the church, together with the former abbey lands that he himself held, to a certain Freothegar, who was later described as a monk and styled 'abbot'.[13] It is possible that Freothegar was a former Abingdon monk of that name, who was later remembered as the abbot of an unspecified house.[14] It is not clear whether Ælfhere or Freothegar intended to restore monastic life at Evesham, but if Ælfhere's action was that of a dying man afraid for his soul, and if Freothegar was a monk, then that may have been their hope. Abbot Freothegar tried to gain possession of those abbey estates that the Evesham priests still held, which suggests at least that he wanted the priests to go. He was unable to make them part with their lands, however, and soon agreed to give the church, with Ælfhere's former lands there, to Godwine, 'a man of great influence', who was probably Ealdorman Ælfhere's nephew.[15] In exchange Godwine gave Freothegar an estate at Towcester in Northamptonshire and paid King Æthelred 300 gold mancuses (£37 10s) for his consent to the transaction. It was a good sum of money for a mere portion of the abbey's lands and confirms that the estate as a whole had once amounted to an enviable endowment. The priests continued to serve the church under Godwine's patronage and to enjoy their portion of the old abbey lands. Godwine afterwards relinquished control of the church to the king but he remained in possession of his portion of the lands, formerly Ealdorman Ælfhere's. King Æthelred then granted the patronage of the church to Æthelsige bishop of Sherborne, but Æthelsige left the country on royal business in 991 and apparently never returned, whereupon the king entrusted it to a Bishop 'Æthelstan', probably Ælfstan bishop of London. Why Æthelred should have given the patronage to those bishops instead of to Oswald, who had founded the Benedictine abbey c.970 and who would remain as bishop of Worcester until his death in 992, is an interesting question. Money may have been paid by the new patrons; and Æthelred may never have been reconciled with Bishop Oswald, who had opposed his claim to the crown in 975. We can only be sure that everything

12 T. Marlb. pp. 142–5; Cox 1975, p. 40.

13 This paragraph is based on T. Marlb. pp. 144–7.

14 Knowles et al. 2001, pp. 298–9.

15 Williams 1982, pp. 170–72.

positive that might happen at Evesham continued to be conditional on the will and competence of the king.

The monks reinstated

Evesham had therefore much to hope for when King Æthelred, after years of apparent negligence, was persuaded from the early 990s to lavish favours on the English Church. He had eventually come to believe that his largesse would help to secure God's protection from the Viking attacks that his own measures had failed to prevent.[16] It was evident by then that his father Edgar, a godly king, had enjoyed a period of respite from the Vikings that Æthelred could only long for. With that realization and change of heart Æthelred reinstated the church of Evesham as a Benedictine monastery soon after the death c.995 of Ælfstan bishop of London, who had probably been the church's latest patron. The king's action proved to be no temporary expedient, for Æthelred did not withdraw his support from Evesham abbey during the twenty years of life that remained to him. The king placed the revived abbey under the patronage of the bishop of Worcester, Oswald's successor Ealdwulf, and the Evesham priests were finally replaced by monks under an abbot called Ælfric,[17] presumably appointed by the bishop in his role as patron. Ælfric was in office by 997 when he was at Wantage in Berkshire to witness, at the same time as the bishop, one of the king's charters relating to Wiltshire.[18]

It was probably Abbot Ælfric who began the practice of recording the day and month of death of each monk or friend of the abbey in a written necrology (a list of notable deaths) with a view to the perpetual commemoration of their anniversaries. A local record of that kind had been enjoined c.970 in the *Regularis concordia* ('Monastic Agreement'), the national agreement of King Edgar's time that guided the conduct of the reformed Benedictine monasteries in England.[19] In the only surviving copy of the Evesham necrology the earliest abbot of Evesham mentioned is Ælfric's successor Ælfgar, but deaths in November have been omitted from the copy;[20] and since Ælfric died in November he may have appeared in the original necrology. None of the abbots before Ælfric was commemorated in

16 *ODNB.*

17 T. Marlb. pp. 146–7.

18 S891.

19 *Regularis concordia*, p. 67.

20 J. Gerchow, *Die Gedenkenüberlieferung der Angelsachsen, mit einem Katalog der Libri Vitae und Necrologien* (Berlin, 1988), p. 359. See ibid. pp. 292–9 on the list as a whole (British Library, Lansdowne MS 427, fols 1r–19v, copied from British Library, Cotton MS Vitellius E.XII, fols 73r–83v, before its destruction by fire).

November[21] so none of their names was ever there. It therefore seems reasonable to suggest that Abbot Ælfric instituted the list and that when he died he became the first abbot to be entered in it. A place in the necrology could be represented to potential lay benefactors as a meaningful reward for supporting the revived monastery, because the abbey promised those to be named in it that they would be prayed for every year until the end of the world. It was thus a powerful instrument of persuasion and remained so, for it was still being kept up to date in the fourteenth century. Moreover, by starting a necrology of its notable associates, Evesham had found another way to preserve the best of its past. By also completing the list of abbots and venerating Ecgwine's remains, the revived abbey was able in a short time to build a reputation for ancient and venerable spiritual power.

Ælfric was buried at Evesham and he happens to be the earliest of the abbots of whom any physical remains have been identified. It is not clear whether the grave originally lay inside a building or in the open, but the remains were disturbed about 100 years after his death, during construction of the Romanesque abbey church. They were still identifiable as his, perhaps by an inscription, and were then reverently reburied in the north transept of the new church, with the inclusion of a new lead plate inscribed HIC REQVIESCIT DOMNVS ABBAS ÆLFRICVS HVIVS LOCI ANIMA SVA REQVIESCAT IN PACE AMEN ('Here rests Ælfric lord abbot of this place. May his soul rest in peace. Amen'). The bones rested there until 1823, when they were uncovered again during archaeological excavations[22] and fragments of his grave-clothes and boots were removed; they and the inscribed plate later passed to the Almonry Museum (now the Almonry Heritage Centre) in Evesham. One other surviving fragment of the tenth-century abbey has been identified, having been discovered at the site in the early nineteenth century. Now kept in the Almonry Heritage Centre, it is a small flat piece of oolitic limestone irregularly broken from a panel, and is carved on the face with an interlace pattern in shallow relief. It dates from the ninth or tenth century but its original setting cannot be determined.[23] It may conceivably be a fragment of a screen, a sarcophagus, or a shrine.

Abbot Ælfric was succeeded by Ælfgar, presumably the abbot of that name who witnessed two charters of King Æthelred in 1002, one relating to Gloucestershire and Worcestershire and the other to Sussex; the bishop of Worcester also attests in both documents.[24] It would seem that Ælfgar, like Ælfric before him and like

[21] British Library, Lansdowne MS 427, fols 20r–38v (where Ælfric's commemoration appears on fol. 37v), copied from British Library, Cotton MS Vitellius E.XVII, fols 241r–246v (formerly fols 243r–248v) before the fire.

[22] Cox 2010a, pp. 60–61.

[23] Bryant 2012, p. 357 and illus. no. 634.

[24] S901, S904. No other Abbot Ælfgar of that date appears in Knowles et al. 2001 or in PASE.

Abbot Eadwine more than sixty years before them, was sometimes called far from Evesham on royal business and that he, like them, acted in association with his bishop. With an abbot so well placed the abbey may have attained a strong position, for when Abbot Ælfgar died Abbot Brihtmær succeeded him and after several attempts obtained a court judgment that he could buy back from Godwine the estates that Godwine had received from Abbot Freothegar, and for the same sum as Godwine had then given the king, 300 gold mancuses.[25] At some time between 1002 and 1014 the bishop of Worcester (either Ealdwulf or his successor Wulfstan I) seems to have given to Evesham a relic of Bishop Oswald, an arm bone that Ealdwulf had removed from Oswald's grave at Worcester in 1002. The gift recalled the fact that Oswald, now a saint, was Evesham's founder and heavenly patron on a level with St Ecgwine, but it also reminded the abbey in a tangible way that it was subject to the current bishop as an arm is to the body.[26]

Abbot Brihtmær's successor was Æthelwine, who left to become bishop of Wells in 1013;[27] it was a distinction that reflected well on his standing as abbot of Evesham. As a result of his departure, however, the abbacy was vacant in January 1014 when King Æthelred took refuge in Normandy during the invasion of England by Swegn Forkbeard king of Denmark. Godwine seems to have taken advantage of the vacancy and the king's absence to recover the Evesham abbey lands that he had formerly held. When Æthelred returned a few months later, however, the king was able to fill the vacant abbacy by appointing Ælfweard, a monk from St Oswald's foundation at Ramsey in Huntingdonshire.[28] The right to appoint the abbot, or at least to approve his election, had passed from the bishop of Worcester back to the king, with whose successors it would remain until the Dissolution. In 1014, however, the affairs of the abbey and the kingdom remained disturbed by the Danish threat, and it seems that Evesham abbey was directly assailed around that time by Danes in search of tribute or booty. The shrine of St Ecgwine was a tempting object, not for its contents but because of its covering of precious stones and golden-yellow metal, which probably consisted of applied silver-gilt plates. Such was their value that some Danes 'in the area' (*circumcirca*) robbed the abbey to get them. But the spoliation at Evesham cannot be securely dated and its circumstances are not well recorded. The likelihood is that it occurred in or immediately before Abbot Ælfweard's time, for he was the first abbot that sought to replace the damaged shrine.[29] If so, there were at least

25 T. Marlb. pp. 146–9.
26 Cox 2002.
27 Knowles et al. 2001, p. 46.
28 T. Marlb. pp. 148–9.
29 Ibid. pp. 72–3.

two occasions when the damage could have been done. One was in 1013, when the church of Worcester was stripped of precious metals in order that it could pay its share of an 'almost insupportable tribute' to Swegn the Danish king, who had invaded England that summer;[30] Evesham abbey may have been forced to pay a share of the same tribute and to allow Ecgwine's shrine to be stripped. Another possible occasion for the damage was at the beginning of 1016, when the Danish leader Cnut son of Swegn crossed the Thames into Mercia with a large body of horsemen. Entering Warwickshire, they plundered and burned and killed wherever they went[31] and they may have attacked Worcestershire at the same time, for the Danish earl Hákon was later accused of taking lands from the church of Worcester 'after that region had been plundered and most cruelly laid waste'.[32] Ecgwine's shrine could have been despoiled then, and Ælfweard powerless to prevent it.

30 Hemming, I, pp. 248–9; J. Worc. II, pp. 474–5.

31 ASC (DEF); J. Worc. II, pp. 480–81.

32 Hemming, I, p. 251.

CHAPTER 7

Abbot Ælfweard and King Cnut

IN 1016 Evesham's affairs were about to take a turn for the better. King Æthelred had enabled Abbot Ælfweard to retrieve control of the estates that Godwine had taken, and although Æthelred's support for Evesham came to an end with the king's death in April 1016, while the affairs of the kingdom were still in crisis, Godwine's claim on the abbey's estates was finally extinguished later that year when he was killed in battle against Cnut at Ashingdon in Essex.[1] The battle, and the death soon afterwards of Æthelred's son King Edmund, resulted in Cnut becoming king of England and in a gradual return to relative peace and order. A succession of capable abbots and supportive kings would then give Evesham abbey decades of stability and, with it, the opportunity to prosper.

Cnut's reign began particularly well for Evesham because Abbot Ælfweard was already a kinsman (*consanguineus*) of the new king.[2] The connection was probably through Cnut's first wife Ælfgifu of Northampton, an English noblewoman whom Cnut had married on an earlier expedition to England. It was presumably to Ælfgifu and not to Cnut that the English abbot Ælfweard was related by blood[3] and it may be relevant to observe that the first element of the names Ælfweard and Ælfgifu was the same; that was the English custom among close relatives. If Ælfweard and Ælfgifu were related, both may also have become allied by marriage to Leofric, who was earl of Mercia by 1032, for Leofric's son Ælfgar seems to have married a kinswoman of Ælfgifu, perhaps in the late 1020s.[4] When Cnut, as the abbey's royal patron, decided to place Evesham under the personal protection of the 'Lady Ælfgifu' some time before 1023[5] he may have been mindful that she had a family connection with the abbot. In any case, Ælfgifu of Northampton would have been a fair choice for the position. By 1023 Cnut had been married for some

1 T. Marlb. pp. 148–51.
2 T. Marlb. pp. 150–51.
3 A. Williams, '"Cockles amongst the Wheat": Danes and English in the Western Midlands in the First Half of the Eleventh Century', *Midland History* 11 (1986), 1–22 (at 8).
4 P. H. Sawyer, ed., *Charters of Burton Abbey*, Anglo-Saxon Charters 2 (Oxford, 1979), pp. xlii–xliii; A. Williams, *Kingship and Government in Pre-Conquest England c.500–1066* (Basingstoke, 1999), p. 135.
5 S1423.

years to Emma of Normandy, his second wife, who was also known in England as Ælfgifu, but Cnut had never repudiated the first Ælfgifu; on the contrary, he continued to hold her in high regard and in 1030 entrusted her with the regency of Norway. There is, therefore, much to suggest that it was she who held the delegated patronage of the abbey in 1023.

Danish people had been settled in England for many years before the whole country received a Danish king in 1016, and though there was a sudden change of regime when Cnut acquired the throne, there was no social revolution. Ælfweard's personal connection with Cnut was of course an advantage to Evesham after the transition of power, but it was not crucial to the abbey's wellbeing, for Cnut was more anxious to be accepted by the English as a godly benefactor like Edgar than to be feared as the bloodthirsty aggressor portrayed by his court poets in Denmark.[6] Cnut was therefore conspicuously generous to English monasteries and was said to have given Evesham abbey the estates of Badby and Newnham, which adjoined each other in Northamptonshire. The gifts seem in fact to have been made through English intermediaries. Thus the Newnham estate was acquired c.1023 through the Evesham monk Æfic, Ælfweard's deputy, whose family had held it. The Badby estate came later, through Earl Leofric at the request of the earl's spiritual adviser and Æfic's kinsman, the anchorite Wulfsige, to whose family it had likewise belonged. It thus appears that Ælfweard, Ælfgifu of Northampton, Æfic, and Wulfsige all had Northamptonshire connections. That would help to explain why Cnut enabled Evesham to acquire estates there, even though they lay more than fifty miles away by road. Cnut was said also to have given plots of land to Evesham abbey in the towns of Gloucester, Winchcombe, and, of course, Northampton.[7]

King Cnut and Earl Leofric were able to help in the partial fulfilment of Abbot Ælfweard's ambition to add Bengeworth and Hampton to Evesham's central core of estates. Bengeworth and Hampton lay side by side directly across the river from Evesham, with Bengeworth at the immediately opposite end of the crossing from the abbey. Geographically they belonged to the abbey's closest hinterland (Fig. 3). Historically, however, Bengeworth and Hampton had been part of the church of Worcester's Cropthorne estate;[8] moreover, the Cropthorne estate had coincided with the bishop's hundred of 'Cuthburgehlaw', which had become part of his triple hundred of Oswaldslow.[9] Thus Bengeworth and Hampton, though on the

6 e.g. *EHD c.500–1042*, pp. 335–41.

7 T. Marlb. pp. 134–5, 152–3; S977.

8 DB, fol. 174r.

9 S731 (spurious but believed to contain authentic topographical information, on which see *DB Worcs.* (Williams), pp. 16, 35).

abbey's doorstep, were outside its ownership and its hundredal jurisdiction. There was the added inconvenience that traffic between the abbey and its nearest estates across of the river had to pass through Bengeworth. By the 1030s, however, the position had changed, for Hampton had come into the possession of Earl Leofric through Cnut, and some time between 1033 and 1038 the earl seems to have granted it to Evesham abbey.[10] Cnut had also acquired half of Bengeworth and he tried to convey it to the abbey in or before 1030 by granting it to one of his thegns for life with reversion to Evesham;[11] Cnut's precise intentions were thwarted, however, for before 1066 the church of Worcester was somehow able to retrieve that half of Bengeworth and to keep its hold on the other half.[12]

Even before Godwine's death in 1016 the overlordship of Evesham's lost estates had been restored to the abbey, but Abbot Ælfweard was not immediately free to manage them all as he wished because at least some were still in the hands of Godwine's former tenants. Ælfweard had to buy out the tenant if he wanted to resume direct management of such an estate and turn it to the abbey's profit. Thus it was that, some time before 1023, he had to appear at the shire court of Worcester before Earl Hákon and Leofric, who was then the sheriff, and buy back an estate at Norton by Evesham, which had been so neglected or despoiled as to be 'lying waste'. Ælfweard was then able to sell a lease of the Norton estate for three pounds to a certain Æthelmær for a term of three lives. The lease was strictly framed, defining the lessee's obligations to the abbey and to the king and stipulating that the estate must have on it at least one man, six oxen, twenty sheep, and twenty acres of sown corn by the time it reverted to the abbey.[13] One may not be reading too much into a single document to suggest that Ælfweard was eager to respond to the challenges both of resuming control of the abbey estates and of improving their management, in some cases after years of neglect or abuse, and that the health of the abbey's economy as a whole was a matter that received his serious attention.

Saints and relics

Evesham's advantage in having Cnut's favour and protection and in attracting the support of Earl Leofric and of his wife Godgifu ('the Lady Godiva') was matched by Abbot Ælfweard's aspiration to make the monastery not only a wealthy landed

10 T. Marlb. pp. 154–7; S1223 (spurious but may have some authentic basis).

11 S991 (suspect but believed to have an authentic basis).

12 Hemming, I, pp. 269–70.

13 S1423, on which see the commentary in A. J. Robertson, ed., *Anglo-Saxon Charters*, 2nd edn (Cambridge, 1956), pp. 403–5.

institution but also a respected place of learning and pilgrimage. The time was right for such ambitions, for the church of Evesham had outlived the kingdom of Mercia and the under-kingdom of the Hwicce, had survived the interference of regional ealdormen, and had emerged from the tutelage of bishops to become by the 1020s a permanent part of the Church and nation and one already grounded in 300 years of history. To enhance the abbey's prestige now would not only be a noble aim in itself but would also help to secure the future.

The possession of saints' relics made their resting places especially holy to the outside world and Ælfweard was active in promoting awareness of Evesham's relics, especially those of St Ecgwine, and in acquiring the remains of other saints — the more the better in Ælfweard's view. The Ecgwine of history, however, was little known, even at Evesham, and his remains would hardly have been capable of attracting public interest by themselves; he needed a written biography, and one that was as detailed and flattering as it could be. Thus Ælfweard commissioned the learned monk Byrhtferth of Ramsey to compose a *vita* for St Ecgwine. Byrhtferth was the obvious choice, not only because Ælfweard had known him at Ramsey but also because Byrhtferth had already written a *vita* of St Oswald of Worcester, Evesham's second founder.[14] Byrhtferth finished the biography of Ecgwine with much creative imagination and in his usual grandiloquent style, and its success was remarkable. At a stroke the *vita* established Ecgwine's saintly reputation for the rest of the Middle Ages and created for posterity the story of Evesham's foundation as the outcome of a personal meeting between Ecgwine and the Virgin Mary. Thus by 1023 we already find Ælfweard and the community leasing the estate at Norton by Evesham 'with the blessing of God and St Mary and of the holy man St Ecgwine'.[15] Thanks to Byrhtferth, Ecgwine had become more than a revered founder and heavenly intercessor; he was being portrayed as a daily presence who, with God and the Virgin Mary, validated all the abbey's transactions, secular as well as religious, and bestowed on them an authority that no reasonable person could challenge.

Ælfweard was not content to enhance the inherited cult of St Ecgwine. As far as the abbot was concerned Evesham could never have too many relics and he used his lofty contacts to bring in other cults whenever he could. Through King Cnut he was able to obtain from the church of Repton in Derbyshire the relics of St Wigstan,[16] a member of the Mercian royal family, who was murdered in 849. Afterwards Wigstan's relics were especially valued at Evesham for his supposed

14 Byrhtferth, pp. lxxiii, lxxxii–lxxxiii.

15 S1423.

16 T. Marlb. pp. 150–53. I have been unable to verify that the transfer took place in 1019, as is sometimes stated.

family connection to King Coenred of the Mercians (704–9), an early benefactor of the minster.[17] To Ælfweard, however, relics did not need an Evesham association to make them desirable; a relic was a treasure simply because the saint was then in heaven. For instance, Ælfweard needed no special justification for acquiring the relics of St Odulf (d.855), founder of the Frisian church of Stavoren (now in the Netherlands), whence they had allegedly been stolen by Vikings. He simply bought the relics for Evesham from some merchants who were taking them to London, apparently in 1035.[18]

A little later Ælfweard decided to make a new reliquary for St Ecgwine's bones to replace the one harmed by Danes. He did so in 1040 and reputedly in unusual circumstances. In that year Ælfweard had been part of the delegation that was sent to Flanders to invite Harthacnut (son of Queen Emma and the late King Cnut) to come to England as king in succession to his recently dead half-brother Harold Harefoot. During the crossing to Flanders Ælfweard's ship was caught in a storm but he was said to have subdued it by praying to St Ecgwine and vowing to make a new shrine of gold and silver for his relics. Harthacnut arrived safely in England in June 1040, Ælfweard rapidly made good his vow, and Ecgwine's relics were translated to the new shrine on 10 September of that year.[19] The shrine was probably made under the direction of Manni, an Evesham monk of outstanding creative skills; he was well versed in religious literature and excelled in the arts of liturgical chant, calligraphy, painting, and work in precious metals.[20]

Discipline and worship

Byrhtferth of Ramsey's imaginative account of the funeral and posthumous miracles of St Ecgwine, written in the eleventh century, probably bears little relation to what actually happened at the early minster but it does tell us about the Benedictine abbey of Ælfweard's time. Byrhtferth admitted that his knowledge of the miracles was confined to what he could glean from local informants and from alleged 'ancient writings',[21] and it seems fair to assume that he knew nothing about the minster's liturgical arrangements and internal organization in Ecgwine's time; he would thus have had no alternative but to depict Evesham's usual practices as they were in his own day. From such glimpses as Byrhtferth provides, it would appear that Ælfweard's Evesham conformed in some degree to the precepts of the

17 *Evesham Chron.* pp. 325–6.

18 T. Marlb. pp. 152–3; *Evesham Chron.* pp. 313–14 (after Ælfweard became a bishop in 1035, and before Cnut's death on 12 November that year).

19 T. Marlb. pp. 70–73; *Ramsey Chron.* pp. 149–50.

20 T. Marlb. pp. 156–7.

21 Byrhtferth, pp. 280–303.

Regularis concordia of c.970, the national agreement that supplemented the 'Rule of St Benedict' with a programme of internal discipline and liturgical practice that was designed to be followed by all the monastic houses in England.

At Evesham the abbot's role in public affairs meant that he often had to travel some distance from the house and so was absent for significant periods. Naturally, then, he had a deputy and for that man Byrhtferth uses the Latin title of *senior* ('elder'). We know that the *senior* mentioned at Evesham was not the abbot because Byrhtferth in an undated story tells us the *senior*'s name, Wigred, and we know that he was the abbot's deputy because the Evesham monk Dominic revised Byrhtferth's miracle stories after the Conquest and substituted the term *prior* for *senior*.[22] In the later tenth century the *senior* at Evesham is found in charge of organizing a celebratory meal on the feast of St Ecgwine, of appointing 'officials' (*ministri*), and of undertaking the abbey's case in a local dispute about a piece of land. Byrhtferth also mentions the sacrist, whose duties at Evesham included the ringing of bells for the services.[23]

It was presumably through Wulfsige the recluse that Earl Leofric and his wife Godiva formed a friendship with Wulfsige's kinsman the monk Æfic and became frequent visitors to the abbey.[24] Æfic, who died in 1037, was described in later sources as 'prior' of Evesham, the abbot's deputy, but in his own day his post at Evesham carried the title of 'dean',[25] as at other great monasteries.[26] The title remained in use at Evesham until shortly after the Conquest[27] and then gave way to 'prior'.[28] The dean's role became especially important in 1035 when Cnut appointed Ælfweard to be bishop of London concurrently with his abbacy at Evesham.[29] Ælfweard evidently lived in London most of the time after that[30] and relied on the dean to manage everything at Evesham.

Leofric and Godiva were benefactors to a number of monasteries but it was almost certainly their special affection for Dean Æfic that induced them to build a church of the Holy Trinity at Evesham. It presumably stood near the abbey church and may even have been attached to it. Within the new Trinity church they provided a large crucifix with figures of St Mary and St John, all in silver and

22 Byrhtferth, pp. 290–91; Dominic, *V. Ecgwini*, p. 96.

23 Byrhtferth, pp. 288–9. See *Regularis concordia*, pp. 16, 24, 26.

24 T. Marlb. pp. 154–5.

25 ASC (C) 1037; T. Marlb. pp. 156–7.

26 e.g. Bury (S1468), Christ Church Canterbury (S1234, S1400, S1471, S1473), Worcester (S1058, S1475).

27 *Worc. Acta 1062–1185*, p. 6.

28 As at Christ Church Canterbury and Worcester: Tinti 2010, pp. 70–73.

29 T. Marlb. pp. 150–51 ('sub Cnutone rege', i.e. before Cnut's death in 1035); S974 (dated 1035) is witnessed by Ælfweard's predecessor as bishop of London.

30 T. Marlb. pp. 156–7; *Ramsey Chron.* p. 157.

gold, and in 1037 Godiva herself attended the funeral of Dean Æfic in that building. She and her husband also gave the abbey a green chasuble (a priest's liturgical vestment), a black cope, and many other costly things; and those were in addition to a black chasuble 'with other precious things belonging to it' that King Cnut had given.[31]

From Byrhtferth we learn that the offices of nocturns, matins, lauds, terce, and vespers were in daily use and one may therefore infer with confidence that the rest of the offices prescribed by the 'Rule' — prime, sext, none, and compline — were also observed. That terce was followed by a mass is indicated by Byrhtferth's reference to the Gospel and the Agnus Dei.[32] On one occasion Wigred, the *senior*, is said to have chanted the seven Penitential Psalms privately on entering the church to pray.[33] Funeral rites included chanting over the body while it was awaiting burial, and a mass for the deceased.[34] The hymn *Te deum* is mentioned as being sung on occasions of special rejoicing. Visually impressive ritual is suggested by Byrhtferth's reference to crosses, candelabra, lamps, chalices, horns (perhaps for holy oil), and vestments. At least some of the bells (called by Byrhtferth *tintinnabula* or *cloccae*) could be heard outside the church;[35] evidently they were in a tower or turret.

In Ælfweard's day the church of Evesham had been for 300 years the religious centre for those of its estates that lay immediately around, but most of them still had no local church buildings of their own.[36] The core estates were served as one large parish by priests appointed by the abbey, and the inhabitants paid the church of Evesham various recurring and substantial dues in return for the pastoral care that they received. The payments included a tenth of the farmer's annual produce (his 'tithes'), and some of the tenants owed an annual render of grain called 'churchscot'.[37] Because the abbey had the only convenient church for most of the local population, there was a weekly influx to Evesham of people coming for Sunday worship. Their numbers, which were augmented by the occasional visits of pilgrims to the shrine of St Ecgwine and by the arrival from time to time of distinguished guests, could turn the abbey into a crowded place. It had not been designed to accommodate many people and Ælfweard decided that he should ease the overcrowding by providing a group (*praedium*) of costly buildings at the abbey ('apud monasterium'); their precise location is not recorded. Once built

31 T. Marlb. pp. 152–7.

32 Byrhtferth, pp. 284–5, 288–9. See *Regularis concordia*, pp. 13–14, 16, 22, 53–5.

33 Byrhtferth, pp. 292–3. See *Regularis concordia*, p. 12.

34 Byrhtferth, pp. 280–81. See *Regularis concordia*, p. 65.

35 Byrhtferth, pp. 286–7, 296–7.

36 Below, ch. 11.

37 S1423.

they were used by numerous wealthy visitors in the course of a year.[38] Evesham's reputation as a holy place and as a seat of authority was certainly a burden — but one that the abbey had willingly taken upon itself.

Learning

The abbey seems to have been a school of the visual arts in Ælfweard's later years, under the monk Manni, and it was also a place of learning. Evesham is not known to have enjoyed any such reputation before then but one assumes that some 'sacred reading' was carried on after the tenth-century monastic revival, for it was prescribed in the *Regularis concordia*.[39] If any manuscripts were written or kept at Evesham before the revival they have not been identified, unless the eighth-century copy of the 'Rule' at the Bodleian Library (MS Hatton 48) can be said to have belonged to Evesham, but early books from Evesham may easily have been dispersed between the 940s and 1014. That had been a period of abrupt changes in the patronage and personnel of the minster and it may have resulted in useful manuscripts being taken away to other houses of religion. Even at the very beginning of Ælfweard's abbacy the monastery was not without intellectual resources, for it was able to provide elementary education to children destined to be monks and to young boarders. One of those was Wulfstan, the future bishop of Worcester, who was sent to Evesham for a while by his father and mother, who lived at Long Itchington in Warwickshire.[40] Although Evesham abbey was more than thirty miles from Long Itchington by road, it was their nearest monastic house and that may have been an important consideration for Wulfstan's parents when choosing Evesham for the education of their son. As bishop of London from 1035 Ælfweard is known to have improved the abbey's literary resources by sending many books from London, both sacred works and grammatical ones.[41] Books of grammar were essential for teaching Latin to boys at Evesham, whether as private boarders or as future monks, and those pupils that would be monks could then progress to reading the religious books that Ælfweard had also taken pains to provide.

With Manni in charge of calligraphy and manuscript illumination, with a sought-after grammar school for boys, and with a growing collection of books, Evesham clearly had a healthy literary life in Abbot Ælfweard's time. It is no

38 T. Marlb. pp. 120–23.

39 *Regularis concordia*, p. xxxiii.

40 R. R. Darlington, ed., *The* Vita Wulfstani *of William of Malmesbury*, Royal Historical Soc. Camden Third Series 40 (London, 1928), p. 4.

41 T. Marlb. pp. 152–3.

surprise, therefore, to find that Evesham's domestic chronicle the *Gesta abbatum* ('The Deeds of the Abbots') was begun during his abbacy. It took the form of a narrative continuation of the tenth-century list of abbots and covered the period from the secularization of the minster c.941 up to 1016; that is to say, it ended soon after the appointment of Ælfweard as abbot. The *Gesta abbatum* to 1016 were later incorporated in Thomas of Marlborough's thirteenth-century history of the abbey, and Thomas gives the *Gesta* some subtle reworking there to minimize the historic role of the bishops of Worcester at Evesham. Nevertheless, Thomas's redacted version of the *Gesta* to 1016[42] preserves a characteristic of the original that enables it to be distinguished from the next continuation, which covers 1016–78; the narrative to 1016 does not date the abbots' deaths but the continuation to 1078 does so. In fact, there can be no doubt that Thomas recognized the original narrative from c.941 to 1016 as a distinct work because he chose to round off his version of it with a passage of his reflections on the whole story up to that point. The absence of any dates in the pre-1016 narrative is consistent with it having been put together from oral testimony, and there should have been people alive in 1016 who knew about the changes since c.941, even if they could not recall exact dates. The resulting text is no piece of fine literature but it is notable as an early example of English monastic local history and it places firmly in Abbot Ælfweard's day the beginning of such writings at Evesham.

Ælfweard's Evesham abbey may also have been the place at which were begun the lost national annals for 1035–66 that seem to underlie the narratives for those years in the extant manuscripts 'C' and 'D' of the great national record known as the 'Anglo-Saxon Chronicle'. The direct references to Evesham in 'C' and 'D' during that period and the favourable attitude of those versions to the family of Earl Leofric both suggest the possibility;[43] one may add that Ælfweard's standing as bishop of London and as a relation of King Cnut would have given him an interest in national events, and that his abbey of Evesham provided a cultured environment in which the annals could have been written up.

The death of Ælfweard

Ælfweard continued to have a special concern and affection for Evesham,[44] but he lived in London, and it was as bishop of London that he witnessed charters of King Harthacnut (d.1042) and of his successor King Edward ('the Confessor'). He was

42 T. Marlb. pp. 140–51.

43 S. Baxter, 'MS C of the Anglo-Saxon Chronicle and the Politics of Mid-Eleventh-Century England', *EHR* 122 (2007), 1189–1227.

44 T. Marlb. pp. 152–3.

still bishop at the beginning of 1044[45] but he resigned the see later that year when it was clear that his life was coming to an end. Ælfweard had developed symptoms that were likened to those of leprosy; pustules broke out all over his face, and when they dried the skin was left rough and pale. But it was not leprosy, or leprosy alone, that would kill him, because it is not a fatal disease. Ælfweard sent word to Evesham abbey that he would like to end his days there, and he set out towards Evesham with a number of gifts including books, chasubles, copes, other ecclesiastical treasures, and, of course, relics: the jawbone of St Ecgwine, which Ælfweard had presumably removed from Evesham to London, and the bloodstained cowl of St Ælfheah, the archbishop of Canterbury murdered in 1012.[46] Some of Ælfheah's belongings had been taken from his body before its burial at St Paul's London, and other relics had become available when his tomb was opened by permission of King Cnut in 1023.[47] It was rumoured that Ælfweard's well-known lust for saints' relics had eventually brought about his sickness, for some interpreted that as a punishment for removing remains of St Osgyth from the church of Chich (now St Osyth) in Essex; he may have been particularly tempted to take them because Osgyth was said to have been the mother of Offa of the East Saxons (fl.709), one of Evesham's greatest benefactors. When the Evesham monks heard that Ælfweard had leprosy they were overcome by fear and sent a declaration that they would all leave the abbey if he tried to come there. The personal bond between the community and its abbot had probably become loose during his years away in London, but Ælfweard was bitterly disappointed at the abbey's disloyalty and he made instead for Ramsey, his first monastic home. The Ramsey monks welcomed him with honour and he gave them the treasures that he had intended for Evesham. Ælfweard never saw Evesham again and he died on 25 July 1044.[48]

45 S994, S1001, S1044.

46 *Ramsey Chron.* pp. 157–8.

47 A. R. Rumble and R. Morris, ed. and trans., '*Translatio sancti Ælfegi Cantuariensis archiepiscopi et martiris* (BHL 2519): Osbern's Account of the Translation of St Ælfheah's Relics from London to Canterbury, 8–11 June 1023', *The Reign of Cnut: King of England, Denmark and Norway*, ed. A. R. Rumble (London, 1994), pp. 283–315 (at pp. 296, 304, 306); J. Flete, *The History of Westminster Abbey*, ed. J. A. Robinson (Cambridge, 1909), p. 70.

48 T. Marlb. pp. 156–7; *Ramsey Chron.* pp. 157–8; J. Worc. II, pp. 540–41.

CHAPTER 8

Abbot Manni, the town, and the Vale

WITHIN three weeks of Ælfweard's death the artist and craftsman Manni had been appointed to succeed him as abbot of Evesham; because the death was expected, it is likely that Manni had been designated some time earlier. Manni was a Danish name that the English spelt 'Mannig' and he seems in fact to have been of mixed Danish and English blood because he also had the English name Wulfmær, though it was rarely used. At a council held in London King Edward appointed Manni as the new abbot and he was consecrated on 10 August 1044.[1] It may seem odd that an artist–craftsman, albeit a monk, should have been chosen to manage a wealthy abbey, but Manni could draw on strong support both outside the abbey and within. Earl Leofric continued to favour Evesham until his death in 1057, and Manni had in Æthelwig a deputy whose exceptional talents lay in law and administration.[2]

It was perhaps to be expected, however, that Manni would make less of a mark in public life than his predecessor, and the few surviving records do leave that impression. Abbot Manni occurs as a witness to deeds of two bishops of Worcester, Lyfing (in 1045) and Ealdred (in 1046×1053 and c.1053). Between 1053 and 1055 he also witnessed, as the first among six abbots, an agreement between Wulfwig bishop of Dorchester on the one part and Earl Leofric and the Lady Godiva on the other concerning the monastery at Stow in Lincolnshire.[3] Being on good terms with the bishop of Worcester and with the earl of Mercia was important but the abbey would try to profit from the goodwill of anyone that had local influence. When the young son of a prosperous person was admitted to Evesham as a potential monk the grateful parent might be expected to mark the occasion with a gift to the house. Thus in 1046 or 1047 a certain Wulfgeat gave the abbey an estate at Witton near Droitwich when his son Ælfgeat joined the community, and Wulfgeat placed his deed of grant on the altar of the abbey church to confirm the donation publicly.[4] The abbey was glad to recruit from prominent local families,

1 ASC (D); J. Worc. II, pp. 540–41; T. Marlb. pp. 156–7.

2 Below, ch. 9.

3 S1397, S1406, S1407, S1478.

4 DB, fol. 177v.

not just because they made immediate donations such as Wulfgeat's but also because they were likely to provide steadfast support for the abbey in its future dealings with the outside world.

Art and architecture

Although Abbot Manni had other calls on his time he continued the artistic work that he had pursued under Abbot Ælfweard. He personally produced a missal and a large psalter, both of which he illuminated. He also began work on a shrine for the bones of St Odulf, having appointed a team of lay craftsmen to make it under his supervision. The shrine was covered in gold, silver, and precious stones, three of which were said to be so brilliant that when the shrine was displayed in the church they shone at night, by reflection and refraction from lamps or candles. The master of the goldsmiths that fashioned the shrine was called Godric and he is represented as making small figures (*imaginulae*) that were designed to be attached to it. As St Odulf's shrine progressed it was seen to surpass that which Abbot Ælfweard had created for St Ecgwine. Manni therefore decided to put Ecgwine's relics in the new shrine and to use Ecgwine's former shrine for those of St Odulf. Manni also made a shrine for St Credan's relics,[5] which suggests that Manni was the unnamed abbot who had first exhumed the remains. We have no description of Credan's shrine and it was perhaps comparatively modest given the saint's obscure credentials; it is not even clear what justification the monks had for treating the eighth-century Abbot Credan as a saint. The monk Dominic alleged only that an abbot had been told in dreams to translate Abbot Credan's remains to a shrine, and that when his grave was opened they had been found to lie between two other persons and were shining like the finest gold.[6] It was probably for want of better information about Abbot Credan's sanctity that the monks chose not to commission a *vita*. The exhumation had taken place long after Abbot Credan's death and the monks may simply have confused him with the obscure Irish or Cornish saint of that name, a man who had had no connection with Evesham.[7] The confusion may even have been wilful, for it provided Evesham with another home-grown saint whose presence could be expected to contribute something to the house's standing.

During Manni's time Evesham's shrines were attracting pious visitors but they were also receiving the attention of unscrupulous and highly placed relic collectors. In the two episodes that were afterwards written about the culprits were

5 T. Marlb. pp. 84–5, 158–9.

6 *Evesham Chron.* p. 324.

7 Farmer 2011, p. 105.

women, and they may have been singled out for that reason; one of them was said explicitly to have been led astray by 'feminine greed'. She was a noblewoman called Ealdgyth and was a frequent visitor to the abbey. She approached two of the young boys there and bribed them to steal for her some small part of St Ecgwine's relics. The boys entered the church by night and came away with a tooth and part of an arm. After Ealdgyth had taken the relics home, however, she was said to have woken one morning to find that she was blind. Still unwilling to give the relics back, she promised Abbot Manni that she would have a small shrine made for them, adorned with gold and silver, and that it would be given to Evesham at her death together with an estate at Swell in Gloucestershire. Her sight never returned and Manni never received the reliquary or the whole of the estate, though his successor eventually did so.[8] In another incident that took place in Manni's time Queen Edith, King Edward's wife, invited several monasteries to send their relics to Gloucester so that she could choose the best ones to keep for herself. When the request reached Evesham the monks decided to send only the relics of St Odulf. They calculated that by doing so the more precious relics, which included those of St Ecgwine, might be kept safe. The king and queen came to Gloucester to celebrate Christmas — the year was probably 1052[9] — and while there Edith had a goldsmith open up the various shrines so that she could examine the contents. It was said that when the goldsmith opened Odulf's shrine and put his hand in it the queen was miraculously struck blind. Whatever really happened, Edith gave up her plan to take away any relics from Gloucester. Moreover, she gave Evesham a precious covering of cloth for St Odulf's reliquary, which accompanied it safely back to the abbey. In return the queen was said to have recovered her sight.[10]

Manni rebuilt the abbey church on a larger scale than before and had it consecrated on 10 October 1054[11] in a ceremony that seems to have included the translations of St Ecgwine and St Odulf to their new reliquaries.[12] The splendour of the occasion, which was probably under Manni's artistic direction, can only be imagined: the inside of the church brightly painted,[13] the ornaments gleaming, and Manni in his finest vestments. Ealdred, as bishop of Worcester, would normally have performed the consecration, but he was on an extended visit to Germany and had given permission for Leofwine bishop of Lichfield to conduct the ceremony.[14]

8 T. Marlb. pp. 86–9, 170–73; S1026 (spurious). See Finberg 1972, pp. 71–2.

9 J. Worc. II, pp. 572–3.

10 *Evesham Chron.* pp. 317–18.

11 T. Marlb. pp. 158–9; ASC (D).

12 By 1100 both had translation feasts on 10 October: below, ch. 11.

13 For examples elsewhere see W. Rodwell, 'Appearances can be Deceptive: Building and Decorating Anglo-Saxon Churches', *JBAA* 165 (2012), 22–60 (at 47–50).

14 ASC (D).

Leofwine had been the first abbot of Coventry (c.1043–53),[15] founded by Earl Leofric and the Lady Godiva, and was presumably a special friend of Evesham because Manni, whose artistic skills were valued at Canterbury and other places, had helped at Coventry with work on the new building.[16] There were other links, too, between Coventry abbey and Evesham in the eleventh century; the many monks who travelled annually from their various houses to Evesham for the principal feast of St Ecgwine included one from Coventry called 'Sperckulf' (the recorded name is perhaps a scribal corruption of 'Sþertwulf'). Indeed, he regularly attended all the feasts of the Evesham saints.[17] Like him, monks who made the journey to Evesham from other houses evidently had permission to travel, at least for approved religious purposes, and one has the impression that they experienced a measure of brotherhood with the monks of Evesham years before any of their houses had joined Evesham in a formal fraternity agreement.[18]

Because of Manni's association with Coventry abbey it is possible that his new or enlarged church at Evesham resembled the new one at Coventry or was even modelled on it. One can hardly speculate as to its appearance, however, because no-one knows what the Coventry church looked like and only disparate details of Manni's church at Evesham have been preserved in written sources. There was a crypt dedicated to St Ecgwine and a church of St Mary, perhaps over the crypt,[19] and in Manni's day there was a tower,[20] although its age is not recorded. Before the Conquest the churches of St Mary and the Holy Trinity, whether or not they were joined together, probably formed an east–west alignment of distinct buildings such as was then usual at monastic sites. The precinct also included a chapel of St Kenelm,[21] and a chapel of St Nicholas was to be added under Manni's successor.[22] There was thus a complex of churches within the precinct before 1080, but it would be correct to admit that their precise positions and functions remain to be discovered. The possible vestiges that have so far been found by excavation are too fragmentary and disjointed to make sense.[23]

15 Knowles et al. 2001, p. 40.
16 T. Marlb. pp. 156–9.
17 Ibid. pp. 96–7.
18 Below, ch. 9.
19 T. Marlb. pp. 96–9.
20 *Evesham Chron.* p. 321.
21 *Crowland Continuatio*, p. 122.
22 T. Marlb. pp. 170–71.
23 Cox 1990, pp. 124–5; Cox 2010a, pp. 26, 30, 47–9, 58–61.

The precinct boundary

By Abbot Manni's time or thereabouts the monastic enclosure is said to have been marked by a great and high thorn hedge.[24] It may have been already ancient; there had been such a hedge round the minster at Oundle (now in Northamptonshire) in Bishop Wilfrid's day[25] — that is to say, at the period when Evesham minster was founded. Evesham's hedge was, to judge from its reported size, more than a boundary marker. In the eleventh century the abbey needed it to be stout enough to mitigate some of the nuisances created by the settlement outside, such as straying animals, unwanted visitors, and the noise of traders and craftsmen. Moreover, the abbey's accumulation of valuables had brought with it a need to discourage prospective thieves. But the hedge was not only a physical defence; it would have given outsiders to understand that the abbey wanted to keep itself socially aloof and to be shown deference.

The line of the mid-eleventh-century precinct boundary could not have been completely ignored when new precinct walls were built in the twelfth century, because long-established boundaries cannot be shifted without disruption to the delicate network of old property rights and tenancies. Something about the early precinct boundary may therefore be inferred from what we know of the later one. If the early Evesham precinct was like others that have been studied, it may have been in the form of a rough rectangle or circle between 150 and 300 metres across and its line should be traceable today in street patterns and property boundaries.[26] Such features at Evesham suggest that the pre-Conquest monastic enclosure may be represented by a rough square (Fig. 5) that was defined on the north along the same line as the twelfth-century precinct wall and at the same length;[27] on the west by the line of the east side of Vine Street (the precinct boundary in the fourteenth century);[28] and on the south by the line of Little Abbey Lane, which lay slightly above the 100ft (30.5m) contour and was roughly parallel to it. On the fourth (east) side the boundary line may be imagined as keeping a little above the same contour and thus passing across what is now open ground called the Upper Abbey Park (formerly the Cross Churchyard); outside the suggested east boundary the ground falls away to the flood plain, which means that the boundary could hardly have lain much farther east. The early enclosure would thus have been square with sides about 180 yards (about 165 metres)

24 T. Marlb. pp. 122–3.

25 Stephen, *V. Wilf.* pp. 146–7.

26 Blair 2005, pp. 196–8.

27 Below, ch. 17.

28 Cox 1990, pp. 133–4.

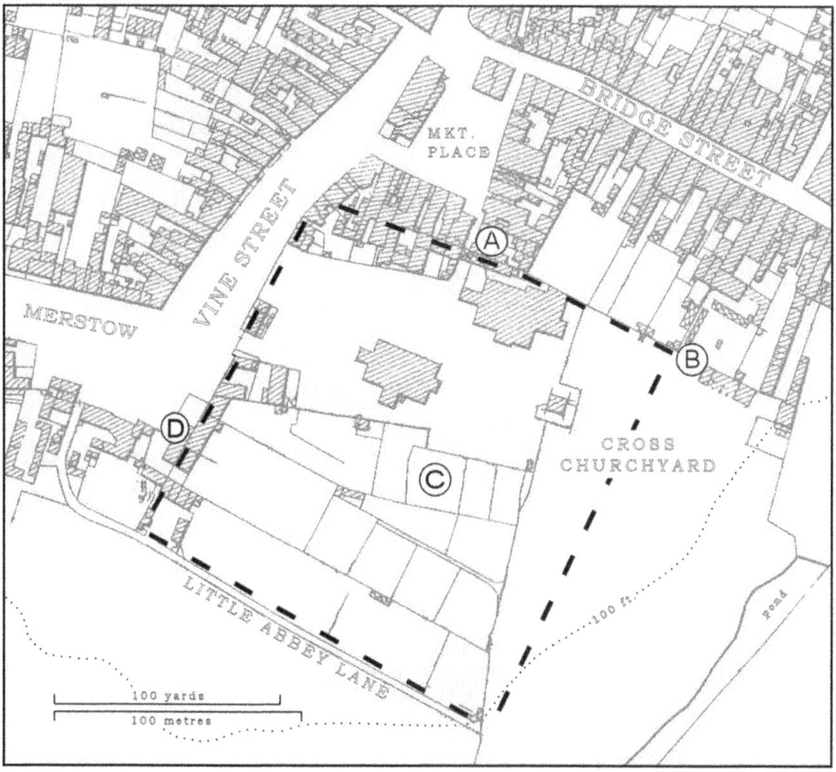

Fig. 5. Conjectural boundary of the pre-Conquest minster precinct. *A*. Site of twelfth-century graveyard gateway. *B*. Eastern limit of twelfth-century precinct wall. *C*. Approximate site of pre-Conquest minster church. *D*. Site of fourteenth-century great gateway. Superimposed on OS Plan 1/2,500, Worcs. XLIX.3 (1904 edn).

long and would have occupied a level area that lay next to the edge of the plateau.

There were probably two main entrances to the pre-Conquest precinct, one on the north and the other on the west. A gateway would have been needed somewhere along the north side in order to provide access on foot from the outer world to the graveyard, which lay on that side, and thence onward through the graveyard to the church. If one were to suggest an early gateway roughly half-way along the conjectured north boundary its position would coincide with the surviving remains of the graveyard gate of the twelfth century. One's best guess is, therefore, that an early north gateway stood on the same site. The other supposed gateway was presumably on the west side of the square precinct and would have been placed there in order to allow access to the minster yard for carts and animals making deliveries, and to the western side of the cloister for important guests and other people having business at the abbey. Access by such a route prevented the inevitable traffic from disturbing the quiet of the church or of the eastern parts of the cloister. The 'great gate' was mentioned c.1100[29] and the fourteenth-century great gatehouse, of which some remains survive, is likely to have been built on or near the same site, for it would have been inconvenient to put it anywhere else (Figs 5 and 11). The suggested pre-Conquest west gateway was not central to the conjectured west boundary as a whole but was roughly central to the part of it that was south of the graveyard — that is to say, the part that fronted the minster yard.

The early town

In Abbot Manni's time the abbey had long ceased to maintain any illusion of geographical isolation. The material world was impinging more and more on the monastic life and only the precinct boundary stood between the community and everything that it was supposed to shun. The first firm indication of what had been happening immediately outside the gates dates from 1055, when King Edward is said to have granted Evesham the status of a 'borough' (*porth*) and market.[30] He was recognizing formally that a trading settlement had already grown up next to the church of Evesham, and that the abbey would now have the legal right to profit from the development by regulating the conduct of the market, by fining those who broke its rules, and by taking payments from those who wished to transact business within it. The gradual formation of a market town had been natural enough because the church of Evesham drew people weekly from the surrounding countryside to worship; most of them had no other church. The regular Sunday gathering of churchgoers was therefore the best opportunity of the week for anyone with surplus produce to find a buyer for it. We must infer that by 1055 there had been such agricultural improvements since the eighth century on the lands surrounding Evesham that there were surpluses to be sold. People who supplied services and craft goods in wood, leather, pottery, and metal — in fact anything that farmers could not do or make for themselves — likewise had an ideal gathering of potential customers every Sunday and it made sense for craftsmen in everyday wares to set up their workshops near the point of sale. That was enough to create a town next to the market. Because the market was associated with churchgoing the market place and the town that formed around it were immediately outside the gate by which churchgoers entered and left the minster precinct, and were thus on the precinct's north side. In other words, the market

[29] T. Marlb. pp. 570–71. On the date see Cox 1990, pp. 142–3 n. 118.

[30] T. Marlb. pp. 134–5.

place began where it may still be seen, at the south end of the present High Street (Figs 5 and 11).[31]

The way in which the approach roads to the market place developed before the twelfth century seems to imply that the produce, livestock, and goods available at Evesham market had mostly been brought in from the church of Evesham's own estates instead of from others that were equally close. Thus the roads from the church's estates north of the town, and from Worcester on the north-west, approached the market place down the ancient route that formed the High Street. At the same time the road from Evesham's estates on the other side of the river, and from its more distant possessions in the Cotswolds, approached the market place by a route that formed Port Street on the Bengeworth side of the river and crossed over into Evesham to form what is now Bridge Street. A bridge is not mentioned there until c.1150[32] but could easily have been present in the eleventh century. That was also the route that connected Evesham to London and the continent, a consideration of some personal importance to the abbot. By contrast, the other early Avon crossing at Evesham, probably called 'Eibbesford', connected the church of Evesham only to places that did not belong to it. The road from the church to the ford seems to have been part of a long-distance route that had existed before the minster was founded (Fig. 1) but by the eleventh century the abbey and its market had little need of a road to the ford, or of the ford itself. As a result the road did not develop into a street, the crossing never acquired a bridge, and that part of the route was eventually abandoned on the Evesham side except for a ferry that was mentioned near the old crossing in 1827.[33]

Traffic to the minster and abbey from the north could reach the west gate by following the High Street along the west side of the precinct. Those travellers from the north that wished instead to approach the graveyard gate, or the market place that lay outside it, could reach them from the north end of the High Street by deviating gradually leftwards from the main street. An effect of making the deviation was the creation of a triangular space defined by the High Street on the west, the deviation on the east, and the precinct boundary on the south. The whole triangle constituted the early market place, and traffic entering or leaving the town by Bridge Street would also pass into and through it.

31 Slater 1996, pp. 79–80. Alternative arguments, for regarding the Merstow as the first market place, are in Bond 1973, pp. 44–7; Bond 1975, pp. 56–7.

32 T. Marlb. pp. 104–5.

33 Izod, 'Plan', parcel no. 7 ('Boat Meadow'); Baylis 2008, p. 120.

Common fields and villages

The local charter bounds that were carefully written up at the end of the Anglo-Saxon period seem to indicate that arable furlongs, each of which was a block of strips, had been formed in the Vale of Evesham by the eleventh century, particularly on the fertile left bank of the Avon, and that in some places the furlongs were at the very edges of the estates in which they lay.[34] The furlongs can be interpreted as elements of open fields, and the existence of arable furlongs at the boundaries of estates in some parts of the Vale by the mid eleventh century suggests that much of the land suitable for cereal crops had by then been brought under cultivation. Nevertheless, clear references to open fields in the Vale of Evesham are hard to find in the records of the earlier Middle Ages, though there were certainly two large fields at Bretforton by 1206.[35]

Open fields could be managed collaboratively by the inhabitants of each estate in comprehensive common-field systems, which allowed a more productive use of the land to the advantage of the tenants and their lord the abbot, and at some period common fields superseded the discrete land holdings of scattered farms that had been usual in the Vale since Roman times. The formation of common-field systems cannot be closely dated but it may have come after the early subdivision of estates, because each subdivision acquired at some point its own common-field system. For instance, Bretforton Upper End, a subdivision of the Bretforton estate, had common fields in 1617,[36] as presumably did the Lower End, but as usual there are no records early enough to indicate when they were formed.

The development of common-field systems of husbandry based on large open fields, through which a tenant's strips would be evenly dispersed, would have been accompanied by the nucleation of settlement. The process meant the tenants in each township leaving their isolated farmhouses and hamlets to make their homes in a central village, where they could have convenient access to all parts of the surrounding fields. In the Vale of Evesham in the eleventh century nucleation may have been in progress for some time — we cannot tell for how long — but it had a way to go, for there were still some small outlying settlements that would disappear only later.

The church of Evesham had, of course, a vital interest in the movement towards common-field systems and nucleated settlements in the Vale, and it may have

[34] This section is based on Monkhouse 1971, pp. 240–42, 245, 247, 270–71; Hooke 1985, pp. 140–41, 215–19.

[35] T. Marlb. pp. 522–3.

[36] W. H. Shawcross, *The Story of our Ancient Village: Or Historical Memorials of the Parish of Bretforton* (Evesham, 1890), p. 70.

been the prime mover in those changes, for the arable improvements directly enhanced the church's income as landlord and contributed to the success of its market at Evesham. Nevertheless, open fields and nucleation were not appropriate to every kind of landscape. By the mid-eleventh century arable farming had not been developed so fully on the Evesham side of the river, where much of the hilly terrain continued to be set aside as woodland; preservation of the natural resources and products that were to be derived from the woods remained important to the abbey's economy.

CHAPTER 9

Abbot Æthelwig under English and Norman rule

IN 1058 Abbot Manni was forced to resign because he had developed a form of paralysis and could no longer carry out his duties. Manni recommended King Edward to appoint as his successor his own deputy (*prepositus*) Æthelwig,[1] who had entered the monastery as the son of a Worcestershire thegn called Ordwig.[2] In addition to his local knowledge Æthelwig had acquired by 1058 such experience and skill in matters of law and administration that he had managed the see of Worcester for a time on behalf of Bishop Ealdred, perhaps during Ealdred's absence in Germany 1054–55. The king agreed to Manni's request and at Easter 1058 Bishop Ealdred consecrated Æthelwig as abbot of Evesham in a ceremony at Gloucester, while the king was holding his court there. Manni stayed at Evesham and was to live nearly eight more years. During that time Æthelwig made sure that he was looked after day and night by two of the best people available and with help from the abbey servants. Manni remained of sound mind and Æthelwig was careful to follow his advice on important matters.[3] Nevertheless, when Bishop Ealdred resigned in 1062 Æthelwig was a strong and willing candidate to succeed him at Worcester, and thus to leave Evesham. But he was passed over in favour of the more spiritual and more reluctant Wulfstan, the dean of Worcester, whose advocates included the pope.[4] Thereafter Æthelwig directed much of his exceptional energy and skill to increasing the wealth and reputation of his abbey, and the result was that Evesham would emerge from the Norman Conquest not merely unimpaired but actually enhanced. Deeply involved in public affairs, however, he had to leave daily management of the abbey largely in the hands of his deputy, the dean. The monk Ælfric occupied that position in 1070, and by 1077 the holder was called Æthelwine.[5]

During Æthelwig's twenty-year abbacy the number of monks at Evesham increased from twelve to thirty-six;[6] there had probably been twelve, the number

1 T. Marlb. pp. 158–61.

2 S1479.

3 T. Marlb. pp. 160–61.

4 E. Mason, *St Wulfstan of Worcester, c.1008–1095* (Oxford, 1990), pp. 77–84.

5 T. Marlb. pp. 166–7; *Worc. Acta 1062–1185*, p. 6.

6 T. Marlb. pp. 174–5.

of the Apostles, ever since the reform of c.970. The manner in which the twenty-four new places were filled is not known but it is clear that the Norman Conquest brought no immediate influx of recruits from the continent; the abbey had no foreign monks at all in Æthelwig's time. It is possible that Æthelwig allowed the community to grow gradually in parallel with the acquisition of new estates; that much is perhaps to be inferred from the account of Gilbert fitz Thorold's gift of land at Lench (later Sheriffs Lench) near Evesham, for it was in accordance with Gilbert's gift that a monk was placed in the abbey.[7] It would seem that the new monk was not Gilbert's son but a beneficiary of his sponsorship, perhaps a promising boy whose parents could not afford to give the usual endowment on his admission to the abbey. Unlike the donor, a Norman, the recruit was apparently English, for even near the end of Æthelwig's life all the monks were English, like himself, and Æthelwine was still called by the pre-Conquest title of 'dean'.[8]

Æthelwig in public life

Such were Æthelwig's proven abilities that his Englishness did not impede his progress after 1066; it may in fact have been the quality that helped him to be so useful to the new king. Having enjoyed the confidence of Edward the Confessor and King Harold, Æthelwig now received that of William the Conqueror and his new archbishop of Canterbury Lanfranc (1070–89). William gave Æthelwig authority over the shire courts of Worcestershire, Gloucestershire, Oxfordshire, Warwickshire, Herefordshire, Staffordshire, and Shropshire,[9] possibly as early as 1068,[10] and his role there in smoothing the transition of estates from English to Norman lordship can hardly be overestimated. It gave him great power and it was said that even the Normans feared him.[11]

Æthelwig's authority in post-Conquest Mercia also enabled him to increase the abbey's estates in various ways. He took legal action to obtain lands that he alleged had been taken away unlawfully in the past. On other occasions he acquired lands by direct purchase,[12] such as the two hides at Lench (Sheriffs Lench) for which he paid King William a gold mark (£6 13s 4d); evidently Æthelwig had a personal income from which to buy the estate, for it was only afterwards that he gave the land to the abbey for the salvation of his soul. Sometimes he received lands as a gift in the time-honoured way; such were the other two hides at Sheriffs Lench, given

7 DB, fol. 176r.

8 *Worc. Acta 1062–1185*, p. 6.

9 T. Marlb. pp. 160–65.

10 Darlington 1933, pp. 17–18.

11 Hemming, I, p. 270.

12 T. Marlb. pp. 172–7.

by Gilbert fitz Thorold. Gilbert was a Norman baron prominent in Herefordshire, Gloucestershire, and Worcestershire and he gave the land for the salvation of the soul of William fitz Osbern, who had died in 1071.[13] Æthelwig gained other lands by inducing the English holders to commend themselves to him, which meant making him their overlord; they did so in the hope that Æthelwig's personal protection would secure them against possible ejection by Normans.[14] Æthelwig's acquisitions were mostly in parts of Worcestershire, Gloucestershire, Warwickshire, and Oxfordshire that were at some distance from the monastery, and they eventually amounted to some fifty-one manors.[15] His remarkable success as an estate builder was of course resented by powerful local rivals, including the church of Worcester and the Norman sheriff of Worcestershire Urse d'Abbetot. While Æthelwig lived, however, they were unable to match his personal influence over proceedings in the Mercian shire courts where matters of land tenure were decided, and so they had little choice but to bide their time.

Negotiations over the disputed Bengeworth estate, which lay immediately across the river from Evesham, showed with what effect Æthelwig could use his public position to the abbey's advantage. In 1066 Bengeworth still belonged to the church of Worcester, from which it was held in two halves by English tenants called Atsere and Ærngrim. After the Conquest Atsere's half came into the possession of Sheriff Urse, who ejected him. Ærngrim, who still held the other half from the church of Worcester, observed Atsere's misfortune and commended himself to Æthelwig instead. Ærngrim afterwards lost the tenancy, however, allegedly through Æthelwig's machinations,[16] and thus left the abbey in unencumbered possession of that half of the estate. Æthelwig also obtained Urse's tenancy of the other half of Bengeworth by giving Urse two distant Worcestershire estates, one of which, Acton (later Acton Beauchamp), had belonged to Æthelwig's father.[17] In Æthelwig's lifetime and through his personal intervention Evesham thus came to possess both halves of the manor of Bengeworth, even though Worcester might still claim to be the tenant-in-chief (the overlord under the king).

Æthelwig was not only active in the law and in administration but he was also able to muster a considerable body of soldiers, probably from the men of his hundred of 'Fissesberg'.[18] In 1075 his force joined those of Bishop Wulfstan, the lord of Oswaldslow hundred; of Sheriff Urse, whose authority extended over five

13 DB, fol. 176r.

14 Hemming, I, pp. 271–2; T. Marlb. pp. 170–71.

15 T. Marlb. pp. 172–5; Clarke 2012a, p. 134.

16 DB, fol. 174r; Hemming, I, pp. 269–70.

17 T. Marlb. pp. 172–5.

18 See R. P. Abels, *Lordship and Military Obligation in Anglo-Saxon England* (London, 1988), pp. 182–4.

other Worcestershire hundreds; and of Walter de Lacy, the second most powerful baron in Herefordshire. The purpose and achievement of their joint forces was to bar Roger de Breteuil earl of Hereford from crossing the Severn eastwards to join a rebellion against the king that was being planned by Roger's brother-in-law Ralph earl of East Anglia.[19] By that time Evesham abbey may also have been under an obligation as a feudal tenant-in-chief to provide a small quota of fully equipped knights, probably five of them, to fight for the king when required.[20]

Good works

Æthelwig let out some of his new estates to influential men in order to build up the abbey's local support but the income derived from his estate-building policy was not all put to secular uses. He spent some of it on ornaments for the church, including vestments, a large cross, and an altar worked in gold and silver, and he built the chapel dedicated to St Nicholas. Had Æthelwig lived longer he would have built a great new abbey church in the latest Norman style; he had accumulated five chests of silver especially for the purpose before he died.[21] There is some evidence, however, that he did not spend much on books. Although a very detailed account of Æthelwig's abbacy was written in the time of his successor, it conspicuously lacks any reference to books acquired or produced, and in that respect Æthelwig's record is unlike those of the other eleventh-century abbots of Evesham. There is more than one possible explanation for the omission and a charitable view might be that Æthelwig's biographer was not interested in books and so neglected to mention them; but that would be strange in someone who was himself a writer. It seems more likely that Æthelwig had really been too busy with immediate matters to think about any literary or intellectual legacy.

Lest it should be thought that Æthelwig's policies were essentially materialistic, it must be pointed out that part of the abbey's income from its growing estates was used in his time to fund a system of internal and external poor-relief that exceeded by far the requirements of the *Regularis concordia*.[22] Records of charitable work at Evesham before Æthelwig's day have not survived, though it was later mentioned that a poor stranger in Abbot Manni's time had been allowed to lodge in the tower of the church.[23] But Æthelwig's policy is well documented. He appointed

[19] J. Worc. III, pp. 24–5.

[20] *Regesta Wm I*, pp. 449–52 no. 131. The date and authenticity of this document have been debated, but evidence remains that Evesham did owe five knights by 1104 and probably by 1078: Clarke 2012b, pp. 2–3, 6, 8–10.

[21] T. Marlb. pp. 170–71, 174–5.

[22] *Regula Benedicti*, chs 53, 56; *Regularis concordia*, pp. 61–2.

[23] *Evesham Chron.* p. 321.

his deputy, the young dean Ælfric, to welcome all the travellers and poor people that came to him and to give them what they needed, and he ordered the cellarer and all the abbey's reeves (estate managers) to provide Ælfric with whatever he required for that purpose. Travellers (*peregrini*) came from Ireland and from Aquitaine in west-central France, neither of which was yet under English rule, and they arrived from other foreign places too. Although *peregrinus* can sometimes mean 'pilgrim' as well as 'traveller'[24] it may be unsafe in this instance to assume that 'pilgrims' were seeking out Evesham's shrines from so far afield.[25] At Christmas and Easter in particular, crowds of paupers and travellers would descend on Evesham and the abbot would then wash their hands and feet and give them clothing, footwear, and money. Every day of the year the abbey provided food for another fifty poor people, while the abbot fed thirteen poor people every day at his table. Twelve other paupers, including 'lepers', lived permanently in the monastery, and when one of the twelve died the dean appointed another to their place. Early every morning the abbot or his deputy would wash and kiss their feet and hands and give them food and clothing. In return those of the twelve that were fit enough had to attend matins every night as well as the daytime offices and the two daily masses, and on feast days they also had to pray all night in the church for the abbot and the brethren. In the period from All Saints Day (1 November) to Christmas and in the nine weeks from Septuagesima to Easter each of the twelve received a penny three times a week, and pennies were given to them and to other poor people on all the principal feast days.[26]

Æthelwig's charity was not merely formal or intended only to impress. That is clear from what happened between 1069 and 1070, when large areas of the north of England and the north Midlands were devastated by King William during his campaign to suppress rebellion there. His forces destroyed livestock and food indiscriminately, and desperate survivors made their way southwards. Many refugees from Yorkshire, Cheshire, Shropshire, Staffordshire, and Derbyshire arrived at Evesham and Abbot Æthelwig made it his business to meet their needs as best he could. That the fugitives should have chosen to make for Evesham is evidence of Æthelwig's widespread reputation after 1066 as one of the few Englishmen of authority and wealth that other Englishmen could still turn to for support. Many of the incomers lay exhausted about the town, both indoors and out in the open, even in the abbey graveyard. Some had arrived in the last stages of starvation and

24 *Dictionary of Medieval Latin from British Sources*, fasc. 10, ed. D. R. Howlett (Oxford, 2006), p. 2201.

25 Cf. G. Beech, 'England and Aquitaine in the Century before the Norman Conquest', *ASE* 19 (1990), 81–101 (at 82, 84).

26 T. Marlb. pp. 166–71.

were beyond help; the dean had to bury five or six of them every day. The plight of the orphans attracted Æthelwig's special concern and he ordered the abbey's lay servants and officials and certain of the monks each to take personal care of a destitute child. It was said that some of the rescued children grew up to become worthy adults and in various ways to be helpful to the brethren.[27]

Near the very end of his life, in 1077 or early in 1078, Æthelwig and the monks of Evesham joined all the independent religious communities of Worcester diocese in an association promoted by Bishop Wulfstan.[28] Also parties to the agreement were the monks of Bath, which lay just outside the diocesan boundary, and the monks of Chertsey in Surrey, whose abbot ruled Bath in plurality.[29] Soon afterwards two monks of Malmesbury and a brother of Taunton minster were added. The signatories promised to be faithful to God and to the king and queen and to sing masses twice a week for the members of all the participating houses and for their deceased brethren. The religious heads promised to obey their bishops and to give alms lavishly to the poor. Æthelwig's participation in the group demonstrates again that he was interested in religious matters and was not always preoccupied with worldly affairs. The inclusion of men from outside Worcester diocese suggests that it was a voluntary association between all the parties and not something imposed by Wulfstan upon his own diocese. Thus the agreement was founded, like the old *Regularis concordia*, on principles of voluntary participation and mutual support, and, like the *concordia,* it required prayers for the king and queen and the giving of generous alms. Since the document was written in English, not Latin, it was conservative in form as well as in outlook. But it was not reactionary; it did not conflict with the new 'Monastic Constitutions' devised by the Conqueror's appointee Archbishop Lanfranc. Nor was the confederation a narrowly English one. Admittedly the named monks, those from Evesham, Chertsey, and Bath, were almost all English, but two of the participating religious heads, Ralph abbot of Winchcombe and Serlo abbot of Gloucester, and one of the Bath monks, Herluin, had foreign names. Æthelwig was an upholder of English interests after the Conquest but he could see that neither the English nor the affairs of Evesham abbey would be served by stubborn insularity. In fact he had already given welcome advice and practical support to the foreigners Serlo and Lanfranc in the affairs of their houses as well as to his English neighbour Bishop Wulfstan.[30]

[27] T. Marlb. pp. 166–7.

[28] *Worc. Acta 1062–1185*, pp. 5–7.

[29] Knowles et al. 2001, pp. 28, 38.

[30] T. Marlb. pp. 164–5.

The call of the desert

At Æthelwig's Evesham it was no longer possible for an ordinary monk, still less the abbot or the dean, to live a life of undisturbed seclusion. Such a life could be read about in the works of Bede and his contemporaries and in the *vitae* and sayings of the Desert Fathers, but Evesham abbey had so grown in size and complexity that its advanced Benedictine regime offered little to those members who might yearn for primitive simplicity. From the mid-twelfth century they could expect to find a home in England under the new Cistercian order, but at Evesham in the eleventh century the only choice for brethren seeking withdrawal seemed to be that of remaining on the abbey site while living as recluses in solitary self-denial; it was an alternative way of life that was understood and approved by the 'Rule'.[31] In the mid-eleventh century there were no fewer than three anchorites at Evesham. One was Wulfsige, Dean Æfic's kinsman and the spiritual adviser of Leofric and Godiva. It was said that by 1062 he had been a solitary more than forty years.[32] Another was called Basing and the third was Ælfwine. All three had chosen to be recluses at a very young age and had been solitaries at other sites before coming to Evesham, which seems therefore to have been recognized as a particularly favourable retreat for men of their disposition. Wulfsige is said to have arrived about 1036 from Crowland and to have lived at Evesham in a cell that he built next to a chapel dedicated to St Kenelm.[33] According to another account he is said to have devoted himself to the service of God at Evesham in an 'underground cavity' (*specus subterraneus*).[34] As far as possible the anchorites avoided human contact but they would sometimes agree to be consulted by people in search of guidance. Ælfwine, we know, lived in a cell at which visitors were allowed to speak to him through the window.[35] Wulfsige seems to have been even more in demand, and by the time of Abbot Æthelwig he was an adviser to the highest in the land and did not always wait to be consulted. He was said to have written to Edward the Confessor urging him to rebuild Westminster abbey[36] and it was Wulfsige who, we are told, finally persuaded the humble Wulfstan to accept the bishopric of Worcester.[37] Whatever the truth of the stories about Wulfsige they are certainly a measure of his reputation. By about 1077 Basing had gone but Wulfsige and Ælfwine seem to have been still at Evesham, and listed as

[31] *Regula Benedicti*, ch. 1.

[32] J. Worc. II, pp. 590–91.

[33] *Crowland Descriptio*, p. 61; *Crowland Continuatio*, pp. 121–3.

[34] O. Clare, *V. Edw.* p. 81.

[35] *Evesham Chron.* pp. 322–3.

[36] O. Clare, *V. Edw.* pp. 80–81.

[37] J. Worc. II, pp. 590–91.

'brethren';[38] Wulfsige was later described as an 'enclosed monk',[39] which likewise suggests that he was recognized as a member of the Evesham community. He was the last of the male anchorites to remain there[40] and was said to have died in 1104 or early in 1105.[41] About 1100, however, the Evesham precinct also housed five female solitaries,[42] and two religious women bearing the continental names of Cecily and Ameline were listed c.1104.[43] Although the first Evesham solitaries had been men, by the end of the century they were apparently outnumbered by women; there would be no nunneries for religious women in Worcester diocese until the mid-twelfth century and, meanwhile, Evesham offered them a secure and private place.

While the monks served as the spiritual conscience of the local laity, the recluses were the ascetic conscience of the monks, who were finding themselves too busy to spend the whole day in contemplation and prayer. The anchorites were therefore not regarded as awkward dissidents or parasites at Evesham abbey, but were held by the monks in great reverence, and when Wulfsige died his tomb was placed in the midst of the choir as a daily reminder to them of true holiness.[44] Few could hope to emulate him. Nevertheless, there were some monks of Evesham who, while not prepared to live as solitaries, felt that communal observance of the 'Rule' was not sufficient for their spiritual needs. A choice open to them in the eleventh century was to remain as ordinary monks but to inflict special privations on themselves. One such was Ælfsige the sacrist. Since he was not listed among the monks c.1077 or c.1104,[45] one assumes that he lived in or before the abbacy of Æthelwig. Ælfsige was given to fasting and on winter nights would stand barefoot on the freezing church pavement throughout matins.[46]

William I's devastation of the north, and the ascetic and nostalgic yearnings of some of the Evesham monks, came together at Evesham c.1073 to inspire a small expedition that had modest aims but would soon lead to a revival of monasticism in northern England, a region that the tenth-century Benedictine reforms had never reached. The party that left Evesham consisted of three men. One was Reinfrid, a Norman soldier. While serving in the north he had been moved by the ruins of Whitby abbey, St Hild's seventh-century foundation, which had

[38] *Worc. Acta 1062–1185*, p. 6.
[39] O. Clare, *V. Edw.* p. 80.
[40] *Durham Liber vitae*, I, p. 104.
[41] *Peterborough Chron.* p. 72; Licence 2011, p. 176 n. 10.
[42] T. Marlb. pp. 570–71.
[43] *Durham Liber vitae*, I, p. 104.
[44] Cox 2010a, p. 60.
[45] *Worc. Acta 1062–1185*, p. 6; *Durham Liber vitae*, I, pp. 103–4.
[46] *Evesham Chron.* p. 321.

been destroyed by the Danes c.857. After that experience he had made his way to Evesham and had entered the abbey as a monk. Reinfrid was there when some of the brothers were approached by Ealdwine ('Aldwin'), the prior of Winchcombe, which lay only ten miles from Evesham and in the same diocese. Ealdwine was probably already known at Evesham because Abbot Æthelwig had been in temporary charge of Winchcombe abbey in the late 1060s after the retirement to Evesham of its Abbot Godric.[47] Although Ealdwine had probably never been to Northumbria he had read Bede's 'Ecclesiastical History', in which the golden period of Northumbrian monasticism is chronicled. Ealdwine had ascetic leanings of his own and had formed a plan to visit the abandoned Northumbrian religious sites and to settle there in a life of poverty. Two of the Evesham monks said they would like to join him. They were Reinfrid, who had never read Bede but knew the north at first hand, and an Englishman called Ælfwig. The two English monks and one Norman shared the same longing for privation and solitude that was felt by the anchorites and ascetics who were already settled at Evesham, and their desire to restore ascetic religion to places in which it had once flourished probably appealed to Æthelwig's well-known respect for English traditions. In any case he gave the three his permission to go, with the condition that they accepted Ealdwine as their leader; he was the highest ranked and probably the most educated. And so, in 1073 or early in 1074, the group set out from Evesham on foot with a donkey on which were borne a few books and religious vestments. Their story after that belongs to the ecclesiastical history of the north. Suffice it to say that their arrival there was so well received that it led within fifteen years, and contrary to their austere intentions, to the foundation of the great new abbeys of Whitby and St Mary's York and the cathedral priory of Durham.[48]

47 Knowles et al. 2001, pp. 79, 257.

48 Knowles 1963a, pp. 166–71 and sources cited there; L. G. D. Baker, 'The Desert in the North', *Northern History* 5 (1970), 1–11 (at 4–6).

PART II

Abbot Walter (1078–1104)

CHAPTER 10

A new regime

FOR much of his life Æthelwig had been troubled by an intermittent form of gout. It was very painful and he was said to have been 'worn out' by it before he died.[1] That was on 16 February 1078[2] and within three months a page was turned when the king appointed Walter as the new abbot. It was the first time since 1014 that someone not a monk of Evesham had taken up the position and Walter was, of course, the first foreigner ever to be chosen. When he arrived at Evesham he was completely unknown to the community, but the personal contrast between Walter and Æthelwig was immediately obvious to the all-English monks, for Walter was a cultured Norman and was younger and physically fitter than Æthelwig had been in recent years. He had been promoted to Evesham from Canterbury, where he had been a chaplain to Archbishop Lanfranc, and his association with the learned Lanfranc went back to the 1060s, when Lanfranc was abbot of Caen in Normandy and Walter was his pupil there. Before Caen and Canterbury Walter had been a monk at the abbey of Cerisy-la-Forêt,[3] thirty miles west of Caen. A fellow pupil and friend at Caen was Gundulf, later bishop of Rochester (1077–1108); they were able and ambitious young men and Lanfranc was evidently grooming them for high office. The chronicler William of Malmesbury relates that Walter and Gundulf were one day at Caen studying a gospel-book with Lanfranc, and while Lanfranc's attention was momentarily distracted they decided to play a game. They said 'Let us turn the pages and see which of us is to be abbot and which bishop.' They came to the gospel of Matthew, and in the twenty-fourth chapter Gundulf's finger alighted on the words 'a faithful and wise servant, whom the lord hath appointed over his family', while in the next chapter Walter found the line 'good and faithful servant, … enter thou into the joy of thy lord'. They began laughing over these promising words and when Lanfranc asked them what they were so happy about, they confessed. Without hesitation Lanfranc is then said to have predicted that Gundulf would become a bishop and Walter an abbot.[4]

1 T. Marlb. pp. 174–5.
2 Knowles et al. 2001, pp. 47, 248.
3 T. Marlb. pp. 176–7.
4 W. Malmesb. *GP* I, pp. 218–21.

By 1078 Walter's ideas about the religious life were naturally those of Lanfranc's Canterbury, where he had spent the last few years, and therefore they owed little to those of Worcester diocese, where the saintly Englishman Bishop Wulfstan was still in office; long after the Conquest Wulfstan and Æthelwig, at Worcester and Evesham, had naturally remained sympathetic to the English traditions into which they had been born and trained. It is therefore possible that the English solidarity that characterized the monastic body at Evesham in 1078 changed more slowly during the twenty-six years of Walter's abbacy than one might have expected. A list of the Evesham community produced c.1104 contains seventy-two names and thus about twice as many people as were there when Æthelwig died in 1078. Of the seventy-two persons c.1104, two were religious women and one was the male recluse Wulfsige.[5] Twelve of the sixty-nine monks were living at the abbey's Danish daughter-house at Odense[6] and that left fifty-seven monks at Evesham; there would have been fifty-eight, but they had no abbot at the time because of Walter's recent death.

Eighteen or more of the seventy-two names listed c.1104 were English. At least nine of those seem to have been held by survivors from Abbot Æthelwig's time but the others must have been those of Englishmen who had been recruited under Abbot Walter; he evidently had no policy of taking in foreigners only. More than thirty monks, however, had continental baptismal names c.1104; among them were perhaps some from overseas, but others may have been English or half-English and born since 1066 to parents who had given the child a Norman name to help him blend into the Norman elite. The total number of Walter's English recruits may therefore have been significantly greater than nine; and the baptismal names listed c.1104 are not a sure guide to whether any of the others was born abroad.

Another difficulty in trying to estimate the number of foreign monks c.1104 is that some of the community had given up their baptismal names and had taken assumed names of a religious character, thus making their national identities impossible to determine. At the end of Walter's abbacy at least nineteen monks bore the names of figures from the Old Testament (Moses and Samuel), apostles (Andrew, Paul, and Philip), martyrs (Alban, Clement, Maurice, Protasius, and Vincent), Church fathers (Ambrose, Augustine, and Hilary), or exemplars of monasticism (Anthony, Benedict, Ecgwine, Macarius, and Martin); Dominic ('belonging to the Lord') was, likewise, an assumed name. A new name would announce clearly that the bearer had abandoned his secular identity on entering

[5] *Durham Liber vitae*, I, pp. 103–4. The list is dated (ibid. III, p. 123) on the basis of Atkins 1940, pp. 217–18.

[6] T. Marlb. pp. 570–71. For Odense see below, ch. 11.

religion. Such names also helped to remove possible confusion between monks with the same baptismal name, a difficulty that was becoming more marked as the convent grew in size. Nevertheless, some duplication of baptismal names remained at Evesham c.1104: the names Adam, Deormann, Nicholas, Peter, Ralph, Richard, and Wigod all occur twice in the list of monks, and Robert and Roger three times each. The renaming process was evidently not applied consistently. A proportion of those with new names c.1104 could have been foreigners. Likewise, any of the assumed names could have been held by an Englishman, and some of the new names were undoubtedly taken by monks of English or half-English parentage; for instance, Clement was a son of the Englishman Godric who had been one of Abbot Manni's goldsmiths,[7] and Dominic had English sympathies and may have been a native speaker.[8]

Whether the recipients of new names were English or foreign, each of the names was evidently chosen by Walter, for none is that of an English saint except in the cases of Alban and Ecgwine. Special considerations applied to them; St Alban was in fact Romano-British and his cult was among the very few from these islands that had acquired a following on the continent; St Ecgwine was internationally obscure but at Evesham his saintly status was vital to the abbey's current standing and would therefore be proclaimed at every opportunity. The giving of assumed names that were not English would have helped Walter to make Evesham more aware of the European history and culture to which the chosen names belonged. It was one way in which he may have hoped to coax the monks towards a broader view of the world than their predecessors had known under Abbot Æthelwig. The need had apparently passed by the 1130s; the monks Ambrose, Macarius, and Vincent are known to have been still alive then[9] but assumed names like theirs have not been found at Evesham after that. The names listed c.1104, whether baptismal or assumed, are of little value as a measure of the continental element, if any, among Walter's monks. What they do suggest, however, is that Walter would accept English recruits on the understanding that Evesham could not remain forever a stronghold of Englishness.

When the Evesham chronicler wrote that Walter 'increased the firmness of the order'[10] he was evidently referring among other things to the influence of Archbishop Lanfranc's 'Monastic Constitutions', which had been produced for Canterbury cathedral priory, probably c.1077. The 'Constitutions' replaced the

7 T. Marlb. pp. 84–5.

8 Dominic, *V. Ecgwini*, p. 67; M. Lapidge, ed., 'The Digby-Gotha Recension of the Life of St Ecgwine', *VEHS Res. Pap.* 7 (1979), 39–55 (at 53).

9 Harley 3763, fol. 93v. Datable temp. Abbot Reynold and before the death of Godfrey abbot of Winchcombe 1137×1138 (Knowles et al. 2001, p. 79).

10 T. Marlb. pp. 178–9.

100-year-old *Regularis concordia* with a set of customs that were based, like the *concordia,* on continental practice and, this time, especially on the customs of the abbey of Cluny in Burgundy.[11] The instructions were thorough and were set out in two parts: for the conduct of services and for the internal management of the monastery. A copy was brought to Evesham, presumably by Walter, and elements of the 'Constitutions' remained in use at the abbey in the fourteenth century.[12] One therefore assumes that those elements, at least, were observed at Evesham from the late eleventh century and throughout the twelfth. Although the 'Constitutions' were idealistic they were not revolutionary and were no affront to Walter's monks, some of whom had been trained in a different tradition. Indeed, if one were prepared to venture beyond the sparse records of religion at Evesham in the twelfth century, the 'Constitutions' would probably serve as a detailed guide to the complex procedures of its church and cloister during that time.

Abbot Walter was an innovator but he knew that the abbey had been raised to its current eminence by his English predecessors and that Evesham would continue to draw strength from them if their achievements were actively broadcast. He therefore encouraged the writing of a continuation of the Evesham *Gesta abbatum* to cover the years from 1016 to 1078, and it was fashioned to culminate in a very full account of the career of Walter's mighty predecessor Æthelwig.[13] The unknown continuator was interested in Greek medical learning because he shows the reader that he knows the Greek names for the illnesses of abbots Manni ('infirmitatem quam Greci paralisin appellant') and Æthelwig ('dolorem … quem Greci podagra appellant').[14] No such references occur in earlier or later parts of the *Gesta* and that is how one can tell that the continuation 1016–78 was once a separate piece of work. From 1044 onwards it also mentions the abbots' dates, a refinement never found in the earlier *Gesta.*

Unlike Æthelwig, Walter had acquired a fine education in liberal and grammatical studies before he came to Evesham, and during his time there he made sure that copies were made of many of the books that the abbey was lacking.[15] Among the manuscripts that were made for Evesham in Abbot Walter's time, a fragment of a service book may have survived as Oxford, Jesus College, MS 51, fol. 1 (Fig. 6). It is a single leaf from an antiphoner (a book of chants) and contains chants for the feast of St Stephen (26 December). It has been described as the

[11] Lanfranc, *Const.* pp. xxxiv–xxxv, xxxix–xlii.

[12] Lanfranc, *Const.* pp. 160 n. 362, 182 n. 393, 190 n. 398; *Penwortham Docs*, pp. 90–93, 105–111; *Evesham Officium*, pp. xiv–xv.

[13] Darlington 1933, pp. 1–10.

[14] T. Marlb. pp. 158, 174.

[15] T. Marlb. pp. 176–9.

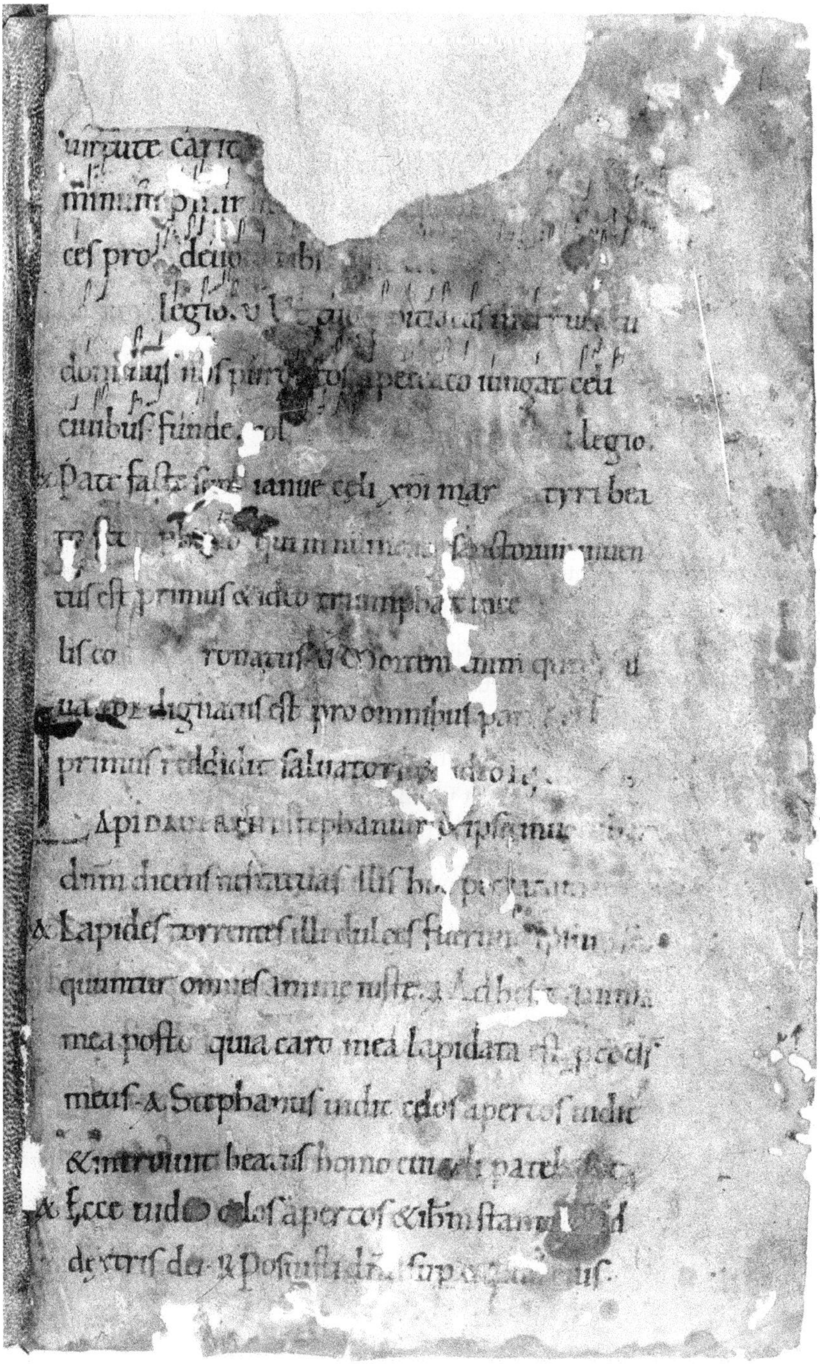

Fig. 6. Leaf from an antiphoner, possibly from Evesham. The vertical marks above the first six lines are neumes, an early form of musical notation. Height 26cm. Oxford, Jesus College, MS 51, fol. 1r.

work of 'an expert scribe writing pure late Anglo-Caroline minuscule'.[16] Though the manuscript seems to have been written after the Conquest, the script is characteristically English and appears not to have absorbed any continental features;[17] moreover, one of the chants is accompanied by musical notation in the form of Anglo-Saxon neumes. The volume with which it is bound seems to have been at Evesham in the late Middle Ages and the leaf was already in place then.[18] If one is correct in assuming that the antiphoner was produced after 1066 at Evesham, the surviving leaf provides some additional evidence that English culture was slow to be superseded there; it is one of several indications that Walter, while embracing European ideas, was careful to avoid a clean sweep of Evesham's inheritance.[19]

A growing establishment

There are signs that by the end of the eleventh century some items of estate income were being allocated to specific needs within the monastery. Thus a suspect charter from Abbot Æthelwig's early years allocates the profits from Acton to 'the brothers' food' and the income from an estate at Dorsington to 'the brothers' clothing'.[20] It was also said that Æthelwig ordered c.1070 that the dean should be given 'his tithes', which may mean that the dean had some discrete income; and his successor the prior was entitled in the early thirteenth century to the great and small tithes of Bengeworth.[21] It was likewise alleged that before c.1078 Acton and Bransford had been intended for 'the food of those serving God' at Evesham abbey;[22] and by the 1080s the Lench (Sheriffs Lench) estate was deemed to have been assigned to 'the monks' table'.[23] Writing in the late eleventh century the monk Dominic states that in Ecgwine's time a small proportion of the minster's landed endowment, twelve hides (*mansae*), was set aside for the monks' food.[24] The information need not be true of the eighth century but it is yet another indication that in Abbot Walter's day the permanent allocation

16 Gullick 1998, p. 18 n. 32.

17 T. Webber, 'The Norman Conquest and Handwriting in England to 1100', *The Cambridge History of the Book in England*, I, ed. R. Gameson (Cambridge, 2012), pp. 211–24 (at p. 222).

18 K. D. Hartzell, *Catalogue of Manuscripts written or owned in England up to 1200 containing Music* (Woodbridge, 2006), p. 507 no. 301.

19 Below, ch. 11.

20 S1479.

21 T. Marlb. pp. 168–9, 392–3, 540–41.

22 'ad uictum seruorum dei illius ecclesie': Darlington 1933, p. 188 (from 'Evesham N').

23 'ad mensam fratrum': *Regesta Wm I*, pp. 460–62 nos 136–7.

24 Dominic, *V. Ecgwini*, pp. 90, 103.

of a certain source of income to a particular purpose would have seemed appropriate.

If the prior had some discrete sources of income in the late eleventh century, so presumably did the abbot. There seems to be no evidence that in the time of Abbot Walter there was yet a strict separation of the abbot's revenues from those of the convent, but one detects in his day the first tangible signs that the abbot's personal status had grown with his abbey and had drawn him further apart from the community. The 'Rule' had always placed the abbot in authority over his monks and thus at some remove from them. Moreover, Walter's predecessors had often been absent on business, and while at Evesham they would have needed access to a private room in which confidential matters could be dealt with. In such ways the abbot had always been separate from the convent. About the time of Walter's death, however, we hear of the 'abbot's chamber' manned by four lay servants and of the 'hall', perhaps also his, with three more servants. Even if he often joined the monks at their meals, one assumes that the abbot worked and slept in those quarters, the existence of which would have visibly confirmed that he had become permanently detached from the convent's everyday life. Contact between the abbot and the individual monk would in any case have become ever more distant as the brethren based at Evesham increased in number from twelve in 1058 to fifty-seven by the end of Walter's abbacy.[25]

The establishment had so grown in physical size by c.1100 that it required a staff of sixty-three lay servants. Some of them were attached to particular buildings, which included the abbey church, the infirmary, the cellar, the kitchen, the bakehouse, and the bath-house. Others worked out of doors in the orchard, the garden, or the vineyard, or were employed as fishermen. Yet others manned the great gateway or served as watchmen. If the monks were to preserve something of their fundamental dedication to prayer they needed more than ever to seclude themselves from the worldly distractions that the success of their institution had generated. Thus the great gateway continued to exclude the general public from the courtyard while an inner doorway that led from the yard to the cloister had its own paid keeper and helped to prevent the monks' comparative stillness from being disturbed by the horses, carts, servants, tradesmen, and visitors that had their proper business outside in the yard.[26]

Some administrative duties were so important that they were better assigned to professionals than left to unworldly monks or uneducated servants. The most senior of such posts was that of the abbey steward. It was a position of much

[25] *Durham Liber vitae*, I, pp. 103–4; T. Marlb. pp. 174–5, 570–71.

[26] T. Marlb. pp. 570–71.

importance to the abbey and of high prestige to its holder. Wisely or not, Abbot Walter soon dismissed the current steward and gave the office to one of his relatives; the position was at the same time made hereditary.[27] The steward probably presided over the court of 'Fissesberg' hundred and over the abbot's manorial courts in the Vale of Evesham and perhaps already over other aspects of secular management outside the monastic precinct.[28] By 1086 the manorial geography of the Vale estates did not necessarily respect the integrity of townships — the land units that had evolved before the Conquest. For instance, Lenchwick manor included Norton township; Offenham manor included Aldington, Bretforton Lower End, and South Littleton; Wickhamford manor had Bretforton Upper End; and part of Wickhamford township was in Willersey manor.[29] The abbey had evidently devised the manorial pattern after the Bretforton and Littleton land units had been divided. The grouping of townships into manors seems to have been a matter of administrative convenience, because it avoided the proliferation of manor courts that would have resulted from every township having its own; the abbey's policy may have been to put the smaller townships with the larger. We do not know exactly when the pattern was formed, however, or by whom, though the abbey's steward was presumably responsible for making it work.

By the end of Walter's abbacy there were three resident secular clerks[30] whose duties perhaps included the preparation of documents and the handling of monetary receipts and payments. In that respect Evesham paralleled Worcester, where Bishop Wulfstan's leading chaplain seems to have been supported by a body of clerks, who were sometimes also called chaplains.[31] Walter had probably performed writing duties during his time as chaplain to Archbishop Lanfranc and, if so, would have appreciated the importance of such work. But the steward's remit was extensive and he probably called on the services of the clerks at least as much as the abbot did, even though the business was done in the abbot's name. In order to authenticate and close the abbot's letters, the clerks may have used a special seal so that they could not be read until the wax was broken. The matrix of such a seal came to light in 1982 at Great Hampton, near Evesham (Fig. 7). It is circular and is made of a fine-grained stone or possibly of a fired ceramic. Skilfully engraved, it portrays a dignified figure seated and robed, probably an abbot; any wax impression from the matrix would show him holding a pastoral staff in his

[27] T. Marlb. pp. 178–9.

[28] Brand 1992, pp. 155, 161.

[29] DB, fols 166r, 175v. For identification of the Bretforton and Littleton divisions see Cox 1975, p. 27.

[30] T. Marlb. pp. 570–71.

[31] *Worc. Acta 1062–1185*, p. lvi.

Fig. 7. Seal matrix found near Evesham. Diameter 58mm. Thickness 13mm. Evesham, Almonry Heritage Centre. Photo by D. C. Cox 1982.

right hand and holding out his open left hand, perhaps in greeting. There was also an inscription round the circumference of the design but it is now lost except for traces of what may have been a final *A*. An Evesham provenance cannot be demonstrated beyond doubt but it is credibly inferred from the place of discovery, and it has therefore been concluded that the matrix was probably made for Abbot Walter or inherited by him from his predecessor Æthelwig. Not far beyond Great Hampton, however, is Pershore, and the final *A* of the inscription could be the ending of … DE PERSORA ('… of Pershore'), which would make Pershore abbey the original owner. The matrix's nearest known parallels are the seal of Bishop

Wulfstan, which he was using by 1089, and the seal matrix of Peter bishop of Chester (1072–85); and the 'Evesham' design is unlike that of any known seal of an abbot or prior of later date.[32]

[32] D. C. Cox and T. A. Heslop, 'An Eleventh-Century Seal Matrix from Evesham, Worcs.', *Ant. Jnl* 64 (1984), 396, 419 nn. 102–5, and pl. LII; Zarnecki et al. 1984, p. 315 no. 363; J. Cherry, 'The Lead Seal Matrix of Peter Bishop of Chester', *Ant. Jnl* 65 (1985), 472–3 and pl. CVI; E. Okasha, 'A Second Supplement to Hand-List of Anglo-Saxon Non-Runic Inscriptions', *ASE* 21 (1993), 37–85 (at 45 no. 191 and pl. II); Bryant 2012, pp. 373–4 (Evesham no. 2) and illus. nos 722–8.

CHAPTER 11

God's work

A new abbey church

ONE of Walter's personal priorities on arrival at Evesham was the building of a new abbey church in the grand Romanesque style (Fig. 8).[1] He had come to Evesham with architectural ideas that were inspired by his mentor Lanfranc's great new churches at Caen in Normandy and at Canterbury, and by St Augustine's abbey, also at Canterbury; all of them Walter had seen being built. He was eager to begin at Evesham and there was no need to delay because he had enough money to make a start, with the five chests of silver that Æthelwig had left for the purpose. Walter and his master mason planned an east arm three bays long, which would consist of a broad central space that was flanked by arcades of columnar piers, was roofed in timber, and ended in an apse. The east arm would have side aisles groin-vaulted in stone, each of which would have its own apse. The central space of the east arm would be where the high altar was to stand and thus where the monks' conventual masses would be held daily. On or above the altar would be placed the relics of St Ecgwine, which had been housed in the crypt of the pre-Conquest church. Underneath the east arm would be a groin-vaulted crypt of three parallel compartments that corresponded in plan to the east arm above. The central compartment of the crypt would be subdivided by two east–west rows of colonettes that would help to support the floor above. The aisles of the crypt were to be divided from the central compartment by rows of massive rectangular piers, each of which would support one of the columnar piers above. The purpose of the crypt would be to house the altar of St Mary. West of the east arm and its crypt would be a square crossing defined by four tall compound piers supporting a tower. The monks' stalls would stand in the crossing, two rows of them on the north side of it and two on the south, and that is where the convent would gather at intervals during the day and night to sing the monastic offices required by the 'Rule' and its supplements. Flanking the crossing would be north and south transepts, each of them with an apsidal chapel on its east side, and west of the crossing would be a timber-roofed nave of eight bays with arcades

[1] This section is based on Cox 2010a.

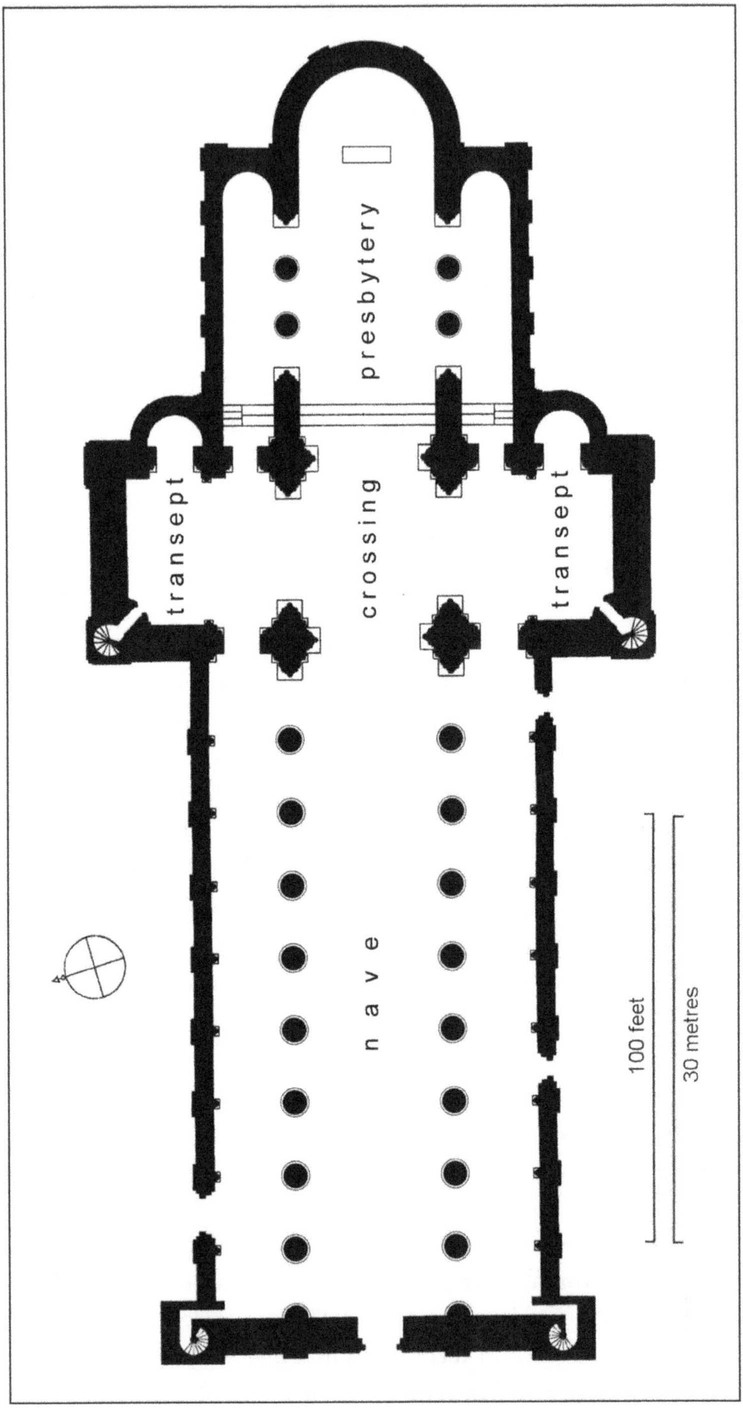

Fig. 8. The abbey church begun c.1079. Ground plan, partly conjectural, based on excavations and documentary sources.

supported on compound piers and with groin-vaulted side aisles. The whole design would give Evesham the first great church in Worcester diocese to be built in the continental style. There was no other until 1084, when Bishop Wulfstan started to follow Walter's example by building a new cathedral at Worcester. The design of Walter's church would provide for all the essentials of the liturgy but it was conceived on a scale that went far beyond what was practically necessary; and it had plan elements that served no essential purpose but which the Romanesque architectural tradition regarded as indispensable — transepts and a nave. It should be understood that the abbey church was intended to be much more than a working building; after all, the Anglo-Saxon abbots had already met that need, with a church that the monk Dominic described nostalgically as 'at that time one of the most beautiful in England'.[2] The new church had greater ambition. It was meant to strike its users and visitors with religious awe and to put them in mind of God's glory and omnipotence. It would also proclaim to everyone that Evesham abbey was among the great monasteries of the Anglo-Norman realm because it was built like them. Moreover, its great size would remind the local people that within its own territory the abbey was all-powerful under the king.

The plan of the whole building was first marked on the ground and laid out in such a way as to avoid for as long as possible the eventual demolition of the last remnant of the principal Anglo-Saxon abbey church; that had to be preserved until enough of the new church was built and ready for use. In no other way could the essential daily offices and masses of the monastic community be continued without interruption. Oolitic limestone was brought in from the Cotswolds for the dressed wall surfaces of the new building. For the rubble cores of the walls and piers the masons used blue lias limestone, which was a hard but friable material unsuitable for being squared or carved. The abbey had its own supply of it from quarries at Cleeve hill, which was then in the manor of Offenham, and oxen from that manor were used to haul it to Evesham. Once each functioning part of the church was finished the corresponding part of the old church could be pulled down, but its materials might still be useful; the rubble of the old east arm was used to fill in the crypt beneath it.

Progress was sometimes hindered by difficulties in getting the right stone and timber, and it was seriously delayed when Æthelwig's money ran out. We do not know whether Æthelwig had expected his five chests of silver to cover the cost of the entire church, but Walter had wanted everything to be as beautiful as possible and his own scheme may have exceeded in size and fine detail whatever it was that Æthelwig had provided for. It was time for Walter to draw a pecuniary advantage

[2] T. Marlb. pp. 102–3.

from St Ecgwine's growing reputation, so he sent for two monks and instructed them to carry Ecgwine's relics through England and to preach to the people; one of the monks, called Heremann, had joined the abbey in Walter's time[3] and may have been chosen because he was young and fit. The purpose of the tour was to persuade the public that they could receive Ecgwine's help in their personal difficulties if they made donations. We hear of Heremann and his companion, accompanied by their attendants, travelling to Oxford, London, Rochester, and Winchester, and to Lewes priory in Sussex, and we also find them much farther north, crossing the Trent. As they journeyed they accumulated stories of miracles that had been bestowed by Ecgwine on particular donors, and they were able to use them to elicit more contributions as they progressed. On their return to Evesham bearing a great deal of money, a written record was made of the donations received and of the miracles that were reported to have been the donors' rewards.[4] It had been a straightforward exercise in the open exploitation of relics for money, and with the new funds Walter was able to finish the east arm, crypt, crossing, transepts, and the first stage of the central tower. Everything was thus in place for the monks to conduct their services in the new building, and at that point Walter decided to call a temporary halt. It meant postponing construction of the planned nave, which was a part of the building that would eventually impress the world but was not immediately wanted for monastic worship. Since Walter did not live to begin the nave of the new church, however, that of its Anglo-Saxon predecessor had to remain standing for a time so that the local people could continue holding their services in it.

The cult of saints and the liturgy

The range of historical reference embodied in the religious names that were taken by Evesham monks under Walter's direction suggests that he had a broad view of Evesham's place in the Christian tradition and was not wedded to the place's local associations. Walter nevertheless valued sincerely the status that Evesham derived from the remains of its local saints, and it was in that spirit that he took Lanfranc's advice to test any Evesham relics of which the genuine holiness might be doubted, so that the credibility of the rest should not be compromised. Walter decided to test by fire the bones of Credan and Wigstan,[5] who at the time were virtually unknown as saints except at Evesham.[6] According to eyewitnesses of the tests their bones

[3] He occurs c.1104 (*Durham Liber vitae*, I, p. 103) but not c.1077 (*Worc. Acta 1062–1185*, p. 6).

[4] T. Marlb. pp. 102–17.

[5] *Evesham Chron.* pp. 323, 335.

[6] Farmer 2011, pp. 105, 455; Rollason 1981, p. 4.

emerged from the flames completely untouched,[7] and as a result Walter was able during the rest of his abbacy to take confident steps towards magnifying the reputation of all Evesham's saints, having established beyond doubt that their worth could not be challenged again. Walter's greatest ally in that policy was the monk Dominic. Probably of English parentage, Dominic was recruited to the abbey some time after the ordeal by fire had taken place. He was to excel as a hagiographer, and during the abbacies of Walter and his two successors Dominic produced works that were designed to spread the fame of Evesham's saints, especially Ecgwine and Odulf, and that of the Virgin Mary, who was the abbey's earliest dedicatee. By 1100[8] Dominic had rewritten Byrhtferth's *vita* of St Ecgwine in a style that was more accessible to contemporary readers, especially by avoiding the esoteric vocabulary and elaborate verbiage that were characteristic of Byrhtferth's writing but which had become disagreeable to current taste. And Dominic enhanced the *vita* further by adding to it a collection of miracles that Ecgwine had supposedly performed after Byrhtferth's time.[9] Near the end of Walter's abbacy it seems that Ecgwine's importance was acknowledged even more conspicuously by adding his name to that of St Mary in the abbey's formal dedication. In 1086 Domesday referred to the 'church of St Mary of Evesham'[10] but charters produced at Evesham c.1100 begin to name Mary and Ecgwine as joint patrons.[11]

From Walter's close connection with Lanfranc one may reasonably infer that the conduct of the liturgy at Evesham from Walter's day onwards was much influenced by the detailed recommendations in Lanfranc's 'Monastic Constitutions'. Lanfranc's preferred liturgical practices were evidently subject to local variations, at Evesham and elsewhere,[12] but the Evesham ceremonies would certainly have had the same carefully ordered complexity and visual drama as his, and considerable expertise was required of the monks who arranged them. The sacrist was responsible for looking after the church's furnishings, plate, and sacred vessels, preparing the hosts for Mass, and supervising the timetable of services. The services themselves were prepared and directed by the precentor, who was also the musical director. To ensure the smooth performance of the liturgy he coached monks privately in their chants and readings whenever they needed guidance, and before a service gave the abbot notice of the chants that he was to sing.[13]

7 *Evesham Chron.* pp. 323, 335–7.

8 Byrhtferth, p. xc.

9 *ODNB* ('Evesham, Dominic of').

10 DB, fol. 165v.

11 S1026 (a copy c.1100 of a spurious charter), S1214 (probably forged c.1100).

12 R. W. Pfaff, *The Liturgy in Medieval England: A History* (Cambridge, 2009), pp. 107–10, 190–91.

13 Lanfranc, *Const.* pp. 118–25; *Penwortham Docs*, pp. 106–8.

Ceremonial would have been apparent most grandly at the chief festivals of the Christian year and at the feasts of the local saints, the greatest of whom was Ecgwine. By the end of the eleventh century St Ecgwine had two principal annual feasts at Evesham, those of the 'deposition' on the supposed anniversary of his burial (30 December) and the 'translation' on the anniversary (10 September) of the placing of his relics in a shrine in 1040. Ecgwine also had a lesser translation feast on 10 October, presumably to commemorate the move to another shrine in 1054. Ecgwine's deposition was the most important of his three feasts and the only one of the three that is known to have been celebrated at other houses, which included the abbeys of Bury St Edmunds and Crowland and the cathedrals of Salisbury and Worcester.[14] The deposition fell inconveniently, however, at Christmas; the liturgical kalendar was particularly crowded then[15] and the prospective pilgrim could not be sure of fair weather and dry roads for the journey to Evesham.

Oswald bishop of Worcester had refounded Evesham in the tenth century and was honoured there with three annual feasts. That of the deposition was held on 28 February and was celebrated at a number of other houses, including, of course, Worcester. The feast of Oswald's translation was held at Evesham and Worcester on 15 April, which was the anniversary of Oswald's first translation at Worcester in 1002. Evesham also celebrated the feast of Oswald's second Worcester translation, which had taken place on 8 October about the year 1089.[16] As for the lesser Evesham cults, we find that the feast of St Credan, who was supposed to be the eighth-century Evesham abbot of that name, took place annually at Evesham on 19 August and the deposition feast of St Wigstan was celebrated there on 1 June. A short *vita* of St Wigstan may have been written before the removal of his relics from Repton to Evesham and that may then have been the *vita* that was known at Evesham until the 1180s, when Thomas of Marlborough revised it; there is an alternative suggestion, however: that a new version of Wigstan's *vita* was written at Evesham after the relics arrived there and that Thomas's revision was based on that.[17] Odulf's principal feast took place annually on 12 June and had been observed at Evesham ever since the arrival of his relics in Abbot Ælfweard's time.[18] Odulf also had two translation feasts at Evesham, one on 24 November, which was perhaps the anniversary of the relics' arrival at Evesham, and another

14 Unless otherwise noted, Evesham's principal feasts and their dates appear in F. Wormald, ed., *English Kalendars before A.D. 1100*, I, HBS 72 (London, 1934), pp. 100–111, 198–209; R. Rushforth, *Saints in English Kalendars before A.D. 1100*, HBS 117 (Woodbridge, 2008 for 2005), tables I–XII (between pp. 58–9).

15 Byrhtferth, pp. lxxxvi–lxxxvii.

16 For Oswald's translation dates see Byrhtferth, p. lxxiv.

17 Rollason 1981, pp. 8–9; Hayward 1993, p. 82 n. 4.

18 *Evesham Chron.* p. 314.

on 10 October, which was the anniversary of the transfer of his relics to a new shrine in 1054. When one considers all the saints' days that had to be observed at Evesham, and not just the special local ones, it is evident that the liturgical year was a demanding one that required much time and impeccable planning.

The monks took their seats in the choir stalls at several set times through the day and night, whether or not it was a feast day with special ceremonies, in order to perform the Divine Office that had been required of monks since the time of St Benedict. It was a daily round of services that consisted of psalms, readings, and prayers. Twice a day the monks also attended a conventual mass. Thus they spent much of their time inside the church, absorbed in communal worship in the presence of their saints. In that setting their mundane concerns could be put aside for certain periods to allow each monk to think about God. Not all of the monks could be scholars, artists, or craftsmen and some might not even be proficient readers of Latin or able to hold themselves in private prayer and contemplation, but every monk could hope to be sustained by his daily devotions within that deep reservoir of stillness, the abbey church conceived by Walter, its solid walls and arches the very image of Eternity.

Evesham and Denmark

At a date between 1095 and 1100 and with the permission of King William II ('Rufus'), the abbot sent a group of twelve Evesham monks to Odense, the main city of the Danish island of Fyn;[19] their role was to form a monastic chapter for the new cathedral that had been begun at Odense by the late King Cnut IV. What we know of the preceding negotiations suggests that Evesham already had a good name abroad. The party went at the request of Cnut's half-brother King Erik I, and he was acting on the advice of Hubald the bishop there. The Danish Church was drawing freely on its English contacts at the time and the idea of a cathedral staffed by monks instead of secular canons was especially English.[20] King Erik seems to have visited the cathedral priory of Durham at some time during his reign (1095–1103) and it may have been there that he became familiar

[19] This section is based on Knowles 1963a, pp. 163–4, 475; P. King, 'English Influence on the Church at Odense in the Early Middle Ages', *Jnl of Ecclesiastical History* 13 (1962), 145–55 (at 146–8, 153); P. King, 'The Cathedral Priory of Odense in the Middle Ages', *Saga-Book of the Viking Soc. for Northern Research* 16 (1962–65), 192–214 (at 193–200); T. Marlb. pp. 570–71.

[20] M. Münster-Swendsen, 'Educating the Danes: Anglo-Danish Connections in the Formative Period of the Danish Church, c.1000–1150', *Friendship and Social Networks in Scandinavia, c.1000–1800*, ed. J. Viðar and T. S. Sigurðsson (Turnhout, 2013), pp. 153–73.

not only with the concept of a monastic cathedral but also with the reputation of Evesham abbey;[21] the Durham monks held Evesham in special esteem[22] because their first prior, Ealdwine (1083–87), had been leader of the group from Evesham that had travelled to the north in the 1070s.[23] The twelve monks who were sent from Evesham to Odense more than twenty years later were to find themselves part of an enterprise that surpassed Ealdwine's northern expedition in ambition if not in historic consequences. Their purpose this time was quite different from his; it was not to find a haven of humble solitude but to establish fully developed Benedictine monasticism in an urban setting, the city of Odense. They created one of the earliest monasteries in Denmark, and it seems to have conveyed influence and personnel to some later Danish houses.[24] It would have been necessary for the original Evesham mission to bring some books with them, and there is an early-eleventh-century manuscript from Worcester (Copenhagen, Kongelige Bibliotek, Gl. Kgl. Sam. 1595), consisting mostly of liturgical works and sermons, that could conceivably have been taken to Odense or another Danish house as a gift from Worcester or Evesham.[25] Be that as it may, in the earlier twelfth century the cathedral priory at Odense was deemed to be a daughter-house of Evesham abbey and the abbey was expected to confirm the elections of its priors. In the mid-twelfth century, however, such close ties seem to have been neglected. They were renewed in 1174 and a monk of Evesham, William, was then sent to Odense and installed as prior. Nevertheless, it seems that by c.1200 the cathedral priory was considered to be independent; there is no later record of a link with Evesham. The religious body planted with Walter's monks had formed roots and branches of its own.

Pastoral care in the Vale

For most of the people who lived on the abbey's estates in the Vale of Evesham in Abbot Walter's time there was no permanent place of worship but the abbey church. The only other churches that were conveniently available to some of the inhabitants were at Church Honeybourne, over seven miles to the east of Evesham, and at Church Lench, about five miles to the north, but we do not

21 P. Gazzoli, 'Anglo-Danish Connections and the Origins of the Cult of Knud', *Jnl of the North Atlantic*, special vol. 4 (2013), 69–76 (at 72–3). I am indebted to Dr Gazzoli for a copy of his article.

22 *Durham Liber vitae*, I, pp. 103–4.

23 Knowles et al. 2001, pp. 43, 92.

24 L. Abrams, 'The Anglo-Saxons and the Christianization of Scandinavia', *ASE* 24 (1995), 213–49 (at 239).

25 J. E. Cross and J. M. Tunberg, eds, *The Copenhagen Wulfstan Collection*, Early English Manuscripts in Facsimile 25 (Copenhagen, 1993), pp. 60–62.

know whether the abbey had allowed them to provide the full range of sacraments. Church Honeybourne and Church Lench were the only Evesham estates in the Vale on which a resident priest was recorded in Domesday Book.[26] Neither church, however, seems to have been built by the abbey. Each had probably been provided by a former landholder; Evesham would have become patron of the church only when it acquired the estate.

At Church Honeybourne the church had evidently been built before the Honeybourne estate was divided into Church Honeybourne and Cow Honeybourne, and thus at some time before the early tenth century. It had been intended by its builder to serve the undivided estate; in the twelfth century, and therefore long after the division had taken place, the chapel at Cow Honeybourne was held to be dependent on Church Honeybourne church.[27] There is no evidence that the church of Evesham ever possessed Honeybourne when it was undivided or even that it had always possessed the Church Honeybourne division of that estate; the abbey's claim to have acquired Church Honeybourne in Ecgwine's day is a late fabrication.[28] Church Honeybourne was included in the core estates of the abbey by the mid-tenth century when it formed part of the abbey's 'Fissesberg' hundred,[29] but it is excluded from those estates by an undated pre-Conquest set of charter bounds.[30] It seems that Evesham had not always held Church Honeybourne and had not built the church that stood there. At Church Lench the name of the estate included the element *circe* ('church') by 1086,[31] but Evesham had acquired the estate as recently as Abbot Manni's time (1044–58)[32] and it had therefore not been assigned to the abbey's 'Fissesberg' hundred in the tenth century;[33] again the abbey's claim to have acquired Church Lench in Ecgwine's time is spurious.[34] It is therefore probable that the church had been built before Evesham owned the estate.

Abbot Walter was the first to place pastoral supervision of the abbey's Vale estates in the hands of a secular priest called a 'dean'.[35] Those estates still constituted

26 DB, fol. 175v.

27 *Winchcombe Landboc*, I, pp. 216–17.

28 S80, S1250; T. Marlb. pp. 130–31.

29 Cox 1975, pp. 28, 31, 36–40.

30 S1591a, which treats separately the bounds of Poden, a detached estate later included in Church Honeybourne parish. For a map of the Poden bounds in 1652 see F. Allen, 'A Topographicall Discription and a Breefe Relation of the Mannor of Powden': Worcester, Worcestershire Archives, ref. x899:49, BA 10030.

31 DB, fol. 175v.

32 T. Marlb. pp. 158–9.

33 Cox 1975, pp. 28, 31, 36–40.

34 S80; T. Marlb. pp. 130–31.

35 T. Marlb. pp. 178–9.

a single parish and the responsibility for providing pastoral care within it had probably rested until then on the abbot's deputy,[36] a monk who had been called 'dean' until Walter's time.[37] Walter's creation of a secular deanery of the Vale in his own gift may have been intended not only to improve spiritual provision for the inhabitants but also to offer a deliberate challenge to the growing pastoral zeal of the bishop and his archdeacon. The archdeacon was a priest whom a bishop appointed to oversee pastoral care in the parishes of his diocese, and Worcester diocese under Bishop Wulfstan had an archdeacon by 1086, an Englishman called Æthelric.[38] Unless a parish or group of parishes could prove that it had an historic exemption and the means to manage its own pastoral care, the archdeacon would have the right to intervene there on the bishop's behalf. It can hardly be a coincidence that in Walter's time a myth was being propagated that Bishop Ecgwine had resigned his bishopric before withdrawing to Evesham to become the first abbot;[39] the abbey felt that it was becoming increasingly necessary to pretend that no bishop of Worcester had ever had lawful control of the church of Evesham since Ecgwine's day or had ever exercised any pastoral care in the Vale. During the course of the twelfth century, however, the bishops would seek to tighten further their supervision of the diocese, and the conflict of powers between Worcester and Evesham would then become acute.

36 That was the understanding in the early thirteenth century: ibid. pp. 484–5.

37 *Worc. Acta 1062–1185*, p. 6.

38 Ibid. p. 180.

39 S81. For two estimates of the date of this forgery, both falling within Walter's abbacy, see Hart 1975, p. 74 no. 44; Clarke 2012a, pp. 139–40.

CHAPTER 12

The estates under threat

WALTER could not expect to match Æthelwig's experience and aptitude when it came to worldly matters[1] and when he first came to Evesham he also had much to learn about local people and their personal connections. It was almost inevitable that in some respects Walter's abbacy would begin by upsetting them. Matters were especially difficult for him because he had also to contend with the resentment felt by everyone whom Æthelwig had outmanoeuvred to gain estates for the abbey; they nursed a latent bitterness, which Æthelwig's personal authority had forced them to suppress. Among the aggrieved parties the monks of Worcester cathedral priory were the ones most able to put their feelings about Æthelwig into words, and they propagated a story that implied that God shared their hostility towards him. They said that when Bishop Wulfstan heard that Æthelwig was dead his natural charity had moved him to offer prayers for the abbot's soul but that on doing so he had been instantly stricken with the abbot's disease of gout. When Wulfstan's physicians were unable to find a cure, he had resorted to prayer and it was revealed to him one night that it was his praying for Æthelwig that had incurred the affliction. Wulfstan stopped interceding for him and within a few days had completely recovered.[2]

Walter was unable to reverse the local ill-will that Æthelwig's death had released, but his own initial tactlessness made matters worse. Walter had refused to accept as his feudal tenants many of the English people who had commended their estates to Æthelwig's personal protection. Walter did so in order that he could oust the holders and gain unfettered control of their land. Moreover, it was suspected that Walter was acting partly under the influence of young relatives who had followed him to Evesham[3] in expectation of gains for themselves. They were not disappointed, in fact, for in due course Walter would enfeoff his brother Randal, against the monks' wishes, with the manors of Weethley and Kinwarton in Warwickshire and Lark Stoke in Gloucestershire, and probably with the manor of Abbots Morton near Evesham, as well as with substantial estates at Littleton

1 T. Marlb. pp. 176–7.
2 Hemming, I, pp. 272–3.
3 T. Marlb. pp. 176–7.

and Bretforton.[4] Walter's sister Aubrey ('Albreda') was to receive a large portion of Hampton near Evesham, his nephew Hugh an estate in Lenchwick manor, probably at Norton, and his brother Geoffrey an estate at Badby.[5] Walter's family seems to have received twenty-nine hides altogether, more than half of which went to his brother Randal.[6] In order to support a body of knights, however, Walter had to extend his grants of feudal tenancies beyond members of his family; since Abbot Æthelwig's time the abbey had been under an obligation to supply knights, said to have been five, to the king's army whenever required. In Henry I's reign (1100–1135) the equivalent of four and a half knights was owed but the quota was certainly reckoned to be five before 1166[7] and so it remained in 1218.[8] At first the knights had probably been supported by stipends from the abbey in cash or in kind. Under Walter, however, their service began to be secured by grants of monastic land in hereditary right.[9]

The posthumous reaction to Æthelwig's success as an estate builder, which was further inflamed by Walter's treatment of his English tenants and by his actual or intended nepotism, combined within a year of Walter's appointment[10] to bring about the loss of virtually all the estates that Æthelwig had acquired. The discontented had taken their complaints to King William's half-brother Odo bishop of Bayeux, who was acting as regent during the king's absence in Normandy. Odo had thereupon convened a court of the shires in which the disputed estates lay and it met at a mound called the 'gild beorh' ('assembly barrow'), which stood at or near the place where the boundaries of Worcestershire, Warwickshire, Oxfordshire, and Gloucestershire met. The court ruled that the abbey had to give up all but a few of Æthelwig's fifty-one territorial acquisitions. On the basis of that decision Odo confiscated them, kept some estates for himself to hold in chief and distributed others to new chief tenants, including Sheriff Urse and Urse's brother Robert Dispenser.[11]

Although Evesham may have had some genuine charters that had descended

4 Clarke 2012b, pp. 32–6 ('Evesham O' and 'Evesham E'); Wrottesley 1903, pp. 8–20. For Kinwarton see also DB, fol. 239r. For Abbots Morton see DB, fol. 175v.

5 Clarke 2007, pp. 83–4; Wrottesley 1903, pp. 8–20.

6 Clarke 2012b, p. 10.

7 *Regesta Hen. I*, p. 69 no. 831; *Red Bk Exch.* I, pp. 301–2.

8 I. J. Sanders, *Feudal Military Service in England: A Study of the Constitutional and Military Powers of the* Barones *in Medieval England* (London, 1956), p. 114.

9 T. Marlb. pp. 180–81.

10 'eodem anno quo abbatiam suscepit': Darlington 1933, p. 189 (from 'Evesham N').

11 T. Marlb. pp. 176–9; Darlington 1933, pp. 188–90 ('Evesham N'); Clarke 1977, pp. 118–23; Clarke 2012b, pp. 7–8. On the site of the 'gild beorh' see Mawer and Stenton 1927, pp. 124–5.

from the former owners of some of the disputed estates,[12] the abbey seems to have had few deeds, if any, to justify its current possession of those properties. In consequence Walter could make good only a few of the abbey's claims at the 'gild beorh'. The most important that he established was probably Evesham's title to the portion of Bengeworth that Æthelwig had received from Ærngrim, the church of Worcester's tenant; the other portion had to be returned to Sheriff Urse[13] and it would remain with Urse's descendants until it was restored to the abbey in 1268.[14] Having secured the abbey's part of Bengeworth Walter tried afterwards to deny that the church of Worcester was his feudal overlord there and to assert that Evesham's estates in Bengeworth and in Hampton should not, as Worcester claimed, continue to be treated as part of Worcester's manor and parish of Cropthorne or to be subject to the bishop's hundred of Oswaldslow. That particular dispute ran on for some time until a judicial inquiry was instigated by the church of Worcester. It was held at Worcester before the king's representative Geoffrey bishop of Coutances. Following an adjournment Bishop Wulfstan brought with him a number of reliable and distinguished local witnesses to testify on Worcester's behalf, but the abbot had nothing to reinforce his position but the relics of St Ecgwine, upon which he was prepared to swear. They were not enough, however, and the court found against Walter. He dropped his claims accordingly and entered into a formal settlement with the church of Worcester, an agreement that in 1086 was declared to the Domesday commissioners.[15] Until c.1104[16] Evesham acknowledged the jurisdiction of Oswaldslow hundred over Bengeworth and Hampton, but may have neglected to recognize Worcester as manorial overlord in the abbey's part of Bengeworth: the church of Worcester is named as the tenant-in-chief on one page of Domesday Book but on another it is Evesham abbey. Moreover, Hampton and presumably part or all of Bengeworth were deemed to belong to Evesham's minster parish in ecclesiastical matters and not to Worcester's parish of Cropthorne.[17]

Consolidation

Although Walter had failed, almost completely, to keep hold of Æthelwig's new estates the eventual impact of the abbey's huge gains and losses between 1058 and c.1078 ought not to be overstated, for they had more or less cancelled each

12 Evesham had the single-sheet originals S114, S495, and S550.

13 T. Marlb. pp. 178–9; *Regesta Wm I*, pp. 457–9 nos 134–5.

14 *VCH Worcs.* II, pp. 398–9.

15 *Regesta Wm I*, pp. 993–1000 nos 347–50; *Worc. Acta 1062–1185*, pp. 14–15.

16 Below, ch. 14.

17 DB, fols 174r, 175v.

other out and the worst that can be said is that Evesham would never be able to gain from the long-term potential of the estates that it had just lost. It must be borne in mind that the abbey's income remained a good one.[18] The annual value that Domesday Book put on the estates that the abbey was left with in 1086 showed that the total secular income that they produced for the abbey, £129 17s, had increased since 1066, when the same estates were valued at £118 19s, and that in 1086 few of the estates were producing any less than they had done twenty years earlier.[19] In 1086 Evesham's landed endowment was yielding more income than the estates of any other monastery in the diocese, and among west Midland monasteries only Coventry abbey had an estate that was valued higher.[20] That evidence shows that the economy of the abbey was soundly based. But it could never be proof against adverse market conditions or the hazards of mismanagement.

In thirteen places Domesday records that Evesham abbey had corn mills, so there had been at least that much rural investment by 1086;[21] and it was not finished, for Abbot Walter had recently planted a vineyard on a hillside at Hampton, across the river from Evesham.[22] Agricultural improvements were likely to repay the abbey well, for in 1086, as in Roman times, the Vale of Evesham was part of one of the most productive arable regions of England.[23] The Vale never lost its reputation for fertility; it became proverbial and as such was celebrated again and again by the topographers of the sixteenth and early seventeenth centuries. John Leland in the 1530s saw the Vale as 'the *horreum* of Worcestershire, it is so plentiful of corn'.[24] *Horreum* is the Latin for 'granary' and, according to William Camden in 1586, the Vale 'for plentiful fertility hath well deserved to be called the granary of all these countries; so good and plentiful is the ground in yielding the best corn abundantly'.[25] In 1612 Michael Drayton topped the heap of praise with his verse 'Great Evesham's fertile glebe,

18 The distribution of Evesham's estates in 1086 is well represented by the map of 'Principal Estates of Evesham Abbey' in Bond 1973, p. 4.

19 DB, fols 165v, 174r, 175v, 222v, 239r. The figures, calculated in 'PASE Domesday' (online), do not include places where the abbey held a subtenancy that was not mentioned in DB (as at Goldor, Oxon., and Thelwall, Lancs.).

20 Knowles 1963a, pp. 702–3.

21 DB, fols 165v–166r, 175v, 239r.

22 T. Marlb. pp. 178–9; DB, fol. 175v; Bond 1973, pp. 43–4.

23 H. C. Darby, *Domesday England*, The Domesday Geography of England (Cambridge, 1977), pp. 127–8.

24 L. Toulmin Smith, ed., *The Itinerary of John Leland in or about the Years 1535–1543*, II (London, 1908), p. 53.

25 W. Camden, *Britain*, trans. P. Holland (London, 1610), p. 577, from W. Camden, *Britannia* (London, 1586), p. 316.

what tongue hath not extoll'd? / As though to her alone belong'd the garb of gold'.[26]

The general increase in the abbey's estate income before 1086 was more than usually marked at the town of Evesham, where the valuation nearly doubled in the twenty years after 1066, from 60s to 110s.[27] The recorded householders consisted in 1086 of twenty-seven *bordarii* (small tenants), described as *servientes curiae* ('employees of the abbey precinct'), who also cultivated the soil with four ploughs; in addition the abbey received annual cash rents totalling 20s. One therefore infers that the *servientes curiae* and members of their families had jobs at the abbey, their houses and land perhaps tied to it by that service, and that they also worked on the demesne land at Evesham (the land farmed directly by the abbey). Other inhabitants probably did not work on the demesne and were not employed directly by the abbey, but paid cash rents; they may have been tradesmen. The abbey also had twenty-eight houses in Worcester, and the twenty-three of them that were occupied in 1086 yielded total rents of 20s. Those figures may give an indication of the number of rent-paying households in Evesham, too, where the abbey's rent income was also 20s. That suggests a town of at least fifty households in 1086.

In Walter's time a few new estates were acquired, but more by chance than by design. There were elements of the Norman baronial class that had personal reasons for wishing to give Evesham abbey something not too large or expensive, and in Walter's time that resulted in some small grants of distant properties. One of the earliest gifts was that made by Niel, constable of Chester and lord of Halton in Cheshire. Before 1086[28] he gave the abbey a moiety (a half share) of Thelwall in Lancashire and a fishery and a hide of land at Goldor in Oxfordshire.[29] Also in Lancashire Warin Bussel gave three bovates (or hides) of land on the bank of the Ribble at Penwortham. Warin's gift was possibly prompted by his wife Maud, who may already have held land in Evesham.[30] At some time between 1087 and 1102 Roger the Poitevin, lord of Penwortham, gave an estate near there at Howick.[31] Another early gift was that of Robert of Stafford. In 1072 he had given the abbey an estate at Wrottesley in Staffordshire and afterwards, feeling that his end was

26 M. Drayton, *Poly-Olbion* (London, 1612), p. 221 (spelling modernized here). The recently-granted arms of Evesham corporation included a 'garb, or' (a golden wheatsheaf).

27 For this paragraph see DB, fol. 175v.

28 William son of Niel had succeeded to his father's estates by then: DB, fol. 266r.

29 T. Marlb. pp. 136–7. For identification of Goldor see *VCH Oxon.* VIII, p. 152.

30 *Penwortham Docs*, pp. 5–6 (gift dated temp. Abbot Walter in T. Marlb. pp. 178–9); [H. C. Maxwell Lyte, ed.] *Liber feodorum: The Book of Fees commonly called* Testa de Nevill, I (London, 1920), p. 211.

31 T. Marlb. pp. 136–7, 178–9; *ODNB* ('Montgomery, Roger de').

near, he gained permission to enter the monastery as a monk. At Evesham in 1088 he made it one of his final acts to add Loynton, also in Staffordshire, to his original gift, with a request that his body and those of his wife and son should be buried at the abbey.[32] Between 1102 and 1104 Miles Crispin lord of Wallingford in Berkshire[33] gave a minor estate at Hillingdon in Middlesex.[34] It lay on the main road between Evesham and London by way of Oxford[35] and the gift was solely designed to provide the abbot with somewhere of his own at which to stay while travelling to and from the capital,[36] a journey that he evidently had to make from time to time. Evesham was not the only monastery to receive such a gift from Miles; in 1106–7 he gave to Abingdon abbey a lodging-house on the Abingdon–London road at Colnbrook in Buckinghamshire.[37] Such small and isolated estates can hardly have been of much economic value to Evesham abbey, but they seem to have been given and accepted for special or personal reasons of which we know little. In scale and purpose they had nothing in common with the great landed endowments that had been conferred on the minster at its foundation or with those that Abbot Æthelwig had managed to acquire. Indeed, nothing of such magnitude would ever come the abbey's way again.

Muniments created

In an increasingly sophisticated legal environment Evesham was in great want of documents to prove title to its rights and possessions, and Walter's abbacy accordingly saw a local revolution in the making and keeping of records. The lawsuits in which Walter had been forced to appear had been conducted on the basis of sworn testimony on both sides. Neither Walter nor his opponents had produced current documents in court to back up their claims to disputed lands; they had relied instead on the verbal statements of sworn witnesses. In the matter of Bengeworth and Hampton, Walter made his claim by swearing on the relics of St Ecgwine and he nominated his brother Randal to defend by battle the ensuing agreement if its provisions should be challenged.[38] If Evesham had had some relevant title deeds one might expect them to have been produced in court but the

32 R. W. Eyton, ed., 'The Staffordshire Chartulary: Series I', William Salt Archaeological Soc. *Collections for a History of Staffordshire* 2, pt 1 (Birmingham, 1881), pp. 178, 182–3.

33 *VCH Mdx.* IV, p. 70 n. 18.

34 T. Marlb. pp. 136–7.

35 *VCH Mdx.* IV, pp. 58–9; Ogilby 1675, pls 1, 2, 44.

36 Tindal 1794, p. 77n.

37 J. Stevenson, ed., *Chronicon monasterii de Abingdon*, Rolls Series (London, 1858), II, p. 97.

38 *Regesta Wm I*, pp. 997–9 no. 349.

records of the hearings in which Walter was involved mention no such evidence. The abbey had probably possessed some title deeds until the mid-tenth century, only to lose most of them when the estates were taken into secular hands. Only three genuine single-sheet originals from the period to AD 949 are known to have been held in the Evesham archive and they relate only to the titles of grantees that preceded the abbey in the particular estates; they could not serve as evidence of any grant made directly to Evesham.[39] It seems likely, too, that Abbot Æthelwig had made his extensive acquisitions in the eleventh century without the benefit of written records, for after his death nothing relevant was produced in court to defend the estates before Bishop Odo. The findings of the Domesday commissioners depended on the verdicts of sworn juries and although earlier charters were sometimes produced in evidence to the inquiry, the current relevance of the deeds could be discounted by the court, as happened in the case of the abbey's Ombersley estate. There the commissioners concluded that the estate was rated for the geld (a royal tax) at fifteen hides by 1066 even though, according to the abbey's deeds, Ombersley had only three hides and they were free of geld.[40]

Domesday was a sworn record of the actual possession of an estate but it did not necessarily pronounce on its rightful ownership. After the commissioners had done their work the abbey may therefore have nurtured a hope that when Bishop Odo was dead Evesham would be able to reclaim those of its estates that he had taken before 1086, for the abbey still maintained that his confiscations had been unlawful. It may have been with that in mind that the abbey drew up a list of the estates taken away by Odo, a compilation that was probably made soon after his death in 1097.[41] Evesham still needed deeds, however, if it was to construct a title to those estates and to any others that might be disputed in the future. It therefore seems probable that Walter instructed his clerks to carry out a programme of forgery, either soon after the losses of c.1078 or near the time of Odo's death.[42] That seems to be the reason why the copies of pre-Domesday charters that have come down to us from the Evesham archive are almost all suspect to some degree.[43] It would be fair, however, to regard some of the doubtful deeds as well-intentioned reconstructions of lost or non-existent documents, or as enhancements of genuine but unhelpful ones. In the light of recent experience Evesham did not see the act of forgery as criminal, but as a matter of defending, by whatever means, that which the monks considered to be the moral truth about

39 S114 (dated 779), S495 (dated 944), S550 (dated 949).

40 DB, fol. 175v.

41 Darlington 1933, pp. 186–90 ('Evesham N'); *DB Worcs.* (Thorn), app. IV, 'Evesham N', introduction.

42 Hart 1975, pp. 63, 74, 79; Clarke 2012a, pp. 135–42.

43 F. M. Stenton, *The Latin Charters of the Anglo-Saxon Period* (Oxford, 1955), p. 11.

their right to particular estates. Responsibility for creating the forged muniments seems to lie inevitably at the door of Abbot Walter. The monks of Worcester had portrayed his predecessor Æthelwig as cunning and deceitful[44] but they had never said that he used forged documents, and Walter had offered no such documents in court c.1078 or c.1086. On balance, then, it seems that the work of forgery was probably carried out in the later part of Walter's abbacy and after 1086. By the 1090s the desirability of acquiring plausible title deeds that could be produced in court would have been obvious to everyone in authority at the abbey.

The forged pre-Conquest charters did not have to be in the guise of single-sheet originals, for it was the abbey's contention that it had lost its originals in the tenth century — which seems to have been broadly true and generally accepted. At the time it would have been sufficient for the abbey to enter 'copies' of the supposed originals in a cartulary and to produce the cartulary in evidence when required. That may have been what happened at Evesham, for there is some indication that the manuscript of the Evesham *Gesta abbatum*, which were continued up to 1078 under Walter, had charters appended to it. Walter's original manuscript no longer exists but it certainly had at least one document copied at the end. It was a forged grant from Earl Leofric of land at Hampton and was ostensibly datable to the 1030s. The continuation of the *Gesta* to 1078 refers to a full text of Leofric's charter as being present at the end of the manuscript: 'this is clearly shown in his charter which is to be found at the end of this work'.[45] The *Gesta* do not mention any other appended charters but it is difficult to imagine a special reason why only one charter, or the Hampton charter in particular, should have been added to the *Gesta* manuscript. If, then, the aim in Walter's time was to follow the *Gesta* with the full texts of forged grants, the outcome would have been an early cartulary. Only three eleventh-century English cartularies survive, all from Worcester cathedral priory.[46] If Evesham also had a cartulary at that time, one presumes that it eventually contributed texts to the later Evesham cartularies that have come down to us.

Another kind of record that made its first appearance at Evesham in Abbot Walter's time is the survey, a list of estates drawn up as an aid to administration, giving, among other details, the number of hides in each estate. Several surveys were copied out at Evesham and in most such cases were probably written there.[47]

44 Hemming, I, pp. 270–71.

45 'ueluti in carta sua que in fine huius operis habetur per scripta apertissime demonstratur': T. Marlb. pp. 156–7. The charter (S1223) is not included in the present *Gesta* manuscript.

46 G. R. C. Davis, *Medieval Cartularies of Great Britain and Ireland*, ed. C. Breay, J. Harrison, and D. M. Smith (London, 2010), pp. 217–18 nos 1068–9.

47 They are fully edited and discussed in Clarke 1977 and listed in *DB Worcs.* (Thorn), app. IV (where some are also discussed and translated).

Most of the Evesham lists that we know about were derived from Domesday Book or from its 'satellites'. Some of the surveys thus cover the whole counties of Worcestershire[48] or Gloucestershire.[49] Others, however, concern only the estates of Evesham abbey in those counties.[50] Evesham also had copies of lists that may have been produced independently of Domesday but which can be compared with it: county totals of the hidage of Evesham abbey's holdings c.1088,[51] surveys of c.1104 of Evesham abbey manors in Worcestershire and Northamptonshire,[52] and a list of Evesham abbey manors lost to Bishop Odo.[53] Since none of the documents is earlier than 1086 and, since most are related to records that were generated by the Domesday inquest, one may suspect that it was the inquest itself that stimulated Evesham abbey to collect and produce its first surveys.

48 P. H. Sawyer, ed., 'Evesham A, a Domesday Text', *Miscellany I*, WHS [new series 1] (Worcester, 1960), pp. 3–36; Clarke 1977, pp. 534–40 ('Evesham C'), 584–5 ('Evesham Q').

49 Clarke 1977, pp. 553–68 ('Evesham K'), 570–77 ('Evesham M').

50 Ibid. pp. 546 ('Evesham F'), 582–3 ('Evesham P').

51 Ibid. p. 550 ('Evesham H').

52 Clarke 2007, pp. 83–4 ('Evesham J').

53 Darlington 1933, pp. 188–90 ('Evesham N').

CHAPTER 13

Protecting the future

The papacy invoked

IN the eleventh century Evesham abbey was aware of a vague tradition that 300 years earlier the pope had given his support to the newly founded minster. Byrhtferth of Ramsey in the early eleventh century was the first to publish, in a heavily interpolated version, a document that has become known as 'St Ecgwine's Testament'. According to the 'Testament', after Ecgwine had received the lands at and around the *hamm* the pope signified his approval of the gifts by the use of his seal. The implication seems to be that the original grants had been confirmed in writing and that the pope's seal was then attached. The 'Testament', however, does not give the text of such a confirmation deed and does not even quote from it, and does not name the pope whose seal was supposed to have been added. There is thus no suggestion that Byrhtferth or his contemporaries had seen the supposed confirmation deed or a copy of it; had the text been extant at Evesham in the early eleventh century Byrhtferth would probably have reproduced it. Although the 'Testament' does not date the pope's confirmation Byrhtferth does try to add some substance to his version of the 'Testament' by linking the supposed confirmation to an historical event found in Bede's 'Ecclesiastical History': the joint visit to Rome by Coenred (King Æthelred's successor) and Offa of the East Saxons, which Bede (though not Byrhtferth) says took place in 709 and thus during the papacy of Constantine I. Bede's history, however, does not bear out Byrhtferth's story that Coenred and Offa were accompanied to Rome by Ecgwine and that all three met the pope; whereas Byrhtferth has the three returning to England with the pope's confirmation, Bede records plainly that neither Coenred nor Offa ever returned from Rome, nor does Bede say that Ecgwine had gone with them.[1] Byrhtferth's story of a papal confirmation brought back from Rome by Coenred, Offa, and Ecgwine was an ingenious fiction. There could have been some kind of papal confirmation relating to the foundation of the minster but no text of it seems to have been known at Evesham by the early eleventh century and the credible part of 'St Ecgwine's Testament' does not allow one to suggest its putative date or to attribute it to a particular pope.

[1] Byrhtferth, pp. 256–9, 262–3; HE V, 19.

Whereas the matter of papal support for Evesham had been of little practical importance in the early eleventh century, an appeal to ancient papal protection was just what Evesham needed by the end of the century, to reinforce its title to the original endowments and to resist the bishop's current interest in establishing pastoral rights over the abbey and its deanery. If the abbey was to maintain its long-held independence, however, it would need better documentation than had been available to Byrhtferth, and a dossier of relevant papal material was therefore manufactured. It consisted of four related documents: a privilege of papal protection that purports to have been granted by Constantine in 709 but first appears in Dominic's *vita* of St Ecgwine; a deed dated 709 and witnessed by Pope Constantine whereby Coenred and Offa confirmed the landed endowments of the minster;[2] a revised *vita* of St Ecgwine written by the monk Dominic under Abbot Walter, which contains an interpolated version of 'St Ecgwine's Testament' and a text of the 709 papal privilege;[3] and another privilege of Pope Constantine dated 713.[4] The close relationship of the three '709' documents is illuminated by Dominic's new version of the *vita*; but Dominic did not mention the 713 privilege, which one assumes had not yet been invented or discovered when the *vita* was written.

The text of the 709 privilege presented by Dominic does not convince even on a superficial reading. It is inflated with pious verbiage and unnecessary narrative about the founding of the minster, almost to the exclusion of specific clauses; moreover, its purported date and content depend on Byrhtferth's fictional account of a non-existent visit to Rome by Coenred, Offa, and Ecgwine. When we seek the date at which the purported privilege was really composed, the most important clue is that the text agrees with Dominic's *vita*, in which it first appears, and not with Byrhtferth. Byrhtferth's version of the 'Testament' tells us that King Coenred, on returning from Rome, summoned a 'synod' of 'all the leading men and ealdormen' and invited Bishop Wilfrid and Archbishop Berhtwald to attend.[5] In Dominic's text of the 709 privilege, however, the pope commands Archbishop Berhtwald to summon a 'council of all England' attended by the 'bishops and religious of a holy order' and to 'instruct the magnates to attend together with their followers'. The purported privilege of 709 agrees with Dominic's version of events, in which the archbishop summons the council, but not with Byrhtferth's earlier version, in which it is King Coenred who issues the summons. In his own part of the narrative Dominic tells us that Archbishop Berhtwald and Bishop Wilfrid jointly summoned an assembly of the 'bishops

[2] S80.

[3] Dominic, *V. Ecgwini* ('Testament' on pp. 86–7, privilege on pp. 88–90).

[4] T. Marlb. pp. 318–21.

[5] Byrhtferth, pp. 258–61.

and wise men of both orders' together with the 'nobles of the whole kingdom of England'.[6]

The alleged papal privilege of 709 was evidently composed in the eleventh century and its tone and context, as presented by Dominic, suggest that it was written at about the same time as Dominic's *vita* and thus near the end of the century. Dominic's contemporary John of Worcester (fl.1095–1140) also refers briefly to the 709 privilege,[7] having perhaps read Dominic's *vita*. As quoted by Dominic, the invented papal privilege of 709 entrusts the protection of the church of Evesham to the archbishop of Canterbury, who is to have exclusive jurisdiction over any offence committed against the church of Evesham or within it:

> siquod uero sinistre partis inibi compertum fuerit oriri, auribus summi pontificis patrie potius deferatur, quam per alicuius occultam sententiam sanctus locus iniuste deprauetur.[8]

This can be translated as:

> If anything untoward should be found to arise there, it should be brought to the ears of the local archbishop rather than that the holy place be wrongly degraded by the clandestine ruling of anyone else.

By implication the bishops of Worcester are not to intervene. The 709 privilege is thus an instrument devised by the abbey in the early stages of a conflict between itself and the bishop over his authority at Evesham, a matter that was to absorb both parties intermittently until 1205.

Dominic's version of Ecgwine's 'Testament' relates that Coenred and Offa confirmed to Ecgwine the grants ('donationes et priuilegia') so far made to the minster, and that during a joint visit of the three to Rome in 709 the pope, whom Dominic names for the first time as Constantine, put his seal to their confirmation. The earliest extant copy of the confirmation deed dates from the twelfth century and in it Coenred and Offa confirm to the minster nine named estates (including Evesham) that form a block spanning both sides of the Avon; an addendum confirms Coenred's separate grant of an estate that is a little detached from the rest at Abbots Morton. The document bears four attestations: those of Pope Constantine, Bishop Ecgwine, King Coenred, and Offa of the East Saxons.[9]

6 Dominic, *V. Ecgwini*, pp. 88–9.
7 J. Worc. II, pp. 166–7.
8 Dominic, *V. Ecgwini*, p. 89.
9 S80.

The diplomatic form of the document shows it to be a late fabrication[10] and the date of composition can be determined with fair precision because the text contains anachronisms concerning Bengeworth. The document says that the Bengeworth estate contains four hides; in fact that was the hidage of the abbey's portion of Bengeworth after the loss of one hide at some time between 1078 and 1086[11] and not before. Moreover, the bounds of the whole Evesham endowment, which are given in Latin at the end of the document, are inconsistent with the document's attribution of four hides to Bengeworth; they enclose the whole of Bengeworth and not just Evesham's four hides. In fact the Latin bounds recited in the purported confirmation of 709 seem to be only loosely related to the document in which they appear and have more in common with a detached set of Old English bounds of the same estates preserved in a copy of the twelfth century;[12] the Latin bounds of '709' seem thus to have been derived from some late Old English perambulation. Since Dominic does not recite or even summarize the text of the confirmation, it was probably composed after his *vita* of St Ecgwine (which was written before 1100) and before the estimated twelfth-century date of the surviving copy.

One may venture a closer estimate of the date after 1078 at which the confirmation deed was composed, for its dating clause seems to have been derived directly from that of the supposed 709 papal privilege first quoted by Dominic at the end of the eleventh century. The privilege ends with:

> Scripta est hec epistola anno dominice incarnationis septingentesimo nono in ecclesia saluatoris Lateranensi, precipiente et confirmante Constantino apostolice sedis antistite, astantibus et confirmantibus regibus Anglie Kenredo et Offa, rogante uenerabili uiro Ecgwino episcopo coram pluribus archiepiscopis et episcopis et principibus et nobilibus diuersarum prouinciarum, cunctis clamantibus et dicentibus, 'quicquid in hac constitutione uestra sanctitas exercet, laudamus, concedimus et confirmamus'.[13]

In English:

> This letter was written in the seven hundred and ninth year of the Incarnation of the Lord in the Lateran church of the Saviour by the command and with the confirmation of Constantine bishop of the Apostolic See in the presence of

[10] Scharer 1982, pp. 156–7.

[11] Clarke 2012a, p. 139.

[12] S1599. See Hooke 1990, pp. 46–57, 408–17.

[13] Dominic, *V. Ecgwini*, pp. 89–90.

> and with the confirmation of Coenred and Offa, kings of England, and at the request of the venerable Bishop Ecgwine, before many archbishops and bishops and rulers and nobles of diverse provinces, all crying out and saying 'Whatever Your Holiness enacts in this document, we praise, grant, and confirm'.

The pope's supposed confirmation of the minster's endowments ends with virtually identical words:

> Acta sunt haec anno dominicae incarnationis . Dcc°. ix°. in aecclesia salvatoris Laterana. confirmante Constantino Romanae sedis antistite . astantibus et confirmantibus regibus Angliae Kenredo . et Offa . rogante venerabili viro Egwino episcopo cum pluribus archiepiscopis . et episcopis . principibus . ac nobilibus diversarum provintiarum . cunctis clamantibus et dicentibus. 'Nos hanc voluntatem et regiam liberalitatem laudamus . donationibus ac libertati consentimus'.[14]

Thus a comparison of the two fabricated documents, the 709 privilege and the 709 confirmation deed, suggests that they may have been composed within a short time of each other, probably between 1078 and 1100, and thus during the abbacy of Walter.

If Coenred, Offa, and Ecgwine did not really obtain the privilege and the confirmation deed and bring them back from Rome in 709, we may wonder whether any such documents relating to Evesham had ever existed. It is not impossible that they did, for popes had certainly issued privileges for English minsters in the late seventh and early eighth centuries, and by the tenth century Evesham did possess most of the estates listed in the supposed deed of confirmation. As far as the supposed privilege of 709 is concerned, the following conjectures may be made. In the eleventh century, before Dominic came to write his *vita* of St Ecgwine, it may have been known that Evesham had been the beneficiary of an early papal privilege addressed to the archbishop of Canterbury and that Evesham no longer had a copy of it, probably having lost its copy in the tenth century. The date, grantor, and content of the privilege were thus unknown at Evesham by the late eleventh century. Dominic or a near contemporary therefore invented the text of such a privilege, which was given the date 709 to coincide with the known visit of Coenred and Offa to Rome and thus with the papacy of Constantine.

It seems that Evesham may have discovered, after the invented 709 privilege had been recited in Dominic's *vita*, that a version of the original and lost papal

[14] S80, as printed in W. de Gray Birch, ed., *Cartularium Saxonicum: A Collection of Charters relating to Anglo-Saxon History*, I (London, 1885), p. 185 no. 125.

privilege for Evesham had been preserved at Christ Church Canterbury and that it was dated 713. Dominic had known nothing of its existence when writing the *vita* of Ecgwine. Canterbury may at some time have had a papyrus original addressed by the pope to the archbishop, which had become faded and fragmentary or otherwise inadequate to the current concerns of either Canterbury or Evesham. Thus the earliest known copy of the 713 privilege is clearly an enhanced version; for instance, it repeats the fiction that Ecgwine had resigned as bishop to become abbot of Evesham.[15] It was perhaps produced at or for Evesham, and it came to be preserved in a Canterbury manuscript of the 1120s. By then Canterbury, which also had an interest in the document, had not only a copy of the enhanced 713 text but also a copy of the false 709 privilege; both of those texts appear in its manuscript.[16] The opening words of the two privileges are virtually identical, which suggests that the enhanced 713 text took its superscription from the false 709 privilege. Thus the purported 709 privilege begins:

> Constantinus episcopus, seruus seruorum Dei, Brithwaldo Britanniarum ecclesie primati salutem et apostolicam benedictionem.[17]

The enhanced 713 privilege begins:

> Constantinus episcopus seruus seruorum Dei Britwaldo Brittaniarum primati salutem et apostolicam benedictionem.[18]

The enhanced form of the 713 privilege is a more succinct document than the privilege that is dated 709. It places Evesham under the direct jurisdiction of the archbishops of Canterbury and under the sole direction of its own abbot. The abbot is to be freely elected by the monks (a clause that may have been present in the lost original) and he is to be consecrated at Evesham. After the existence of the 713 privilege became known belatedly at Evesham, the abbey could not then disown the alleged privilege of 709 and would have been forced, with Canterbury, to make a case that there had been two such documents, one dated 709 and the other 713. The granting of two privileges by Pope Constantine, though it was inherently unlikely, thus became part of the story presented by Thomas of Marlborough before the papal court in 1205.[19]

15 As in S81 (above, ch. 11).
16 Sayers 1988, pp. 375–7.
17 Dominic, *V. Ecgwini*, p. 88.
18 T. Marlb. p. 318.
19 Ibid. pp. 280–81, 288–95.

While the enhanced 713 privilege may have descended from a lost original, the 709 privilege (in existence by 1100) was probably a complete invention of Abbot Walter's day and may have been produced about the same time as the purported confirmation deed of Coenred and Offa, which cannot be earlier than 1078 in its present form. The textual links between Dominic's *vita* of St Ecgwine, the alleged papal privilege of 709, and the alleged royal and papal confirmation deed of 709 support the idea that there was an ambitious plan in Abbot Walter's day to create a body of documentary evidence with which to defend the abbey's current status and possessions against potential claimants and with which to invoke the support of the pope and the archbishop of Canterbury.

Walter's legacy

Walter's abbacy was more than the mid-point between the foundation of the church of Evesham and its dissolution in 1540; it was the time in which the direction of its final 450 years was first settled. Walter was responsible for introducing the 'Monastic Constitutions' of his former master Lanfranc archbishop of Canterbury, and they were never superseded as an outline of internal practice at Evesham. He planned and began a great new church, which set the scale for its own completion and for whatever alterations were to follow, and he brought the monks up to a number that, as it happened, would never be substantially increased. He also fostered a literary awareness that had been neglected under his predecessor Æthelwig and an understanding of Evesham's proper place in the culture of Europe. Walter set up a body of professional secular officials to manage the abbey's corporate affairs, and with them he introduced a habit of record-making and record-keeping. Where historical supporting documents were lacking he had new versions made, relating both to the abbey's estates and to its relations with the bishop of Worcester. Under Walter the abbey's lands reached what was to be more or less their final extent, and the increasing availability of formal justice under the king meant that the abbey's tenure of them was never afterwards seriously threatened. A permanent scheme for the pastoral care of the Vale of Evesham was established when Walter appointed a secular dean, whose powers in the Vale paralleled and excluded those of the new office of archdeacon, the bishop's agent in other parts of the diocese. The bishops would later try to wrest those powers from the abbot and his dean, and to suppress the abbey's rights of self-regulation, but the development of canon law during the twelfth century would help Evesham to keep hold of its independence. In all those respects it may be said that by 1100 Evesham abbey had reached a secure, if sometimes uncomfortable, plateau from which it would not be dislodged until 1540.

Against that achievement must be weighed a further erosion of the primitive monastic ideal, essentially a private journey towards close personal union with God through the renunciation of worldly concerns. The size of the establishment in 1100, the external links that it generated, the multitude of administrative tasks that it created, its complex internal formalities and the consequent curtailment of time for quiet contemplation, and the increased remoteness of an abbot preoccupied with business made for a great and beneficent institution certainly, but one that was driven more by a corporate desire to sustain itself at a high level of efficiency and visibility than by the personal quest of each of its brethren for spiritual growth through self-denial. A decline of monastic spirituality at Evesham would be difficult to chart but it was already recognized in Æthelwig's time by the recluses who chose to live in isolation from the rest of the abbey community, and by the monks Reinfrid and Ælfwig who felt the need to leave Evesham and seek seclusion in the harsher north. The monastic ideal exerted a timeless attraction, and in future centuries it would sometimes find personal expression at Evesham, but the abbey that Walter left to posterity would no longer be its natural home.

PART III

Twelfth-century themes (1104–1215)

CHAPTER 14

Interested parties

The king and the archbishop

AFTER the Norman Conquest it was only with the appointment of a new abbot that the king or the archbishop of Canterbury normally intervened in the management of Evesham abbey. The archbishop had the right to correct faults at Evesham by virtue of the supposed privileges of Pope Constantine dated 709 and 713 but he was not actually called upon to exercise the power of correction until 1197, and even then he proved to be so irresolute as to achieve no beneficial effect.[1] Between the death of Abbot Æthelwig (1078) and the fall of Abbot Norreis (1213) the abbots continued to be appointed by the king as patron and feudal overlord, but he does not seem to have taken a personal interest in the process; he was content to follow advice, particularly that of the archbishop. Under an agreement of 1107 the king could no longer appoint the abbot of any house unilaterally,[2] but it remained his prerogative as overlord to take homage from a new abbot for his estates, and that gave the king the opportunity to delay his acceptance of homage and in the mean time to enjoy the abbey's temporalities (its income from secular sources). It was undoubtedly Lanfranc who had nominated Abbot Walter in 1078, and Lanfranc's successors continued to nominate until 1190. The monks were allowed to go through the formality of an election in chapter and they would naturally have elected one of their own number, but they knew that the king would not confirm their choice if they did not elect the archbishop's nominee. Thus all the abbots of Evesham appointed during the twelfth century were brought in from elsewhere. An accident of timing meant that there was one exception to that: following Walter's death in 1104, he was succeeded by an Evesham monk, Maurice;[3] Archbishop Anselm was in voluntary exile from 1103 to 1106 and could not present the king and the Evesham chapter with another candidate.

Although all the other twelfth-century abbots were outsiders to the Evesham chapter, only one of them may have come straight from the continent. That was

[1] Below, ch. 21.

[2] M. Rule, ed., *Eadmeri historia novorum in Anglia*, Rolls Series (London, 1884), p. 186.

[3] *Durham Liber vitae*, I, p. 104.

Maurice's successor Robert, who had been a monk of Jumièges in Normandy[4] and arrived at Evesham c.1121.[5] The last foreigner to be appointed abbot of Evesham was the Frenchman Adam in 1161, and he was not brought over directly from France but from Bermondsey priory in Surrey. Some of the abbots are known to have belonged to knightly or baronial families. Reynold ('Reginaldus'), who was abbot from 1130 to 1149, was a close relative (*nepos*) of Miles of Gloucester earl of Hereford (1141–43) and an uncle of Gilbert Foliot[6] abbot of Gloucester (1139–48), who was afterwards bishop successively of Hereford and London. Abbot Adam (1161–89) was a relative, possibly an uncle, of Simon de St Liz earl of Huntingdon and Northampton (d.1184).[7] It was not the custom to draw attention to a monk's family background, however distinguished, and if we knew more about the other twelfth-century abbots of Evesham we might find that they too were well connected.

The death of an abbot naturally roused the monks to speculation and debate about the succession, and the king's appointment of an outsider under the guidance of the archbishop could then be beneficial if it prevented or stifled a divisive internal contest. Moreover, in drawing from a wider pool of candidates than the Evesham chapter alone, the king and the archbishop might introduce an abbot of exceptional ability such as Adam. If the archbishop's candidate was quite unacceptable to a section of the monks, however, his nomination could actually generate disunity in the chapter, and that might need to be resolved through mediation. Moreover, the archbishop, if he was determined to help a loyal protégé, could have the king impose an unworthy abbot upon a submissive chapter, and that is what happened in 1190. The kind of wrangling that could take place over the appointment of an abbot is well attested in the case of William de Andeville. When Abbot Reynold died in 1149 Archbishop Theobald advised the king on the succession. Theobald favoured William de Andeville, who had been sacrist of Christ Church Canterbury (the cathedral) and was currently prior of Dover, which was a dependency of Christ Church.[8] Some of the monks of Evesham objected to William or to the manner of his nomination, and they included the sub-prior Roger. The archbishop therefore sent the late abbot's nephew Gilbert Foliot bishop of Hereford to talk the protesters round. Gilbert succeeded in bringing over Roger the sub-prior and some of the others but there remained a stubborn minority who would not relent. So strongly did they feel that they were preparing to take their case in person to the court of Pope Eugenius III. This they had a right to do under

4 T. Marlb. pp. 180–81.
5 The abbatial dates of Maurice and Robert are discussed in Clarke 1977, pp. 34–7.
6 T. Marlb. pp. 180–81, 564–5.
7 Cox 2010b, pp. 114–15.
8 Knowles et al. 2001, p. 87.

a privilege granted to Abbot Reynold by Pope Innocent II ten years earlier, which says 'let no successor here be proposed through any kind of underhand chicanery or force, but only a man chosen by the brethren of the same place by common consent, or by a company of brethren of wiser counsel'.[9] The monks that were in favour of William de Andeville's appointment therefore had to make haste to send Richard their prior to Rome, in the company of a monk called Samson, in order to make their own representations directly to the pope. At Bishop Gilbert's suggestion they were to go armed with letters of support from the religious houses of the Evesham region, which would inform the pope that the wiser and more numerous part of the Evesham chapter favoured William's election.[10] Whether the rival delegations actually made the arduous journey to Rome is not recorded but William de Andeville was finally appointed and he proved to be an effective abbot.[11] Nevertheless, the awkward circumstances of William's succession together with his subsequent difficulties at Evesham during the civil war of King Stephen's reign[12] may eventually have left him with a nostalgic preference for Canterbury; that could be the reason why he was buried there in the cathedral crypt and not at Evesham.[13] William's short-lived successor Roger (1159–60) was also from Canterbury, a monk of St Augustine's abbey.[14] It looks as if he too had been a nominee of Archbishop Theobald; it was Theobald, with the king's permission, who had ordered the hesitant monks to hold the election of Roger and had sent his own representatives to supervise it.[15] Bishop Foliot of Hereford was called upon again in 1161 after Adam, the Cluniac prior of Bermondsey, was nominated by a church council at Canterbury to succeed Abbot Roger. The king and the archbishop both approved the nomination but it was necessary to ask the prior of La Charité-sur-Loire in France to release Adam; Bermondsey was a dependency of La Charité. Bishop Foliot, acting as vicar of Worcester diocese while the see was vacant,[16] wrote to the prior of La Charité[17] and Adam was released and duly appointed to Evesham.

Soon after Abbot Adam died in 1189 the monks had to accept as his successor Roger Norreis, the former prior of Christ Church Canterbury. The new king, Richard, was influenced in the appointment by Baldwin, the archbishop

[9] T. Marlb. pp. 322–3.

[10] G. Foliot, *Lett.* pp. 123–4 no. 89.

[11] T. Marlb. pp. 182–5.

[12] Below, ch. 17.

[13] T. Marlb. pp. 182–3.

[14] Ibid. pp. 184–5.

[15] W. J. Millor, H. E. Butler, and C. N. L. Brooke, eds, *The Letters of John of Salisbury*, OMT (Oxford, 1986), pp. 173–4 no. 109.

[16] *Worc. Acta 1062–1185*, p. xlvii.

[17] G. Foliot, *Lett.* pp. 177–8 no. 134.

of Canterbury, who owed Norreis a favour. Norreis had intrigued on Baldwin's behalf against the monks of Christ Church during their campaign of opposition to the archbishop's proposed college at Hackington near Canterbury. The Canterbury monks had succeeded in having Norreis deposed as their prior but Baldwin took the opportunity of Abbot Adam's recent death to compensate Norreis by nominating him as Adam's successor.[18] The king gave his consent and the appointment was made without the formality of an election at Evesham. The monks did not appeal to Rome about the irregularity. They were used to having outsiders as their abbots and when they looked back on previous royal appointees they probably found no serious cause to complain about them. Norreis for his part behaved well enough during his first few years in office[19] and the Evesham chapter was not to know how badly he would turn out.

The bishop

Since 1014 the bishops of Worcester had had no formal part in the choice of a new abbot, but from the time of Archbishop Lanfranc (1070–89) all the bishops in Canterbury province had been expected to take a more thorough approach to their pastoral duties, which could be interpreted as including regulation of the monasteries that lay within their dioceses. Meanwhile, ancient abbeys such as Evesham had become accustomed to freedom of action without close supervision by their bishop, and their high status seemed to require that their customary independence should continue. The different aspirations of bishops and monasteries would not necessarily bring about conflict, however, for if a monastery was being properly run the bishop could choose not to intervene unnecessarily in its affairs and there could be peace between them. In the case of Evesham there was much in the pre-Conquest history of the abbey, including its foundation by Bishop Ecgwine, to show that the abbots had been closely bound to the bishops of Worcester, sometimes formally and often by mutual consent. After the Conquest new abbots had continued to be formally consecrated by them; we do not know who consecrated Walter but his successors Maurice and Robert were certainly among those who received their consecration from the bishop of Worcester.[20] At that time the abbots still accepted consecration from Worcester as a long-established custom but there are suggestions that by Abbot Walter's day the bishop was seeking to assert other rights over the abbey and that the abbey was taking steps to resist him. For instance, it is likely that the forged privilege of Pope

18 *ODNB* ('Norreis, Roger').

19 T. Marlb. pp. 190–93.

20 Atkins 1940, p. 227.

Constantine for Evesham, ostensibly dated 709, was created for Abbot Walter in a form that carefully denied the bishops of Worcester any power to correct faults at the abbey. Moreover, King William II was said to have issued a writ at Abbot Walter's request, and dated 4 April 1100, that forbade the bishop to hold synods or ordinations in the abbey unless invited to do so by the abbot.[21] The writ is known only from a cartulary copy and it is likely to be another Evesham forgery because the list of witnesses includes Archbishop Anselm, who was out of the country at the alleged date.[22] By the 1120s the forged papal privilege of 709 had been joined by the enhanced text of what may have been a lost privilege of Pope Constantine dated 713. It alleged that the abbey was to be under the sole rule of its abbot; that his successor was to be elected by the monks; that he was to be consecrated in his own abbey without making any payment; and that he was permitted to wear a ring, one of the *insignia pontificalia* (episcopal insignia), when celebrating Mass.[23]

It was one thing for Evesham to possess such a document but another to see it enforced, and in 1130 Bishop Simon consecrated the new abbot, Reynold, at Worcester, not at Evesham.[24] Later developments show that the bishop's action had been calculated to curb the abbey's aspirations but it was already clear that Reynold did not intend to let them be curbed. At the consecration he broke with established custom by refusing to give to the church of Worcester the vestment that he had worn there at the ceremony.[25] It was a gesture of defiance that was in keeping with the supposed privilege of 713, which required consecration without payment, and it was a portent of further clashes between the two men. In 1139 Abbot Reynold and Bishop Simon both attended the Second Lateran Council in Rome and while he was there the abbot achieved what was later regarded as a partial victory over Bishop Simon, for Pope Innocent II then ruled that no bishop could hold a synod or chapter in Evesham abbey or celebrate ordinations or masses there unless by invitation of the abbot, and that abbots-elect of Evesham could be consecrated at Evesham by any bishop of their choice. At the same time the pope confirmed the requirements of the supposed privilege of 713 that the abbots should be elected by the brethren and should have sole rule over the abbey.[26] Nevertheless, Bishop Simon remained unwilling to give up his claims, which Evesham represented as novel ones that had not been sought by previous bishops. After the Lateran Council Reynold wrote to his kinsman Gilbert Foliot

21 The two printed editions, though from the same manuscript, have minor differences: Dugdale, *Mon.* II, p. 18; *Evesham Chron.* p. xlix.

22 *Regesta Wm I and II*, p. 107 no. 429.

23 T. Marlb. pp. 320–21.

24 J. Worc. III, pp. 190–91.

25 Atkins 1940, pp. 226–9.

26 J. Worc. III, pp. 264–5; T. Marlb. pp. 182–3, 320–25.

abbot of Gloucester that in the past 'Worcester has treated us as free citizens, never as slaves' and that Evesham's position was supported by prescription and by ancient and genuine documents: 'Why do they complain about the owner of things which they never possessed?' asked Reynold. He went on to declare that Evesham would not give in to the bishop's aggression; it would defend its freedom 'with oaths, with arms, by force, by every kind of argument'.[27] Relations between Evesham and Worcester remained tense, and at some time between 1148 and 1160 another dispute arose that involved either Bishop Simon, who died in 1150, or one of his successors John or Alfred. The immediate cause of the trouble is not recorded but it was serious enough for the monks to appeal to Rome against the bishop and for him to retaliate by suspending their holy orders and by trying, it was said, to have them ejected from the abbey and imprisoned.[28] The bishop's threats were not carried out, however, and he made no real progress towards any acceptance of his claims over the abbey.

On the contrary, in 1163 Abbot Adam and Roger the bishop-elect of Worcester attended the Council of Tours[29] and the abbot there received from Pope Alexander III a further privilege that allowed Evesham abbey to choose any bishop to provide holy oils, the consecration of altars, and the ordination of monks, and ordered the bishops of Worcester to abide by precedent in their relations with the abbey.[30] Fortunately Abbot Adam (1161–89) and Bishop Roger (1163–79) were personal friends with shared literary interests and, from 1163, after a conflict that had lasted thirty years or more, it proved possible for the bishop to waive Worcester's claims upon Evesham and for a long truce to begin. It was probably in 1165 that Adam wrote to Roger about the brotherly love that assured peace between the two houses:

> Love is a precious virtue, which, being worthy of God, of the angels, and of the saints, is forever that which it is. It does not perish, it is not altered, and it does not allow division but has always been wont to make one thing out of two. It couples what has been separated, it binds what has been joined up, it calls back what has been sent away, and it joins together what has been divided. It hates division and preserves unity. It loves peace and has no regard for contentious matters. Division, however, does not break it apart and contention does not disturb it; for in preserving unity it never departs from true peace.[31]

[27] T. Marlb. pp. 566–7.

[28] G. Foliot, *Lett.* pp. 124–5 no. 90.

[29] R. Somerville, *Pope Alexander III and the Council of Tours (1163): A Study of Ecclesiastical Politics and Institutions in the Twelfth Century* (Berkeley, 1977), p. 27.

[30] T. Marlb. pp. 324–31.

[31] Cox 2010b, pp. 135–7.

Adam expected a permanent end to any possibility of renewed discord over the bishop's rights, and peace does seem to have endured for many years. In 1189, long after Adam's friend Bishop Roger was dead but not long before his own death, Adam was said to have taken the precaution of obtaining an indult from Pope Clement III that allowed the abbots of Evesham to continue wearing the ring, which had been permitted under the supposed papal privilege of 713, and the gloves, for which the abbot was said already to have permission, and to begin using the rest of the *insignia pontificalia* — the mitre, the dalmatic, the tunic, and the sandals. Pope Clement was also said to have confirmed that the abbot and monks of Evesham were subject only to the direct jurisdiction of the papacy; this time he allegedly used the contemporary legal phrase *nullo mediante* ('with no intermediary'), which firmly excluded the bishop. It was afterwards claimed that Pope Celestine III reiterated Clement's indult in 1192.[32] There is a suspicion that the alleged indults of 1189 and 1192, if they were granted at all, may have been altered afterwards in Evesham's favour and before they reached their surviving form. When the final confrontation between Worcester and Evesham was played out at Rome before Pope Innocent III in 1205[33] the papacy had no record of the indults, and the supposed originals were brought to Rome on Evesham's behalf by Nicholas of Warwick, whom the bishop of Worcester's proctor alleged to be a known forger and about whom even Thomas of Marlborough, representing the Evesham monks, harboured private suspicions.[34] An intriguing possibility is that Nicholas was a relative of Master Thomas of Warwick, whom the unscrupulous Abbot Roger Norreis employed as his clerk and proctor and who was in Rome with Thomas of Marlborough at the time.[35] But whether or not the indults of Clement and Celestine and the alleged privileges of Pope Constantine were entirely genuine as presented in 1205, all that really mattered was that Pope Innocent III was in fact quite ready to acknowledge them.[36]

The successful resistance of Abbot Reynold and his successors to the claims of the bishop of Worcester had furnished Evesham abbey with an array of written papal exemptions that could be matched by few English houses of 'black' monks (the traditional Benedictines),[37] and by 1163 the bishops had stopped trying to circumvent them. In any case, Adam's long and exemplary abbacy from 1161 to 1189[38] gave the diocesan no excuse to intervene in Evesham's internal affairs.

32 T. Marlb. pp. 330–33.
33 Below, ch. 21.
34 T. Marlb. pp. 280–81, 296–9.
35 Ibid. pp. 264–7, 372–3, 376–7, 514–15, 532–3.
36 Sayers 1988, pp. 380–81.
37 Knowles 1963a, pp. 586–91.
38 Cox 2010b, pp. 113–14.

The danger for Evesham then became one of complacency, and in 1190 Abbot Norreis allowed himself to be consecrated by a bishop of Worcester and to make a formal profession of obedience to him;[39] Norreis thereby averted an immediate confrontation but his was a precedent that would later prejudice the abbey's case for independence.

Lay benefactors

The black monks were aware by the mid-twelfth century that they were no longer the sole representatives of the monastic movement. They were not even by then the obvious choice for lay benefactors seeking a worthy home for their donations. New religious orders from overseas that offered striking and novel ideas were attracting the eager support of the king, the nobility, and the landed classes. Meanwhile, the old-established black-monk houses seemed to have more than enough wealth and no need of any more. The most influential of the newcomers were the Cistercian monks, Benedictines who wanted to be free of secular ties and to follow an ascetic interpretation of the 'Rule', and the Augustinian canons, who sought to be an ideal priesthood by living a disciplined communal life. In Worcester diocese alone three Cistercian abbeys were founded between 1138 and 1151: Bordesley by the Empress Maud, Kingswood by William of Berkeley, and Flaxley by Roger earl of Hereford. For the Augustinians four notable houses were founded in the diocese between 1117 and 1153: Cirencester abbey by King Henry I, Studley priory by Piers Corbucion, Llanthony priory near Gloucester by Miles of Gloucester later earl of Hereford, and St Oswald's priory at Gloucester by Henry Murdac archbishop of York. It was to those new houses that substantial endowments accrued thenceforth and not to such as Evesham.

Nevertheless, the rich and pious did not forget Evesham altogether. In the twelfth century the abbey continued to receive small endowments from Anglo-Norman landowners, but they were seldom new donors and never of the highest rank. Some were men that had previously given estates to Evesham in Abbot Walter's time or were the relatives of such men. Thus Warin Bussel enlarged his original Lancashire gift some time before 1130 by granting the advowson (the patronage) of Penwortham church with tithes, lands, and other property there and in the neighbourhood; in return the abbey agreed to maintain three monks and a chaplain at Penwortham church. At the same time the abbey agreed to accept Warin's body after his death and to receive Warin's small son Warin as a monk if he should wish to enter religion. Thus was founded Evesham's

[39] T. Marlb. pp. 250–51.

dependent priory of Penwortham,[40] whose heads would thereafter be appointed and regulated by the abbey without any reference to the bishop of the diocese in which Penwortham lay.[41] Following Warin's example, his descendants would add further endowments in the same area.[42] In another act of family piety Miles Crispin's original benefaction at Hillingdon in Middlesex was enlarged by Brian fitz Count, who was the husband of Miles's widow or daughter.[43] Between 1108 and c.1115 Brian granted to Evesham abbey the advowson of Hillingdon church with tithes, land, and a house there, and in return the abbey gave its confraternity to Brian and his wife, who thus became lay associates of the monks.[44] A family connection with Evesham may explain why Robert Fossard, who died in the 1130s,[45] gave to the abbey the advowson of Huntington church in the North Riding of Yorkshire;[46] there was a Fossard renting a house at Evesham c.1190[47] and an Alexander Fossard held land there in the early thirteenth century.[48] It seems probable that a personal link of that kind, if we knew what it was, would explain why Robert of 'Kikeswic' gave the abbey some tithes at Pixley in Herefordshire,[49] a small parish some thirty miles from Evesham.

The remoteness from Evesham of those new endowments, and the small profits that the abbey could expect to receive from them, were hardly what it would actively have sought. Among the more attractive acquisitions that came its way, however, was a cell or chapel dedicated to St John the Baptist, which stood on top of Southstone Rock in the parish of Stanford on Teme in north-west Worcestershire and was associated with a hermitage. The site belonged to the wife of Hugh fitz Roger and the couple gave it to Evesham abbey with a carucate of land (equivalent to a hide) some time before 1163. The rock itself was composed of tufa, which was recognized as a strong but lightweight building stone and was particularly valued locally. At about the same time Pain de Noyers endowed the chapel with an 'island' called 'Serpham';[50] the name suggests that the 'island' was

40 *Penwortham Docs*, pp. 2–3, where the agreement to maintain monks at Penwortham is dated temp. Abbot Robert (i.e. c.1121–c.1130).

41 *Penwortham Docs*, pp. 97–105. See M. Heale, *The Dependent Priories of Medieval English Monasteries* (Woodbridge, 2004), pp. 79–80.

42 *Penwortham Docs*, pp. 3–7, 40–41.

43 *ODNB* ('Brian fitz Count').

44 Dugdale, *Mon.* II, p. 18. Datable by witnesses Richard of Beaumais (bishop of London 1108–27) and Hugh of Buckland (d.1116×1119): for their dates see *ODNB*.

45 W. Farrer, ed., *Early Yorkshire Charters*, II (Edinburgh, 1915), pp. 326–7.

46 T. Marlb. pp. 136–7.

47 Vesp. B.XXIV, fol. 45v.

48 T. Marlb. pp. 550–51.

49 Ibid. pp. 138–9.

50 T. Marlb. pp. 138–9; Brooks and Pevsner 2007, pp. 7, 602.

in fact the nearby *hamm* ('land hemmed in by water') of which the very pointed ('sharp') outline was defined by a tight bend in the river Teme.[51] Evesham abbey received another more than usually helpful gift in the early twelfth century when Alnoth, a priest, gave the abbey the advowson of St Michael Cornhill in London.[52] In the 1120s the advowson was held of the abbey by Sperling, a priest, and in 1133 Abbot Reynold renewed it to Sperling together with the abbey's other London property (except some that was rented by one Orgar 'the proud'). In return the abbey was to receive from Sperling one mark (13s 6d) a year and lodging, salt, water, and fire whenever the abbot and his people come to London.[53] It was perhaps the first time that the abbots had had a permanent place to stay in the capital.

Even when viewed in the best light, however, the properties that came to Evesham abbey in the twelfth century could not bear comparison with the gifts that were then being made to the new religious orders or with those that had been bestowed on Evesham itself before 1078. In truth, the abbey did not expect its small twelfth-century acquisitions, welcome as they were, to make any noticeable difference to its already large resources.

The sheriff

Between 1086 and 1107, possibly about 1104, the abbey's hundred of 'Fissesberg' was renamed 'Blackenhurst', which is an earlier form of the name Blackminster; Blackminster, between Offenham and Badsey, is the place where 'Fissesberg' ('Fisc's barrow') probably stood.[54] The boundaries of the hundred were extended, perhaps at the same time, to include those estates in Worcestershire that the abbey had acquired permanently since the mid-tenth century, when 'Fissesberg' was last delimited.[55] In 1107 King Henry I granted that the abbey should govern Blackenhurst hundred without any intervention by the king's local agent, the sheriff of Worcestershire; within the hundred it was thus the abbey that would exercise the sheriff's usual powers in matters of law and order, tax-collecting,

51 At OS NGR SO 718642. Cf. J. E. B. Gover, A. Mawer, and F. M. Stenton, *The Place-Names of Devon*, I, EPNS 8 (Cambridge, 1931), p. 315 ('Sharpham').

52 T. Marlb. pp. 136–7, which mentions no date. Alnoth *presbiter* witnessed a deed relating to St Michael Cornhill (Vesp. B.XXIV, fol. 56r), which is said to have been issued in 1133: Stow, *Survey*, I, p. 195. If the Alnoth of 1133 was the original donor of the advowson to Evesham, the unsourced editorial note (Stow, *Survey*, II, p. 304) cannot be correct in dating his gift to 1055.

53 Vesp. B.XXIV, fol. 56r. Date from Stow, *Survey*, I, p. 195.

54 Cox 2006, pp. 79–83.

55 Clarke 2007, pp. 66–8.

and military organization.[56] The charter of 1107, however, was merely confirming what had been the position in 1086, when 'Fissesberg' was already one of the seven Worcestershire hundreds that were exempt from the sheriff's intervention.[57] There is evidence from Evesham sources to suggest that the exemption dated back to the tenth century[58] and there is no indication that the abbey's claim to it had ever been challenged; Sheriff Urse accepted it with reluctance in 1086 and he was a witness to the grant of 1107.[59]

56 *Regesta Hen. I*, p. 69 no. 831. Full text (from an inspeximus) in *Cal. Chart. R. 1226–57*, pp. 257–8.

57 DB, fol. 172r.

58 Cox 1975, pp. 37–9.

59 DB, fol. 172r; *Cal. Chart. R. 1226–57*, p. 258.

CHAPTER 15

Order and governance

THE abbot had complete authority within the monastery as long as he acted within the precepts of the 'Rule of St Benedict',[1] and since Evesham abbey itself enjoyed virtual autonomy in the twelfth century, there was no external check on that. Within the abbey walls it was therefore in the abbot's power to produce a state of tyranny or one of anarchy. In practice, however, neither extreme was reached at Evesham before the 1190s, and then both were suffered at once.[2] For most of the century a middle course was followed, in which the abbot was willing to take into consideration the views of the monks and to act in their best interests. In overall charge under the abbot were the prior, the sub-prior, the third prior, and certain 'keepers of discipline' (*custodes ordinis*).[3] Four tiers of authority thus stood between the ordinary monks and the abbot's household. If the abbot appeared anywhere, all were expected to stand and bow as he passed; an exception was made on those occasions when he entered the dormitory. If he sat down, no-one was allowed to sit next to him unless asked to do so. If one received anything from his hand, or gave him anything, one had to kiss the hand.[4] There were therefore few occasions on which a monk might be able to speak directly to the abbot.

Whenever the abbot was away, the daily running of the monastery's affairs outside the cloister and the claustral buildings was in the hands of the prior. The prior could summon a 'chapter' of all the abbey servants and punish any that were guilty of misconduct. He was owed great deference but was not quite so remote a figure as the abbot; for instance, the monks were not required to stand up when the prior entered the cloister area but, if he sat down there, those next to him had to rise, and any monk whom he came upon seated outside the cloister also had to stand up. The sub-prior (or 'prior of the cloister') was expected to be in attendance on the prior whenever possible and to be responsible for discipline within the cloister area. When the prior was away the sub-prior exercised the prior's powers

1 *Regula Benedicti*, ch. 64; Lanfranc, *Const.* pp. 110–11; *Penwortham Docs*, p. 91.

2 Below, ch. 21.

3 T. Marlb. pp. 516–19.

4 Lanfranc, *Const.* pp. 112–13; *Penwortham Docs*, pp. 90–91.

to make decisions and to punish or pardon offenders, except in serious cases which had to await the return of the prior or the abbot.[5]

Although they owed total obedience to the abbot and his deputies, the monks were not without a voice. Their daily assembly, the chapter, was required by the 'Rule' and its supplements,[6] and had presumably been held at Evesham since the tenth-century reform if not earlier. It was the forum for announcements, discussions of policy, disciplinary hearings, and the admission of new monks and confraters. The 'Rule' expected the abbot to consult the chapter before forming his own judgement on any matter of importance. He was not bound to follow the advice, however, and in the early twelfth century Abbots Walter, Maurice, and Robert (1078–c.1130) were posthumously criticized for granting estates 'without the chapter' or 'against the chapter's advice';[7] it is not clear in the first case whether the chapter had even been consulted. Abbot Reynold (1130–49) seems to have been more careful: in the 1130s individual monks, other than office-holders, are sometimes named as witnesses to his deeds,[8] and in one instance seven of them, 'and the whole convent', are on the witness-list[9] as if it was necessary at the time to proclaim the chapter's consent. It was not vital that the consent should be unanimous; what was needed was the agreement of the 'greater and wiser part' of the monks.[10] Since it could not be taken for granted that the greater part would instinctively be also the wiser, there would presumably be a discussion in which the more persuasive monks would attract enough support to form a majority for their opinion. The potential remained, however, for the abbot to take arbitrary and unjust actions. In 1206, after painful experience, the chapter set out written rules that were agreed by the abbot; they stated that he must consult the chapter on certain important matters including the appointment and dismissal of internal officials and servants, the expulsion of monks, the granting out of property, and the conduct of lawsuits.[11] Yet under the 'Rule' he could still not be bound by the chapter's advice; everything within the abbey would continue to depend on his judgement and conscience. Because of Evesham's exempt status and the interdict of 1208–13, the agreement of 1206 could not be enforced by outside powers and the abbot was able to ignore it with impunity, though at the sacrifice of whatever remained of his community's trust.[12]

[5] Lanfranc, *Const.* pp. 112–15; *Penwortham Docs*, pp. 92–3.

[6] *Regula Benedicti*, ch. 3; *Regularis concordia*, p. 17; Lanfranc, *Const.* pp. 108–9.

[7] Clarke 2012b, pp. 32–6 ('Evesham E' and 'Evesham O').

[8] e.g. Vesp. B.XXIV, fol. 56r. Date said to be 1133: Stow, *Survey*, I, p. 195.

[9] Harley 3763, fol. 93v. Datable before the death of Godfrey abbot of Winchcombe in 1137×1138 (Knowles et al. 2001, p. 79).

[10] T. Marlb. pp. 322–3, 326–7, 472–3, 516–21. See also Lanfranc, *Const.* pp. 108–9.

[11] T. Marlb. pp. 516–21.

[12] Ibid. pp. 446–7, 452–3.

Obediences

Outside the abbot's household the practicalities of life within the abbey were managed by dividing the routine functions into departments called obediences, each of which was headed by a monk. Before the Conquest there had been a sacrist, who was the monk responsible for the abbey church, and a cellarer, who saw to the material needs of the community. By the 1130s the sacrist had been joined by a 'keeper of the church'[13] and in the time of Abbot Roger Norreis (1190–1213) the titles of other obediences begin to emerge from the records: the chamber (which supplied the monks' clothing, footwear, and bedding),[14] the kitchen,[15] the pittancery (which provided extra food and drink on special occasions), and the almonry (which dispensed charity to the neighbouring poor).[16] In 1206 the full list of obedientiaries also included the precentor (who directed church services and saw to the production of books), the infirmarer, the keeper of the vineyard, the garden keeper, the master of the church fabric, and the guest master; by then the office of cellarer, which remained an onerous one, was divided into those of 'outer' (or 'general') cellarer and sub-cellarer. The prior of Penwortham was also regarded as an obedientiary.[17]

Of the monastic officer-holders mentioned during the twelfth century or listed in 1206, most had been specified in Lanfranc's 'Monastic Constitutions' and had therefore probably been in place at Evesham throughout the century. The obedientiaries and monastic officers that were not mentioned by Lanfranc (the kitchener, the keeper of the vineyard, the garden keeper, the master of the church fabric, and the third prior) may have had their posts created at Evesham during the course of the twelfth century in order to help the existing office-holders cope with an increased burden of responsibility. Thus by 1206 about half of the monks, presumably men who were not too young or too old, had some named area of special responsibility within the precinct. Some obediences had greater responsibilities than others, and there was thus an upper tier of officers that included the prior, the cellarer, the sacrist, and the precentor. They were presumably mature monks who had acquired experience and had demonstrated competence while working their way up through one or more of the lesser obediences.

13 Harley 3763, fol. 93v.
14 T. Marlb. pp. 194–5. See also Lanfranc, *Const.* pp. 126–7; *Penwortham Docs*, p. 109.
15 Vesp. B.XXIV, fol. 36v (Tindal 1794, p. 63n).
16 T. Marlb. pp. 196–7, 224–5. See also Lanfranc, *Const.* pp. 132–3; *Penwortham Docs*, p. 111.
17 T. Marlb. pp. 516–17, 529–30.

Accountability

Each obedience had its particular sources of revenue, which sometimes included the income of a whole manor; in the 1190s the chamber had the Gloucestershire manors of Bourton on the Water, Maugersbury, and Swell, and the cellar had Sambourne in Warwickshire.[18] By the same token other revenues were reserved for the use of the abbot and his household; for instance, by c.1190 the Abbots Morton estate rendered 40s a year to the abbot.[19] By the 1190s there was thus an orderly distribution of the abbey's whole income and a separation of the abbot's revenues from those of the convent. The separation was not only a matter of internal convenience; it meant that whenever the abbacy was vacant the king would be able to enjoy the temporal revenues of the abbot but not those of the whole house as formerly. For that reason it was important that any vacancy among the obedientiaries be filled without delay, or the revenues of that obedience would be temporarily the abbot's and so might go to the king if the abbacy suddenly fell vacant. Each obedience collected its income directly from its designated sources, and was free to take unilateral action to improve its own finances, by, for example, ploughing up more land, raising rents, or acquiring new rents. The cellarer received the residue of all the abbey's income not expressly assigned to the abbot or to a particular obedience. From it he had to supply the food and drink of the monks and their servants, and that of the poor and of the abbey's guests. The obedientiaries who prepared or served food — the kitchener, the pittancer, the guest-master, the infirmarer, and the almoner — all drew supplies from him. He also paid all the servants' wages. Every part of the abbey except the abbot's household therefore depended to some extent on the efficiency of the cellarer's department.[20]

The division of income between the abbot and the individual obediences meant that there was no central treasury for general purposes. It seems, however, that the abbot in chapter was able to order the obedientiaries to contribute occasional sums as the need arose, to pay for things that were outside the remit of any particular obedience and that his own income could not meet alone; that is presumably why one finds the obedientiaries in Abbot Adam's time (1161–89) being told to buy liturgical vestments out of their departmental funds.[21] The weakness of the twelfth-century system of financial devolution at Evesham was an absence of central control. There was no formal procedure for a regular central audit so that the abbey's finances could be continuously monitored. The abbot

18 T. Marlb. pp. 194–5.

19 Vesp. B.XXIV, fol. 36v (Tindal 1794, p. 63n).

20 T. Marlb. pp. 516–21, 528–33.

21 T. Marlb. pp. 186–7.

could presumably correct or dismiss an incompetent obedientiary, but that could only have been done after the harm had become obvious. Nor was the allocation of resources among the obedientiaries set down in any binding document. The whole structure depended on mutual trust and co-operation and was probably worked out and adjusted from time to time through verbal negotiation. It assumed that all sides would behave with prudence and goodwill, but under Abbot Norreis (1190–1213) its vulnerability to neglect and abuse would become painfully apparent. It was therefore in the early 1200s that a system of audit was devised, with a written schedule of the agreed resources of each department. The system may not have been securely embedded in practice until 1216, but the need for it had been recognized by 1203[22] and the earliest extant written version is dated 1206.[23] There it is laid down that each obedientiary, other than the prior and his deputies, should render an account quarterly to the abbot or his appointee — not specified but perhaps the steward — and in the presence of the prior and six monks (three appointed by the abbot, three by the monks); the kitchener had to submit accounts weekly, and the cellarer as often as the abbot wished. If possible, accounts found to be in deficit were to be made up from any that were in surplus; if no obedience was in surplus, the deficit would be met by the outer cellarer; if no obedience was in deficit, any surplus was to be given to a department to be chosen by the abbot in chapter. The new system would not increase the abbey's assets but it would enable their use to be better planned.

Employees and lay officials

The enumeration of twenty-seven householders at Evesham in 1086 as 'employees of the abbey precinct' and of sixty-three lay servants working at the abbey c.1100 is enough to suggest the large scale on which the monastery site was being run by the beginning of the twelfth century.

The abbot's household alone was so complex and autonomous as to need a separate staff. By the 1120s we know that the abbot had his own chamberlain (the manager of his household) and apparently his own cook[24] and presumably therefore his own kitchen (distinct from the conventual kitchen, which was mentioned a little later),[25] and those officers would have had lesser servants under their direction. The office of abbot's chamberlain was mentioned again in Abbot

22 Below, ch. 21.

23 T. Marlb. pp. 516–33.

24 Constantine 'abbot's chamberlain' and Ralph 'cook', were witnesses 'on the abbot's side' to a deed temp. Abbot Robert (i.e. c.1121×c.1130): *Penwortham Docs*, p. 3.

25 T. Marlb. pp. 182–3.

Adam's time (1161–89), when the holder of it was one Gerard,[26] and in 1203, when Abbot Roger's chamberlain was Richard of Kent;[27] Richard's surname suggests that he may have accompanied Roger to Evesham from Canterbury in 1190. By 1207 at the latest the abbot's 'chamber' was a distinct department with its own allotted revenue.[28] The household also included the abbot's chaplains, while two of Abbot Adam's chaplains, William and Master Hugh (probably Master Hugh of 'Coleham', witness to a deed in 1177),[29] were mentioned in 1189.[30] The chaplains were not always secular clerks, for in 1205 one of them, Henry of 'Coleham' (perhaps a son of Master Hugh), was a monk.[31] Another member of Abbot Adam's household was probably Payn of Evesham (fl.1178) who witnessed many of the abbot's charters as *clericus* (a clerk);[32] Payn's son Master Ralph of Evesham (fl.1177–89) was also a frequent witness.[33] Abbot Roger Norreis's clerks included Master Robert of Wolvey (fl.1191–1206),[34] Gilbert (fl.c.1197),[35] and Master Thomas of Warwick (fl.1204–6).[36] The abbot's clerks were trained professionals, as their titles of 'Master' suggest, and could have considerable delegated authority; for instance, in the 1190s Robert of Wolvey is named as the plaintiff (purchaser) on the abbot's behalf in final concords (conveyances) relating to some small estates in Badby and Newnham.[37] A clerk's expertise could be passed down whenever a son joined his father in the office and inherited his knowledge of the abbey's affairs. Master Ralph of Evesham, son of Payn the clerk, was one such heir to the office tradition. He rented property in Evesham c.1190 and held a large estate from the abbey at Church Honeybourne.[38] His connection with those properties suggests that he was at least the third generation of his family to serve the abbots as a household clerk, for Abbot Maurice had granted a hide of land at Church Honeybourne before c.1121 to another Payn *clericus* (perhaps Ralph's grandfather), who was

26 Dugdale, *Mon.* II, p. 19.

27 T. Marlb. pp. 236–7.

28 T. D. Hardy, ed., *Rotuli litterarum clausarum in turri Londinensi asservati*, I, Record Commission (London, 1833), p. 84.

29 Vesp. B.XXIV, fol. 22v.

30 Harley 3763, fol. 91v.

31 T. Marlb. pp. 272–3.

32 Vesp. B.XXIV, fols 22v, 35r; Harley 3763, fols 88r, 93v, 94r.

33 Vesp. B.XXIV, fols 22v, 32r; Harley 3763, fols 88r, 91v, 92v, 93v; Dugdale, *Mon.* II, p. 19; *Worc. Acta 1062–1185*, p. 124.

34 Vesp. B.XXIV, fol. 24r; T. Marlb. pp. 236–7, 532–3.

35 T. Marlb. pp. 196–7.

36 Ibid. pp. 264–5, 376–7, 532–3.

37 Vesp. B.XXIV, fols 24r–24v.

38 Ibid. fols 43v, 55r.

also the holder of five *mansurae* in Evesham c.1130.[39] Evidently the abbot's clerks did not have to be celibate, though his chaplains may have been; it is also unclear whether the administrative duties of the chaplains and clerks were mutually exclusive or overlapped in some ways.

Master Ralph and his family were not at all unusual in holding lay offices under the abbey by hereditary right. The practice of making offices hereditary had some merit in a period when documentation was still sparse and much official information and procedure had to be memorized; it could best be passed down within a family. The stewardship of the abbey, which had been made hereditary by Abbot Walter for one of his relatives, remained heritable c.1191 when Philip the steward (fl.1177)[40] was succeeded by William his son;[41] and it continued to be hereditary until 1249.[42] Each succession to an hereditary post was nevertheless subject to the abbot's confirmation, because the lawful heir might not be a suitable person. In one such instance, Abbot Adam accepted the claim of a woman to the hereditary office of head porter but allowed her to succeed only in association with a man called Henry,[43] who was afterwards known as Henry *janitor*.[44]

The holders of lay positions at the abbey often had holdings on the abbey estate, which they could presumably sub-let if they were too busy to work them. Such tenancies were attached to the office, not to the person, but in practice the succession to the holding would often be granted, with the office, to a relative of the previous incumbent. As a result the abbot found that he needed to discourage any deceased officer's family from presuming that they would automatically inherit his holding as well as his office; when Abbot Adam granted a half-virgate at Hampton to Godfrey his *serviens* ('servant' or 'officer') it was on condition that Godfrey, at the approach of death, would surrender the holding to the abbot free of any claim from his family.[45] Instances of holdings that did descend with particular lay offices include that of Hugh *portarius* (a gatekeeper, fl.1175×1189),[46] perhaps the successor of Henry *janitor*. He was paying 12d rent in Evesham c.1190,[47] and in 1206 the almonry was still receiving a rent of 12d a year

39 Clarke 2012b, pp. 32–6 ('Evesham O' and 'Evesham E').
40 *Worc. Acta 1062–1185*, p. 124.
41 Below, this section.
42 Brand 1992, p. 161.
43 T. Marlb. pp. 188–9.
44 Vesp. B.XXIV, fol. 32r. In the fourteenth century Nicholas Porter held the office of gatekeeper 'in fee': *Evesham Chron.* p. 294.
45 Vesp. B.XXIV, fol. 32r.
46 Ibid. fol. 47v, datable temp. Simon abbot of Pershore (appointed 1175) and King Henry II (d.1189).
47 Vesp. B.XXIV, fol. 42v.

from 'the gatekeeper's land'.[48] John *portarius* was paying the same rent a few years later.[49] In another instance the five virgates of land in Badsey held by William the steward c.1130[50] were in the hands of Philip the steward c.1190[51] and of Philip's son William the steward c.1192;[52] Philip, followed by William (fl. 1206),[53] also had three virgates and a mill in Abbots Salford[54] and six pieces of land (probably closes or house plots) in Evesham.[55] An additional perquisite of the hereditary stewards was a daily corrody (food and lodging) at the abbey.[56] As a further instance of an hereditary estate linked to an office, we may note that in the 1120s Abbot Robert granted a virgate of land at Evesham to William the chamberlain,[57] and that Abbot Adam (1161–89) granted a virgate there (perhaps the same land) to Ernald the chamberlain;[58] they were presumably chamberlains to the abbot, because the conventual chamberlain would have been an obedientiary, not a personal holder of land. Richard of Kent, probably Abbot Roger's chamberlain of that name (fl.1203), also held lands in Evesham some time before 1230.[59]

There were lay tenants c.1190, mostly in Evesham but some in nearby Bengeworth and Hampton, who had by-names that suggest that they too worked in the abbey.[60] They included Geoffrey *mareschal* (in charge of horses), William *janitor* (a gatekeeper), two men called *celarius* (cellarmen), four men called *cocus* (cooks), and two called *hortolanus* (gardeners). Such people had been employed at the abbey as early as c.1100, when there already two gatekeepers, two cellarmen, five servants in the kitchen, and three gardeners.[61] Tenants who served the abbey in various ways outside the precinct c.1190 included Ralph *cachepol* (a catchpole — a petty officer of the law or a tax collector), Ralph and Richard, both *decanus* (tithingmen or petty constables), Roger *molendinarius* and William *pistor* (respectively engaged in the abbot's monopolies of milling and baking), and Adam *prepositus* (a reeve). Some tenancies in the town c.1190 were those of ecclesiastics such as Randal *capellanus* (a chaplain) and Giffard and Ralph,

48 T. Marlb. pp. 526–7.
49 Ibid. pp. 400–401.
50 Clarke 2012b, pp. 32–6 ('Evesham O' and 'Evesham E').
51 Vesp. B.XXIV, fol. 50r (Tindal 1794, p. 56n).
52 Clarke 2012b, p. 38 (from 'Evesham G').
53 T. Marlb. pp. 532–3.
54 Dugdale, *Mon.* II, pp. 18–19; Harley 3763, fol. 81v.
55 Vesp. B.XXIV, fols 42v–43r, 44r–45r.
56 Brand 1992, pp. 155, 161. The evidence is dated 1247.
57 Clarke 2012b, pp. 32–6 ('Evesham O' and 'Evesham E').
58 T. Marlb. pp. 188–9.
59 Ibid. pp. 546–7.
60 Vesp. B.XXIV, fols 32r (Tindal 1794, p. 61n), 34v, 42r–45r.
61 T. Marlb. pp. 570–71.

both *clericus*.[62] They were presumably appointees of the abbey and may have been serving in the town chapels of St Lawrence and All Saints. In the countryside the demesne manors also had resident employees c.1190; they might include a reeve, a beadle, a miller, a shepherd, a swineherd, a smith, or a forester, but probably not all of them together, and each man had a small allocation of land in return for his services.[63]

Certain freeholders[64] on the abbey's nearby rural estates c.1190 owed occasional and quite onerous services at the abbey but were not its employees. William Pintelthein of Hampton, John of Wickhamford, and Richard Franceis of Badsey held lands that put each of them under an obligation to carry the baggage of any of the monks anywhere in England at the abbot's expense; in two of those instances it was specified that the tenant should provide his own pack horse. Ralph Wither at Norton had simply to accompany the monks anywhere in England. Evidently the abbey's own brethren were sometimes called upon to visit distant places. Meanwhile, an unnamed freeholder at Adlestrop in Gloucestershire had to carry the abbot's letters and act as his messenger throughout England;[65] there could be no better example of how the local economy and the needs of the abbey had become inseparable.

62 Vesp. B.XXIV, fols 42v, 43r, 45v.

63 Vesp. B.XXIV, fols 31v–32r, 49v, 52v–53r, 66r, 67r (Tindal 1794, pp. 51n, 56n, 60–61n, 67n, 68n); Harley 3763, fol. 75r.

64 Named in Clarke 2012b, p. 38 (from 'Evesham G').

65 Vesp. B.XXIV, fols 31v, 49r, 50r, 53v, 67r (Tindal 1794, pp. 52n, 56n, 57n, 60n, 67n).

CHAPTER 16

Economic realities

DURING the twelfth century the abbey's landed estate, valuable as it was, could not support every possible expense; such was the abbey's standing that its obligations far exceeded the welfare of a few dozen monks and the remuneration of their lay servants. It was a religious house comparable in rank to any in the land and it therefore had a dignity to keep up, and new buildings that would be suitable to its status were costly to provide and needed constant expense to furnish, staff, and keep in repair. The profitability of the demesne estates (where the demesne lands were not in the hands of freehold or feudal tenants) depended partly on physical structures that needed to be enhanced, equipped, and maintained; thus bridges, local churches, manor houses, barns, mills, fishponds, and dovecotes demanded continual expenditure. Moreover, the abbey was expected to make a contribution to the poor that was proportionate to its means. The abbot was a great prelate and lord and had to have the appropriate household luxuries and servants; he had to travel in suitable style to London and other cities; he had to bestow fitting hospitality on guests of a like status to his own; and to manage the many calls on his attention he had to pay for a retinue of secular clerks. An additional drain on the house was the king's entitlement to the abbey's temporal revenues during every vacancy of the abbacy. And from the middle of the twelfth century all the abbey's expenditure had to be carried on against a background of gradual price inflation, which was to become acute in the 1190s.[1] The financial affairs of Evesham abbey could not safely be left to take care of themselves.

Income gained

On the face of things the abbey was gaining in economic strength. The number of people living on Evesham's rural manors in the Vale grew during the twelfth century, as did the number coming to live in the town.[2] That may be the reason, or one of the reasons, why the nave of Bretforton church, originally aisleless,

1 D. L. Farmer, 'Prices and Wages', Hallam 1988a, pp. 716–817.

2 For the town see below, ch. 17.

was enlarged twice c.1200, first by a south aisle and later by one on the north.[3] Population growth throughout the Vale may also be inferred from three written sources.[4] The earliest is Domesday Book (1086), which states the rural population recorded in Evesham's Worcestershire manors south of the Lenches (excluding Evesham and Bengeworth, which were partly urban).[5] The latest of the sources is a collection of extents (rentals and customaries) of c.1190, which is preserved in the Evesham cartularies.[6] They allow one to see the recorded populations of the same manors 100 years after Domesday. Between those sources chronologically are figures for c.1104 in the survey known as 'Evesham J'.[7] The demographic trend is difficult to estimate directly from the documents, for they enumerate only tenants (and perhaps not all of them), and each kind of record does that in a different way;[8] additional family members and other landless people are not counted at all. Nevertheless, an expanding population in the Vale of Evesham during the twelfth century can probably be deduced from those sources because it would explain something plainly recorded in the extents of c.1190 — that is to say, the abbey's move towards taking cash rents from its customary tenants (the peasant farmers) instead of requiring their labour services and their renders in kind. The argument assumes that there were not enough agricultural tenancies available to meet a high demand from a growing population. Under those circumstances there would have been an increase in the number of landless men in need of employment — an expanding pool of labour from which the abbey could derive advantages. By allowing customary tenants to pay cash rents the abbey would have more cash with which to employ landless labourers flexibly on its demesnes instead of its being bound to make use of a predetermined pattern of labour services; the abbey would also have more cash to buy, whenever it needed to and in whatever quantities, the things that would otherwise arrive as fixed renders on prescribed dates. Tenants who were no longer performing labour services and making renders in kind were able to get the cash to pay their rents and dues by

3 Brooks and Pevsner 2007, p. 169.

4 The original sources were consulted here. A published table derived from them (Hallam 1988b, pp. 570–71) includes some totals that differ from mine but it serves to confirm the upward trend.

5 DB, fol. 175v.

6 The extents of c.1190 are in Vesp. B.XXIV, fols 22v–24r, 26v–27r, 31v–32r, 34r–34v, 36v, 46v, 49r–55v, 64v, 66r–67v (many of which are printed as footnotes in Tindal 1794, pp. 50–61, 63, 67–70); most are also in Harley 3763, fols 72r–81r, with extents for Abbots Salford and Sambourne (both Warws.) on fol. 81v.

7 Clarke 2007, pp. 83–4.

8 The Evesham figures are discussed in that light by J. Langdon and J. Masschaele, 'Commercial Activity and Population Growth in Medieval England', *Past & Present*, no. 190 (2006), 35–81 (at 57n, 59–60).

spending more time on their holdings and by selling their surplus produce in the market.

The abbey's gross revenue from its demesne estates certainly increased in the twelfth century. The sources of income included cash rents, payable by freeholders and some of the customary tenants; labour services and renders in kind from the other customary tenants (which one assumes were of equivalent value to the cash alternatives); and annual customary payments in cash, including *wudeselver* (in lieu of carting winter fuel) at the rate of nine pence per virgate held (a virgate was a quarter of a hide), *fissepeni* (to provide fish for the abbey in Lent, when meat was not allowed) at the rate of one penny per virgate, and 'pannage' (*pasnagium*) for the right to feed pigs in the abbey's woodland. Some tenants also had to make contributions towards the occasional taxes payable by the abbey to the king, by way of 'aid', 'toll', 'geld', and 'royal service' (probably scutage, a payment in lieu of knight service). The extents of c.1190 enable one to calculate for each demesne manor the total cash value that was put upon (and sometimes substituted for) the labour services and renders in kind; to that figure can be added the stated cash rents of freeholders. As a result one finds that the demesne manors were usually valued more highly c.1190 than in 1086, even without counting the income from the other dues and taxes, for which we have no totals. Since every such estate valued c.1190 also yielded an unrecorded income from the produce of the demesne, one may be confident that by c.1190 the gross value of each of those demesne manors was well above that of 1086.[9]

Income lost

The abbey's gross income from its demesne estates during the twelfth century had been compromised from the start by the policies of abbots Maurice and Robert (c.1104–c.1130), who, ignoring the advice of their monks in chapter, continued Abbot Walter's practice of letting out demesne estates to relatives, employees, and supporters in return for fixed cash payments or services, which might include knight service.[10] The policy proved to be short-sighted, for the abbey's return from those estates remained fixed from year to year while the grantees received all the benefits that population growth was creating, including an increased demand for their produce and for subtenancies on their land and a diminished cost of employing direct labour. The early twelfth-century abbots had been warned by

[9] For the corresponding manors in 1086 see DB, fols 165v–166r, 175v, 222v, 239r. For explanations of customary payments named in the extents see N. Neilson, *Customary Rents* (Oxford, 1910), pp. 33–4, 51–2, 90–97.

[10] Clarke 2012b, pp. 11–15. Further details are in Clarke 1977, pp. 138–9.

their chapters about letting out demesne estates, but in mitigation it must be stated that neither the abbots nor their officials could easily have calculated the consequences, because they had no contemporary written overview of the abbey's economy by which to form a judgement. As soon as Abbot Reynold took office in 1130 he was presented with a written summary of his predecessors' unwise grants, and the need for a change of direction was immediately apparent;[11] Reynold began a policy of retrieving control of the alienated estates. The loss of demesnes, however, could not be suddenly reversed. The abbey had no right in law unilaterally to dispossess the original grantees or their heirs; unless one of the abbey's freehold or feudal tenants died without an heir, or a lessee's term came to its fixed end, the abbey could resume such an estate only with the tenant's consent. The tenant could not be expected to give consent freely but he might be asked to give the estate back in return for cash or in exchange for another estate that lay farther from the abbey. In his first year Reynold paid twenty marks to William of Melling and his brother Simon to buy back the lands that they held in Hampton and Norton, near Evesham,[12] but the retrieval of other estates granted away before 1130 could only be very gradual. It depended not only on the tenant's consent but also on the abbey's ability to pay him off, and the sums required could be very great; Abbot Adam had to pay William de Waterville 100 marks to give back land at Badby.[13] And the policy could not be pursued with absolute consistency; sometimes a distant demesne estate had to be let out in order to get back a nearer one. By the 1190s the retrieval of estates from their freehold and feudal tenants was therefore far from complete.[14] Meanwhile, the military tenants rendered nothing to the abbey in return for their holdings except knight service, and they did it apathetically.[15]

The abbey's large gross income went some way towards masking the effects of price inflation. In practice, however, the balance between the abbey's income and its spending commitments was always precarious, and unforeseen events could bring sudden crises. For instance, in the civil war that occupied most of King Stephen's reign (1135–54) a large number of the monks were involved at one point in a theft of gold, silver, and precious stones from the shrine of St Ecgwine. Their subsequent claim to have been driven by hunger may have been false,[16] but

[11] Clarke 2012b, pp. 32–6 ('Evesham O' and 'Evesham E'). On the date see Clarke 1977, pp. 225, 229, 289–90.

[12] Vesp. B.XXIV, fol. 31r.

[13] Vesp. B.XXIV, fol 40v; T. Marlb. pp. 186–7.

[14] Clarke 2012b, pp. 17–24. Further details are in Clarke 1977, pp. 155, 158, 444–5, 494–6, 507a–509.

[15] 'et hoc tepide': Clarke 2012b, p. 37 (from 'Evesham G').

[16] T. Marlb. pp. 182–3.

it does seem to indicate that the Evesham monks were experiencing an episode of exceptional hardship. The war led to more than one direct violation of the abbey precinct[17] and there is therefore every chance that the whole neighbourhood, from which the abbey derived most of its income, suffered losses during the conflict. In 1153, near the end of the war, Evesham abbey also had the duty of entertaining Henry duke of Normandy, son of the Empress Maud and soon to be King Henry II, as he and his retinue made their armed progress through the Midlands.[18] A royal visit was an expensive and unpredictable event at the best of times and Henry II and his court were noted for restlessly travelling about his realms. Before Henry II's time we have no record of any visit to Evesham by Henry I, Stephen, or the Empress Maud but Henry II is known to have brought his entourage to Evesham again in 1158, 1175, and 1181,[19] and there may have been other visits during which Henry issued no documents that would have recorded his presence. With no central system of accounting and audit until the 1200s, the abbey's economy was so vulnerable to unforeseen setbacks that it is hardly surprising that by 1206 the reckless actions of one abbot, Roger Norreis, and the litigious zeal of his legal adviser, Thomas of Marlborough, were enough to bring the finances of the abbey close to collapse.[20]

Harnessing the written record

Evesham came slowly to a realization that the abbey was in want of administrative records – surveys, properly authenticated deeds, and cartularies in which to store copies of them. They would serve better than a chronicle to confirm the house's rights, its possessions, and its relations with its tenants, especially in the later twelfth century when the emerging royal and ecclesiastical courts of law preferred verifiable written forms of evidence. The increased need for formal deeds, and an intimate awareness at Evesham of the potential for them to be forged, called for a reliable method of authenticating those that the abbey issued. In the late eleventh century the abbot may have had a seal for sealing up and identifying his letters with a wax impression that was to be broken when the letters were opened. It was for a different purpose, however, that Abbot Reynold began to use a conventual seal, designed to be attached to documents such as grants, leases, and agreements,

[17] Below, ch. 17.

[18] *Regesta Steph.* p. 121 no. 321. On the date see Z. N. Brooke and C. N. L. Brooke, 'Henry II, Duke of Normandy and Aquitaine', *EHR* 61 (1946), 81–9 (at 86–7).

[19] For 1158 and 1181: R. W. Eyton, *The Court, Household, and Itinerary of King Henry II* (London, 1878), pp. 37, 242. For 1175: J. H. Round, *Feudal England: Historical Studies on the Eleventh and Twelfth Centuries*, reprint (London, 1964), p. 385.

[20] Below, ch. 21.

which the abbey would issue in a format that was open for anyone to read. The seal was not to be broken and was to provide the deed with a permanent mark of its authenticity. But the Evesham seal was more than a bureaucratic device. It was a miniature work of art and the matrix for it was produced by a specialist craftsman (Fig. 9). In shape it was an upright oval and it depicted the Virgin seated on a throne and handing a pastoral staff to St Ecgwine, thereby investing him with the authority of abbot of Evesham. A surviving fragment of the inscription reads … [S(AN)]C(T)I EG[WINI] ('… of St Ecgwine'), which is enough to show that it named Ecgwine as joint patron of the abbey.[21] Anyone seeing that seal on a document would be reminded that the contents bore the authority not merely of St Ecgwine but of the Virgin Mary too. The seal also conveyed the urgent political message that Ecgwine's successors, the contemporary abbots of Evesham, owed their authority ultimately to the Virgin and not to any bishop of Worcester. By the late twelfth century each abbot also had a personal seal. He needed one when he acted in matters that did not involve the abbey, as, for example, when he served as a judge-delegate at papal hearings in England. The personal seal of Abbot Adam (1161–89) was oval (Fig. 10) and was only slightly smaller than the conventual seal. It depicted the abbot at full length as a vested figure holding a pastoral staff in his right hand and a book in his left. Adam often acted as a judge-delegate[22] and the single known impression of his seal is attached to a deed that he witnessed in that capacity.[23] Neither the conventual seal nor Abbot Adam's seal had a design on the reverse. By the early thirteenth century there had been a proliferation of seals, in the sense that senior lay officials of the abbey had personal seals, which they might add to documents under the conventual seal if they were named in them as parties; William the abbey steward, whose father Philip the steward had had a personal seal in the time of Abbot Adam (d. 1189),[24] used his own seal in that way in 1206, and so did the abbot's clerks Robert of Wolvey and Thomas of Warwick.[25] They were not official seals, but private ones used in an official context.

[21] Zarnecki et al. 1984, p. 312 no. 355 (Durham University Library, Durham Cathedral Muniments, 2.4.Ebor.26a). For another incomplete impression: R. H. Ellis, *Catalogue of Seals in the Public Record Office: Monastic Seals*, I (London, 1986), p. 33 no. M314 (TNA, PRO E329/83).

[22] K. Christensen, '"Rescriptum Auctoritatis Uestre": A Judge Delegate's Report to Pope Alexander III', *The Two Laws: Studies in Medieval Legal History dedicated to Stephan Kuttner*, ed. L. Mayali and S. A. J. Tibbetts (Washington, DC, 1990), pp. 40–54 (at pp. 51–4).

[23] Westminster Abbey Muniments, no. 2857 (c.1180×1184): G. R. Elvey, ed., *Luffield Priory Charters*, I, Northants. Record Soc. 22, pt 1 (Northampton, 1968), and Bucks. Record Soc. 15 (Welwyn Garden City, 1968), p. 45 no. 39.

[24] Dugdale, *Mon.* II, p. 19.

[25] T. Marlb. pp. 532–3.

Fig. 9. The conventual seal. Original height c.76mm. Impression attached to a deed of 1245. Durham University Library, Durham Cathedral Muniments, 2.4.Ebor.26a.

The seals imply an increasing reliance on written evidences by the 1130s, and some convenient means of reference to a growing archive of such material became more and more desirable during the century. A cartulary was a single book in which the abbey could enter copies of the many separate documents that it had issued and received or had generated for internal use. Evesham may have had a

Fig. 10. Seal of Abbot Adam. Original height c.72mm. Impression attached to a deed of c.1180×1184. Westminster Abbey Muniments, no. 2857.

cartulary since the late eleventh century, created in the first place as a receptacle for 'copies' of forged or lost pre-Conquest charters, and it was not until the end of the twelfth century that the monks took the first steps to making a new cartulary by having their pre-Conquest estate deeds and boundary perambulations copied into a book that was arranged in convenient topographical order.[26] The late appearance of the new cartulary is one sign of how slowly and incompletely Evesham abbey had turned to the production and preservation of written records as internal aids to administration, even though it had long been accustomed to use deeds and to issue them under the conventual seal. For many years after the 1130s there seem to have been no current estate surveys to which the abbey might refer; it was the 1190s[27] before at last it produced up-to-date extents of its demesne estates and a list of its military and freehold tenants.[28] Before then the abbey's officials had probably relied, for current information about particular properties and tenants, on a collective office memory and on title deeds. But without recent surveys or systematic accounts they would have found it hard to form a strategic view of the abbey's whole estate, or on that basis to make the most of its economic potential.

26 Vesp. B.XXIV. On the date see P. A. Stokes, 'The Problem of Grade in Post-Conquest Vernacular Minuscule, c.1060 to 1220', *New Medieval Literatures* 13 (2011), 23–47. The specific palaeographic dating evidence is presented in P. A. Stokes, 'Late Old English at Evesham: The Case of Cotton Vespasian B.XXIV' (TS of a paper given at the conference on 'Writing English 1100–1200' at Leicester, 2007). I am grateful to Dr Stokes for kindly allowing me to cite his unpublished paper here. For the physical and organizational structure of the manuscript and its evolution up to the fifteenth century see Clarke 1977, pp. 20–25.

27 *DB Worcs.* (Thorn), app. IV.

28 Clarke 2012b, pp. 37–9 ('Evesham G').

CHAPTER 17

Investment

Investing in the countryside

An increasing rural population in the twelfth century and a consequent competition for agricultural tenancies seemed on the surface to be working to the abbey's economic advantage. Since the monks did not have a better understanding based on comprehensive and continuous accounts, they may have seen no strong reason at the time to put money into the more efficient exploitation of their estates. It was later admitted that, in the twelfth century, the abbey's demesne lands were never provided with enough oxen to be ploughed to their full potential, and so were less productive of cereals than they might have been.[1] In some places, of course, there had been good reasons for not ploughing. At Lenchwick the abbey had woodland that was valuable enough to require the services of a resident forester c.1190. His remuneration was a house and four acres of land and three sievefuls of seed corn a year;[2] he was unable to grow enough corn to provide all his own seed but the abbey evidently preferred not to clear more land for him by sacrificing some woodland. In other places, however, the abbey was prepared to ignore potential arable land. At Offenham Abbot Adam chose to set aside a large level area between the village and the Avon and turn it into a deer park.[3] The undertaking was ambitious in the amount of labour that was needed to dig a ditch round the whole circuit of the park and to make an outer bank surmounted by a hedge or a wooden pale. The capital cost, however, was not great; no sophisticated buildings were required and local materials and labour were plentiful. The value of the park was in its venison and other game, which furnished the table of the abbot and his guests, especially in winter, when other meats were scarce; in its coverts, which might eventually yield useful timber; and in its grazing areas, which could be rented out. Nevertheless, the park was essentially a luxury, more a sign of lordly status than an agricultural investment. The pleasure and prestige of owning it outweighed the economic considerations and were deemed sufficient to justify relinquishing an opportunity to grow more cereals there.

1 T. Marlb. pp. 502–3.

2 Vesp. B.XXIV, fol. 53r (Tindal 1794, p. 51n).

3 Bond 1973, p. 42; Bond 1975, p. 56.

The lack of drive to increase cereal production on the abbey's demesne estates during the twelfth century was matched by poor investment in their infrastructure. The demesne estates did have some of the mills[4] and barns that were essential to an arable economy, and had the convenience of some artificial fishponds, at least at Evesham,[5] but less was spent on such assets than should have been. Evesham abbey's complacency about them during much of the twelfth century was what Abbot Randal (1214–29) recognized when in the space of fifteen years he created many new fishponds, mills, dovecotes, and manorial buildings and replaced five of the barns in the Vale of Evesham with better ones. By then it was also understood that income could be increased by ploughing up more land and raising rents.[6]

Investing in towns

A market town had formed outside the abbey before the end of the eleventh century, presumably in response to the production of agricultural surpluses and an expansion of the rural population. The same conditions applied with even greater effect in the twelfth century and resulted in a physical enlargement of the town that would not be repeated before the railway age. In the twelfth century the abbey needed to continue housing its lay servants and officials, and in a controlled and profitable way to provide for an influx of people driven by rural population growth and by the attractions of pursuing a trade or craft in a growing town. Immigration from the countryside was to the abbey's economic advantage if only because more rent could be had from an urban building plot than from an equivalent area of agricultural land. By the 1120s the abbey was therefore letting *mansurae* (houses or house plots) in Evesham for cash rents and on special terms described as *de burgo* ('of the borough').[7] Burgage tenure was attractive to applicants because it usually offered freedom from customary services and the right to sell or give away the tenancy. Thus by 1190 the town consisted of at least 200 dwellings, perhaps four times as many as in 1086, and the cash rents alone were producing roughly twice the Domesday value of the whole manor.[8]

Houses may have accrued before the Conquest in the original Evesham streets, which were apparently High Street and Bridge Street, but by 1190 the abbots

4 DB, fols 165v–166r, 175v, 239r; Vesp. B.XXIV, fols 23v, 26v–27r, 32r, 52r, 53r, 66r, 67r (Tindal 1794, pp. 51n, 54n, 59–60n, 61n, 67n, 68n); T. Marlb. pp. 524–7.

5 T. Marlb. pp. 186–7.

6 Ibid. pp. 482–3, 520–21.

7 Clarke 2012b, pp. 32–4 ('Evesham E').

8 Vesp. B.XXIV, fols 42r–45v. A total town rental of £27 6s 8d has been calculated from this record (Slater 1996, p. 81) but I make the total to be £10 13s 6d. For 1086 see above, ch. 12.

had created three new areas of housing attached to the existing town (Fig. 11).[9] One was a large development laid out west of the abbey precinct and called the Barton. It adjoined two ancient open spaces, the Pig Market[10] and the Merstow, both of which lay against the boundary of the abbey and its demesne. The Pig Market (now Vine Street) continued the High Street southwards past the town's original market place and along the west side of the abbey precinct; it broadened out towards the entrance to the abbey's demesne farmstead, at a gateway that became known as the Barton gate.[11] There is excavation evidence to suggest that the west side of the Pig Market (the side opposite the monastic precinct) was not built up before the twelfth century.[12] The Merstow funnelled out at right angles from the end of the Pig Market and thus lay along the north boundary of the abbey's demesne, which was marked by a wall in the fourteenth century.[13] The name Merstow is first recorded at Evesham in the early thirteenth century, as 'Merstowe',[14] and its most probable meaning seems to be 'place of the pool',[15] though we have no other evidence of an early pool there. Another suggested meaning is 'place on the boundary',[16] which would at least be appropriate to the Merstow's position in the twelfth century. The Barton development probably also included Bewdley Street, which led off at right angles from High Street and was built on a westward alignment that continued that of Bridge Street. The name Bewdley Street (colloquially 'the Bewdley')[17] comes from the French *beau lieu* ('lovely place'); Bewdley the distant Worcestershire town received the same name, but independently. At Evesham the name sounds as if it was devised by the abbey after the Conquest in order to attract tenants, and the results of a small excavation at one end of the street do suggest occupation in the eleventh or twelfth century.[18] By 1190 a smaller housing area called the New Borough was established between High Street and Bridge Street. It comprised two new streets, the present Cowl ('coal') Street and Oat ('wood') Street. The last and smallest area to be developed

9 Vesp. B.XXIV, fols 42r–45v. The present paragraph takes into consideration Bond 1973, pp. 44–7; Bond 1975, pp. 56–8; Hilton 1982, p. 3; Slater 1996, pp. 78–81.

10 So called by 1820: Rudge 1820, p. 107 and plan facing p. iii.

11 On the gate see Cox 1990, p. 134.

12 Locket and Griffin 2006, pp. 68–9, 72–3.

13 Cox 1990, p. 133.

14 T. Marlb. pp. 396–7, 542–3.

15 R. Forsberg, 'Old English *burnstōw* and *merestōw*: Two Appellative Compounds in *-stōw* with a Topographical First Element', *Studia Neophilologica* 56 (1984), 3–20 (at 11–15), where other suggestions are also considered.

16 B. Jepson, *English Place-Name Elements relating to Boundaries* (Lund, 2011), pp. 35, 57.

17 Baylis 2008, pp. 92, 131; personal knowledge.

18 'Evesham', *Recent Archaeological Research in English Towns*, ed. J. Schofield and D. Palliser, CBA Occasional Paper [12] (York, 1981), p. 36.

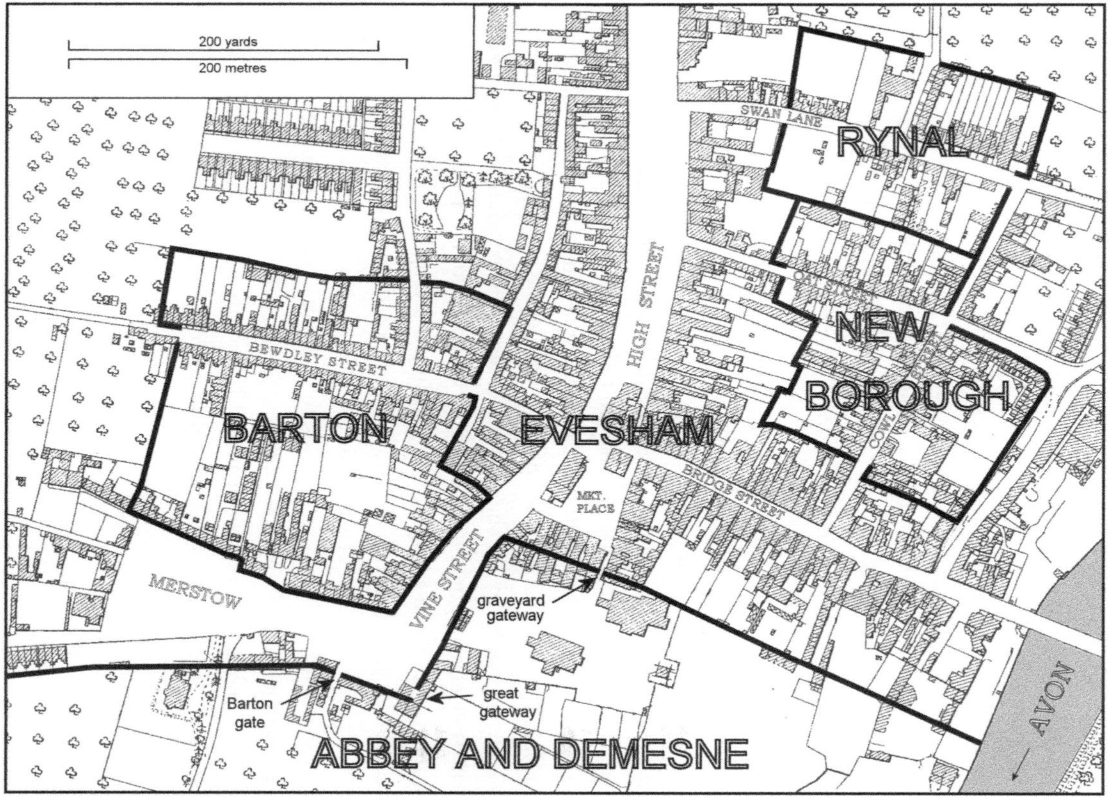

Fig. 11. Evesham town plan elements c.1190. Possible identifications superimposed on OS Plan 1/2,500, Worcs. XLIX.3 (1904 edn).

before 1190 seems to have been the Rynal (along the present Swan Lane),[19] which was laid out parallel to Oat Street. The new streets – that is to say, Bewdley Street, Cowl Street, Oat Street, and Swan Lane, are narrowest where they lead off from High Street and Bridge Street,[20] presumably having been opened up by creating gaps through single house fronts in the original two streets.

The rapid expansion of Evesham created a demand for more water, and by 1265 a public supply had been provided at a conduit or washing-place (*lavour*), which stood in the market place somewhere near the place where Bridge Street enters.[21] The water that filled it was probably the same as that which was feeding pipes to the monks' washing-place, which Abbot Adam had provided in the cloister.[22] In 1189 Abbot Adam had received one of several private donations towards making an 'aqueduct and laver' at Evesham,[23] and it may therefore have been he that made the public conduit that was standing in 1265. If so, it seems to have been a particularly early example of its kind.[24]

Many of the craftsmen and professional people working at Evesham, if not wholly employed by the abbey, probably looked to it for an important part of their business. Among the townsmen of 1190 that must have been true of Reynold *parmentarius* (a parchment maker), and one may also imagine the abbey calling in Robert *le mascun* (a mason) or Edric and Hamelin, both *carpentarius* (carpenters), when small building jobs were needed, or sending for Roger *medicus* (a physician). The mutual dependence of the townspeople and the abbey can only have been strengthened by Evesham's twelfth-century expansion, but there were tenants by 1190 who may have looked beyond the abbey for most of their business. Among them were those engaged in processing or selling cloth, such as Gilbert and Walter, both *fullo* (fullers), Robert *le mercier* (a mercer), and Randal *tinctor* (a dyer).[25] By 1200 a margin of economic independence from the abbey may even have stirred in some of them an aspiration to municipal self-government, though for Evesham that was still a long way off.

The abbey's portion of Bengeworth, which lay immediately across the bridge from Evesham, seems to have been rural in 1086[26] but it was partly urbanized

19 Rudge 1820, p. 106.

20 OS Plan 1:2,500, Worcs. XLIX.3 (1886 edn).

21 O. de Laborderie, J. R. Maddicott, and D. A. Carpenter, 'The Last Hours of Simon de Montfort: A New Account', *EHR* 115 (2000), 378–412 (at 408).

22 Below, ch. 20.

23 'aqueductus faciendi apud Euesham' (Vesp. B.XXIV, fol. 48r); 'aqueductus et lauatorium ... facta sunt' (T. Marlb. pp. 184–7).

24 D. M. Palliser, T. R. Slater, and E. P. Dennison, 'The Topography of Towns 600–1300', Palliser 2000, pp. 153–86 (at pp. 177–8).

25 Vesp. B.XXIV, fols 42v–45v.

26 DB, fol. 175v.

Fig. 12. Bengeworth: early features. *A*. Site of a ditched enclosure. *B*. Moat Orchard. *C*. Chief house of the abbey's Bengeworth estate. *D*. Site of the medieval church. *E*. Site of the Beauchamps' castle. *F*. Burgage plots belonging to the abbey. Superimposed on OS Plan 1/2,500, Worcs. XLIX.3–4 (1904 edns).

by 1190. There were then seventeen virgates of arable in the hands of peasant farmers but also twenty-eight *bordarii* (small tenants), of whom twenty-five paid an annual rent of 12d each; the other three paid 18d, 2s, and 2s 6d. The *bordarii* evidently occupied burgages that were of uniform size as part of a regular scheme.[27] The plot boundaries were probably those discernible in the twentieth century in a rectangular block lining the south side of Port Street, which is the main road as it descends to Evesham bridge; their original number, before they were amalgamated or split, can be estimated at about twenty-five (Fig. 12). It is likely

27 Vesp. B.XXIV, fols 34r–34v. See Hilton 1982, p. 3; R. Holt, 'Society and Population 600–1300', Palliser 2000, pp. 79–104 (at p. 95).

that Port Street marked the boundary between the abbey's part of Bengeworth and that which belonged in the twelfth century to the Beauchamps, whose castle stood on the north side of the street.[28] The original settlement on the abbey's part of the estate was presumably near the medieval churchyard, which lies off the south side of Port Street at the top end, where the ground levels off around the 100ft (30.5m) contour; near the churchyard were ancient ditched enclosures and on the west side of it stood the chief house of the abbey estate, called the Manor House by 1906,[29] which has a twelfth-century doorway with zigzag moulding.[30] The block of burgage plots in Port Street would thus have been on the abbey's side of the street and deliberately sited to take advantage of traffic passing on the main road. That would have caused the older settlement near the church to be eclipsed, as it still is, and the ditched enclosure south of the church seems to have been abandoned at that time. The north side of Port Street, too, has what appear to be medieval plots but they are much longer than those on the south; they may have been laid out independently by the Beauchamps.

Meanwhile, in 1107 the abbey had obtained a grant of a market at Stow on the Wold,[31] a recently founded settlement next to the ancient Foss Way amid Evesham's Cotswold estates. The abbey had a large market place there and during the twelfth century probably began to increase the available building plots at Stow and thus to create a new town.[32] Stow was certainly a town in 1206,[33] though it was always smaller than Evesham. In 1190 there were thirty holdings let for standard cash rents (mostly 6d or 12d a year),[34] which were indicative of a planned town with house plots of regular sizes.

Protecting the precinct

Although the ordinary business of Evesham town may sometimes have been audible within the abbey precinct, especially on market days, that was probably acceptable; the abbey's main courtyard was itself a place of daily activity of a secular kind with much coming and going. But a source of real irritation were some private dwellings that had been allowed within the monastic precinct. Certain of them were held by descendants of Abbot Walter's brother Randal, who

[28] May 1845, p. 164.
[29] *VCH Worcs.* II, p. 397.
[30] Brooks and Pevsner 2007, p. 307.
[31] *Regesta Hen. I*, p. 69 no. 831.
[32] Bond 1973, pp. 47–9.
[33] T. Marlb. pp. 524–5.
[34] Vesp. B.XXIV, fol. 46v.

were hereditary tenants of the abbey by knight service.[35] The unseemly clatter and inconsiderate conduct of armed men living within the abbey enclosure can be imagined, and in Abbot Reynold's time the abbey had begun to feel that the dwellings were intrusive and that it was being unduly hemmed in by them. Reynold therefore decided to have the houses removed. He met with more than token resistance but he was able to break it with the help of his powerful relatives, among them Miles of Gloucester.[36]

Of greater concern than that was the lawlessness that accompanied the civil war between King Stephen (1135–54) and the Empress Maud, because the abbey then became vulnerable to armed raiders. One such threat was no farther away than the Bengeworth end of Evesham bridge, where one of the castles of William de Beauchamp had been built; he was a grandson of the abbey's old rival Urse d'Abbetot, and at Church Lench he was a tenant of the abbey by knight service.[37] There was a history of discord between Sheriff Urse's family and the abbey that went back at least as far as the death of abbot Æthelwig in 1078, and it was unfortunate for Evesham that William de Beauchamp was now the sheriff of Worcestershire and therefore the chief law officer. His castle at Bengeworth was as near to the abbey as it could possibly be and would have enabled the armed men within, if they so desired, to interfere with river traffic to and from Evesham or with goods, livestock, and people crossing the bridge in and out of the town. After the outbreak of war Abbot Reynold, apparently with the advice of Miles of Gloucester, by then earl of Hereford (1141–43), went to great expense to build a wall for the protection of the abbey and graveyard.[38] Vestiges of Reynold's wall have been found on the north side of the precinct and show that it was formidable, with a thickness of about 5ft 3in. (about 1.6m) in at least one place. The remains on the north side suggest that the wall kept to the supposed line of the pre-Conquest boundary all around the precinct, and that originally it did not extend eastwards or westwards from there to the river.[39] On the north side of the abbey the wall incorporates a twelfth-century stone gateway, which still provides access for pedestrians from the market place to the graveyard; the inside surfaces of its passageway are decorated with blind Romanesque arcades. Wheeled vehicles could probably enter the graveyard from the main street by a gateway

35 Clarke 2012b, p. 19.

36 T. Marlb. pp. 180–81.

37 *Red Bk Exch.* I, p. 302; Clarke 2012b, p. 37 (from 'Evesham G').

38 T. Marlb. pp. 180–81.

39 Hughes 1990, p. 161; S. Woodiwiss, 'Survey of Part of Abbot Reginald's Wall Evesham', Hereford and Worcester County Council Archaeology Section internal report (Worcester, 1987), in the 'Online Archaeology Library' of Worcs. Archive and Archaeology Service. Cf. May 1845, p. 168.

on the west, though the first mention of that dates only from 1450.[40] There was presumably another west gateway in the wall to give access from the street to the main courtyard: the 'abbey gate' was described c.1230 as being in the main street.[41] The thickness of Reynold's wall was proportionate to the perceived scale of the immediate threat to the abbey, and its permanence showed that precinct security was expected to be a lasting concern. The wall might have deterred a small army had it been adequately manned, and it could have been even more effective than it was had Reynold not been dissuaded from his idea of providing the whole town with water defences, perhaps by means of a moat across the neck of the river loop in which Evesham lay. Miles, a supporter of Maud, had warned him that such additional fortifications would only tempt King Stephen to seize and occupy the place.[42]

Soon after Abbot Reynold's death in 1149 William de Beauchamp and his armed followers somehow breached the wall into the graveyard and plundered goods from the abbey. Since they had not tried to force a gateway, the intrusion was perhaps intended to take the abbey servants by surprise. Whatever the method of entry it was not an act of war but an opportunistic raid on an unloved and supposedly unarmed neighbour. All Abbot William could do personally was to excommunicate William de Beauchamp and his accomplices, but the raiders could not so easily evade the force of armed men that the abbey immediately got together, which killed many of them the same day. Abbot William was then able to seize the Beauchamp castle at Bengeworth and to destroy it completely;[43] the only known remains have been traces of a moat.[44] There was at least one other incident at about the same time; in 1150 it was reported that Roger of Gloucester earl of Hereford, the leader of the Empress Maud's party, had broken the abbey's sanctuary by capturing some knights of Ralph of Worcester within its walls.[45] Those episodes demonstrate how necessary an investment the abbey wall had become, for if ancient ideas of sacrilege, excommunication, and divine retribution had ever deterred violence against church property, they could no longer be relied upon to do so.

40 Dugdale, *Mon.* II, p. 23.
41 T. Marlb. pp. 546–7.
42 Ibid. pp. 180–83.
43 T. Marlb. pp. 182–5.
44 May 1845, p. 164.
45 G. Foliot, *Lett.* pp. 129 no. 93, 134–5 no. 96.

CHAPTER 18

Worship

Saints and the civil war

ABOVE all the saints stood the Virgin Mary, and Evesham abbey felt especially close to her in the early twelfth century. For 100 years or more the house's existence had been attributed to her original intervention in the days of Eof and St Ecgwine, and the abbey therefore inferred that it would always be under her special protection. Abbot Walter's new crypt became a focus of Evesham's devotion to the Virgin, probably in or before the early twelfth century, and although the abbey had no relics of her she did have her altar, which could stand there in calm detachment from the liturgical activities and saints' relics in the church above.[1] The abbey also sought ways of drawing attention to her in the outside world, where it may have hoped to win some reflected glory.

As a public tribute to its heavenly patron, the abbey produced a compilation of miracle stories associated with the Virgin. It was begun some time after c.1121 by the monk Dominic, who collected together fourteen tales of her posthumous miracles.[2] He culled them from scattered sources, mostly of continental origin, and only one of the stories is associated with Evesham itself. But his intention, as with all his writings, was to celebrate a saint who was especially important to his own house. Dominic is last mentioned in 1133 and probably never knew that by the mid-twelfth century his Evesham collection would be amalgamated with two collections from elsewhere. As a comprehensive 'Miracles of the Virgin' the composite work created a literary genre that would permeate western European culture during the rest of the twelfth century and well beyond. One reason why

[1] Cox 2010a.

[2] The only complete edition is in J. C. Jennings, 'Prior Dominic of Evesham and the Survival of the English Tradition after the Norman Conquest', unpublished B.Litt. thesis, University of Oxford (1958), pp. 145–204. The text has been printed elsewhere, but in sections: C. Neuhaus, ed., *Die lateinischen Vorlagen zu den alt-französischen Adgar'schen Marien-Legenden*, I (Heilbronn, 1886), pp. 9–20, 22–8 [miracles 1–6]; H. Kjellman, ed., *La Deuxième collection anglo-normande des miracles de la Sainte Vierge* (Paris and Uppsala, 1922), pp. 3–5, 23–4, 30–33, 41, 44–5, 47–9, 60–61 [miracles 7–12]; Southern 1958, pp. 179–81 [prologue and miracles 13–14].

the combined collection enjoyed such wide diffusion was that it did not shed glory on any one place, as did the usual saint's *vita*, but instead had a consistent focus on the person of the Virgin.[3] Dominic could not have foreseen the international appeal of the work to which he had unwittingly contributed; his only desire in compiling the miracles had been to glorify the patron of his own abbey.

Evesham was just as intent on attracting attention to its relic collection. The abbey's shrines or reliquaries were essentially boxes covered with precious metals and stones. They contained remains of Ecgwine, Oswald, Credan, Odulf, Wigstan and others and, though portable, were usually kept on the high altar or above it, some of them perhaps on a horizontal beam;[4] and on a saint's feast day his shrine would probably be brought forward for special veneration. Among the feasts associated with the Evesham shrines in the twelfth century, St Ecgwine's deposition and translation remained pre-eminent, and from the 1130s the abbey's conventual seal (Fig. 9) proclaimed Ecgwine as patron of the abbey jointly with the Virgin Mary. Below Ecgwine's feasts in status were those of Oswald and Credan, both of whom had played a part in the history of the abbey. Less prominent than theirs were the feasts of Wigstan and Odulf, and of Wulfsige the Evesham anchorite. In life neither Wigstan nor Odulf had been associated with Evesham, and Wulfsige had only lately been elevated to sainthood.[5]

It is difficult to go beyond appearances to discover what worshippers, monastic and lay, honestly believed about the relics. In the late eleventh century Abbot Walter had clearly appreciated their purely secular value, for he had used relics to raise funds for the abbey from people who looked to the saints for personal favours, and he had brought relics into a court of law to validate oaths made in the abbey's support. The abbey would have been unable to take advantage of the relics in such ways unless the general public of Walter's day had accepted that the remains themselves were holy. One cannot be so sure that the appointed hagiographers or the abbots believed in them wholeheartedly and in private, but an incident in Abbot Reynold's time (1130–49) affords an oblique glimpse into the attitudes of the ordinary monks of Evesham. Many of them were involved in a theft of gold, silver, and precious stones from St Ecgwine's shrine while the abbot was at dinner. Their excuse was that they had been driven by hunger caused by the civil war that was then in progress.[6] Their immediate bodily needs had been more real to them than any expectation of being struck down by God or the saint, which was

[3] Southern 1958, pp. 178–83; J. C. Jennings, 'The Origins of the "Elements Series" of the Miracles of the Virgin', *Mediaeval and Renaissance Studies* 6 (1968), 84–93.

[4] Cox 2010a, p. 59.

[5] Licence 2011, p. 177.

[6] T. Marlb. pp. 182–3.

the invariable fate of such offenders in the pages of Byrhtferth and especially of Dominic; in Dominic's words, 'seldom did anyone scorn him [St Ecgwine] with impunity or inflict injury upon him or his servants without being punished'.[7] The culprits showed little respect for the reliquary but they did not interfere with the actual relics and may still have believed in them as intrinsically sacred. Among the English as a whole, however, it does seem that the war had impaired religious belief, for some people were driven to declare that 'God and his saints were asleep'.[8] Whether or not that view was widely shared one assumes that the twelfth-century monks of Evesham needed to participate in the cult of relics without regard to their private beliefs or to the current level of public enthusiasm; they would have done so in obedience to the abbot and in support of the perceived interests of their house.

At the beginning of the twelfth century St Ecgwine's remains were held in the two reliquaries made for them in Abbot Manni's time (1044–58). The principal one contained most of the bones, while the lesser held part of an arm. Under Abbot Reynold the monkish thieves damaged or stole the top (*culmen*) of the main reliquary and he therefore had a new top made. He also had a new reliquary made for the arm.[9] Evesham then held most of Ecgwine's relics, but not all of them. Others were held at Peterborough abbey;[10] they perhaps included the jawbone that Abbot Ælfweard had taken to London and which he had apparently given in 1044 to Ramsey abbey, only fifteen miles from Peterborough. Moreover, one of Ecgwine's teeth may have found its way to Glastonbury, where it was recorded in the fourteenth century.[11]

Evesham had acquired a relic of St Oswald's arm, probably at the time of Oswald's translation at Worcester in 1002; Abbot Reynold made a reliquary for it. But by then the cult of St Oswald at Evesham carried some risk, for Oswald had been bishop of Worcester when he refounded Evesham abbey about 970. In the twelfth century it was an awkward fact that the Evesham monks did not want to celebrate but to suppress, because the current bishops might try to use it in support of their claim to jurisdiction over the abbey. Thus Oswald's arm-relic was openly venerated at Evesham but the true reasons for the abbey's devotion to Oswald — that he was its second founder and, with Ecgwine and the Virgin Mary, its heavenly patron — were deliberately concealed from outsiders. That was probably why the monk Dominic seems never to have produced

7 Byrhtferth, pp. 290–97; T. Marlb. pp. 80–89, 104–7, 118–21.

8 ASC (E) 1137.

9 T. Marlb. pp. 182–3.

10 W. T. Mellows, ed., *The Chronicle of Hugh Candidus* (Oxford, 1949), pp. 54, 56.

11 J. P. Carley and M. Howley, 'Relics at Glastonbury in the Fourteenth Century: An Annotated Edition of BL Cotton MS Titus D.vii, fols 2r–13v', *Glastonbury Abbey and the Arthurian Tradition*, ed. J. P. Carley (Cambridge, 2001), pp. 569–616 (at p. 583).

a revised *vita* of St Oswald to accompany that of St Ecgwine; such a work could not have avoided proclaiming Evesham's embarrassing debt to Oswald as bishop.[12]

St Credan's shrine was another of those made for Abbot Manni, and its relics had emerged unharmed when Abbot Walter tested them by fire. After that, however, there is no known record of Credan's posthumous miracles, if indeed any were claimed. As for St Odulf, a few miracles were still being reported at Evesham in the early twelfth century, and it was customary to suspend a hanging (*cortina*) in Odulf's honour above or behind the high altar at the time of his feast.[13] St Wigstan's relics, like St Odulf's, were among those that had been acquired by Abbot Ælfweard. They had been brought from Repton in the early eleventh century and had survived Abbot Walter's test by fire, from which time they are known to have been kept in a reliquary,[14] but no subsequent miracles were reported at Evesham.

The festal commemorations of Evesham's special saints occupied only a few days in the course of the liturgical year and most feast days were dedicated to saints with whom the abbey had no direct connection. Some saints were universal and were revered in every church, and in a few such instances Evesham may even have held what passed for a small relic.[15] A lesser saint, however, might be remembered at Evesham because he or she was personally favoured by a particular abbot. The presence of St Vigor in a litany used at Evesham by the mid-thirteenth century requires some such explanation.[16] Devotion to St Vigor bishop of Bayeux was unusual in England and may have been practised at Evesham because he was the dedicatee and reputed founder of the abbey of Cerisy-la-Forêt,[17] where Abbot Walter had been a monk.[18] Later, it was probably Abbot Adam (1161–89) who introduced the feast on 30 March of St Rieul (or Regulus), the first bishop of Senlis, which was rarely observed in England; Senlis was the seat of Adam's family.[19]

12 Cox 2002.

13 *Evesham Chron.* pp. 317–19.

14 Ibid. p. 336.

15 Evesham had unspecified relics of other saints than its own c.1500: Cox 2002, p. 277.

16 N. J. Morgan, ed., *English Monastic Litanies of the Saints after 1100*, I, HBS 119 (Woodbridge, 2012 for 2007), pp. 26, 112, 169.

17 M. Baylé, 'Cerisy-la-Forêt: abbatiale Saint-Vigor', *L'Architecture normande au moyen âge*, ed. M. Baylé, 2nd edn (Condé-sur-Noireau, 2001), II, pp. 65–8 (at p. 65).

18 T. Marlb. pp. 176–7.

19 Cox 2010b, pp. 114–15.

Abbot Adam's reforms

A longing to return to the simple way of life implied by the 'Rule of St Benedict' had ultimately given rise to the Cistercian order of monks. In England their new abbeys had sprung up quickly and in large numbers in the earlier twelfth century. They had drawn benefactors and recruits away from the ancient abbeys such as Evesham and had naturally absorbed the kind of people that, as recluses and ascetics, had formerly served within Evesham abbey as its monastic conscience. Thus by the middle of the twelfth century it had become necessary for the black monks to justify a continuance of the traditional practices that their critics portrayed as self-indulgent. Their established ways were so deeply rooted in the past and in contemporary society that the black monks could not have simply abandoned them in face of the Cistercian challenge even if they had wished to. Nor could they honestly ignore some of the Cistercian arguments for reform.

At Evesham abbey it was probably in deference to those arguments that some changes to the monastic life were introduced by Abbot Adam (1161–89), who was said to have surpassed his predecessors in the 'regeneration of discipline'.[20] The aspects of reform that Adam particularly chose to pursue may probably be deduced from the fact that he had previously been a monk at La Charité and Bermondsey, which were members of the great family of monasteries governed from Burgundy by the abbey of Cluny. Adam would have been aware that in 1147 the abbot of Cluny, Peter the Venerable, had prescribed many reforms for the Cluniac houses by way of response to the rise of the Cistercians. They included injunctions against haste in the performance of the liturgy, against luxury in food and clothing, and against idleness and gossiping.[21] That Adam introduced some such ideas to Evesham is suggested by the tone of a letter that he sent from there to the abbot of nearby Winchcombe in the 1160s: in it he thanks Abbot Gervase for the warm welcome that he has received on a recent visit to Winchcombe but points out the dangers of immoderate hospitality, through which kindness can be marred by fuss and excess.[22] Nevertheless, a letter written to Abbot Adam by Peter of Blois suggests that there was to be no retreat at Evesham from the established tradition of the black monks that God and the saints should be honoured in the grandest possible way. According to Peter an elaborate and drawn-out liturgy of the Cluniac kind was fitting as long as it was based on true devotion, and the demands that it put upon the monks would help them to avoid the sin

[20] 'dicitur pre ceteris ordinem reformasse': T. Marlb. pp. 188–9.

[21] Knowles 1963b, pp. 69–71.

[22] Cox 2010b, pp. 128–30.

of sloth.[23] Similar considerations might have been said to justify the impressive display of fine art and architecture that was characteristic of the black-monk houses such as Evesham and which the early Cistercians condemned wholeheartedly. At Evesham in the later twelfth century there would be no religious scruple about completing the abbey church on a grand scale, enhancing the shrine of St Ecgwine, and adding to the plate, furnishings, and vestments. The only restraints would be financial.

The cult of saints revived

Even before the civil war the older Evesham saints had virtually ceased to excite the people's imagination or stir them to expect and report amazing cures. Even St Ecgwine generated no reports of miracles after 1104, and when Thomas of Marlborough copied Dominic's collection of Ecgwine's miracles in the 1180s he had no new stories to add.[24] The standing of Evesham's saints was not improved when the sensational cult of Thomas Becket, which began in 1170, starkly exposed the want of novelty and drama surrounding the old Evesham cults. In response Evesham made a conscious effort to reassert the claims of its saints, knowing that the alternative was to watch its shrines recede further into obscurity. Evesham was not the only centre seeking to refresh its cults at that time; there was a general revival of interest in the relics of local saints in England, many of which were being translated to new shrines.[25] At Evesham in 1183 Abbot Adam with his own hands transferred the bones of St Ecgwine from his two reliquaries to a single new shrine in a memorable ceremony that was attended by five neighbouring abbots, including those of Gloucester and Tewkesbury, and by the prior of Worcester.[26] It was also in the 1180s that the monks of Evesham invited Thomas of Marlborough, a friend of the abbey but not yet a monk, to write a more succinct version of Dominic's *vita* of St Ecgwine. Thomas completed the new version and submit-

[23] 'Petri Blesensis epistolae', *PL* 207, cols 1–560 (at cols 304A–306C). On the letter see Knowles 1963a, pp. 385–6; E. C. Higonnet, 'Spiritual Ideas in the Letters of Peter of Blois', *Speculum* 50 (1975), 218–44 (at 226).

[24] T. Marlb. pp. 76–125; Dominic, *V. Ecgwini*, p. 75.

[25] P. Draper, 'Bishop Northwold and the Cult of Saint Etheldreda', *Medieval Art and Architecture at Ely Cathedral*, ed. N. Coldstream and P. Draper, British Archaeological Association Conference Transactions 2 (London, 1979 for 1976), pp. 8–27 (at pp. 16, 24 nn. 48–9); J. Crook, *English Medieval Shrines* (Woodbridge, 2011), pp. 170–212.

[26] British Library, Harley MS 229, fol. 25r. See W. A. Wright, ed., *The Metrical Chronicle of Robert of Gloucester*, II, Rolls Series (London, 1887), p. 688; 'Annales de Theokesberia', *Ann. mon.* I, Rolls Series (London, 1864), pp. 43–180 (at p. 53); 'Annales prioratus de Wigornia', *Ann. mon.* IV, Rolls Series (London, 1869), pp. 355–562 (at p. 385).

Fig. 13. Lead ampulla found near Penwortham, depicting on one side (right) St Ecgwine and on the other St Eadwine. Present height c.90mm. From *Transactions of the Historic Soc. of Lancashire and Cheshire* new series 9 (1868–9), pl. facing p. 169.

ted it for the approval of Archbishop Baldwin,[27] one of Abbot Adam's literary friends.[28]

Adam's measures to enhance the cult of St Ecgwine may have served to revive the monks' confidence in the relics, for in the 1190s some of them ventured to remove Ecgwine's arm-relic temporarily to the chapter house and to swear upon it an oath of solidarity against Abbot Roger.[29] That there was also some renewal of popular pilgrimage to the shrine of St Ecgwine at that time is perhaps to be deduced from a lead ampulla (a small phial) of c.1200 that was found in Lancashire in 1863 a few miles from the site of Evesham's cell at Penwortham (Fig. 13). On one side of the ampulla is depicted St Ecgwine and on the other St Eadwine, king of Deira, who died in 633[30] and whose body was at Whitby abbey. Whitby had been refounded in 1078 as a result of the expedition from Evesham to the north[31] and the connection between Evesham and Whitby was

27 T. Marlb. pp. 52–3. The text is printed ibid. pp. 6–53.

28 Cox 2010b.

29 T. Marlb. pp. 460–63. On the date see ibid. pp. 196–7.

30 H. E. Smith, 'Notice of a Mediaeval Signaculum of the Anglo-Saxon Saints, Edwyn and Ecgwyn', *Transactions of the Historic Soc. of Lancs. and Ches.* new series 9 (1868–69), 165–80; B. W. Spencer, 'An Ampulla of St. Egwin and St. Edwin', *Ant. Jnl* 51 (1971), 316–18; B. Spencer, *Pilgrim Souvenirs and Secular Badges*, Medieval Finds from Excavations in London 7 (London, 1998), p. 51.

31 J. Burton, *The Monastic Order in Yorkshire, 1069–1215* (Cambridge, 1999), p. 33; Knowles et al. 2001, p. 77.

remembered and celebrated by both abbeys in the twelfth century. Indeed, they declared before 1125 that 'the two congregations were to be as one',[32] a promise that implied a shared regard for their respective saints, including Ecgwine and Eadwine. The ampulla on which each of those received equal prominence was the kind of keepsake that pilgrims of c.1200 had lately been buying at the shrine of St Thomas of Canterbury in order to carry away water made holy by the saint, and some such practice was evidently being encouraged at Evesham or Whitby, or at both. Before the early twelfth century sick people had been drinking water in which the relic of Ecgwine's arm at Evesham had been washed, and many cures had been claimed then as a result of their doing so.[33] Another source of water made potentially miraculous by St Ecgwine may have been available at Evesham before the 1220s, when there was a mention of the 'third fishpond past St Ecgwine's well'.[34] The well was evidently near the sequence of three aligned fishponds along the spring line near the base of the gravel terraces on which the abbey stood, and it may even have been the source from which the monastic pond-system was fed.[35] However that may be, the ampulla is evidence of a popular cult of St Ecgwine at the end of the twelfth century that consciously emulated at least one practice that was favoured by pilgrims to the shrine of St Thomas.

It was during Abbot Adam's time, in the 1180s, that Thomas of Marlborough accepted the Evesham monks' invitation to write a full *vita* and *miracula* (a collection of miracle stories) of St Wigstan 'free from written mistakes and other faults, which had not been done before'. It has been suggested that the faulty version, now lost, had been written by the monk Dominic,[36] but Thomas did not attribute it to him nor did Dominic mention it among his own works.[37] As with his revised *vita* of St Ecgwine, Thomas submitted his *vita* and *miracula* of Wigstan for Archbishop Baldwin's approval and afterwards produced an amended version.[38] In that text Abbot Walter is said to have dropped Wigstan's skull after testing it by fire, whereupon it had been seen to perspire. But Thomas recorded no further miracles of St Wigstan at Evesham after Walter's death in 1104, and the only others that he knew of were in Leicestershire at the reputed site of Wigstan's murder. Likewise, no-one sought in Thomas's time to add new miracles to Dominic's

32 T. Marlb. p. lxi.
33 Ibid. pp. 114–15.
34 Ibid. pp. 404–5, 552–3.
35 Bond 1973, pp. 31–3.
36 Hayward 1993, p. 82 n. 4.
37 J. C. Jennings, 'The Writings of Prior Dominic of Evesham', *EHR* 77 (1962), 298–304 (at 303–4).
38 T. Marlb. pp. 52–3; *Evesham Chron.* pp. 325–37.

early-twelfth-century *vita* and *miracula* of St Odulf, the text of which seems to have remained current and unaltered.[39]

It is clear that the Evesham monks, despite their desire to attract pilgrims, were not prepared in the late twelfth century to inflate the ancient catalogue of miracles attached to Evesham's pre-Conquest saints by pretending that any such events had been reported within living memory. But they did try to promote the cult of a new Evesham saint, Wulfsige the anchorite. The other local saints had died long before the Conquest and their deeds had inevitably receded from history into legend, but Wulfsige had lived at Evesham until 1104 or early 1105. He was therefore, like Becket, a credible figure of the recent past. He was also different from the other Evesham saints in that his remains were not collected in a reliquary but rested intact in a tomb in the liturgical choir of the abbey church, which was directly under the unfinished central tower.[40] It seems that he had not been declared a saint immediately after his death, for in the early twelfth century neither Dominic nor John of Worcester called him one,[41] and it was not until late in the century that the Evesham monk Master Thomas of Norwich compiled a collection of Wulfsige's miracles. He arranged it in three sections or 'books',[42] a clear sign that the reported miracles were numerous; but the text is now lost. Master Thomas died in late 1206 or in 1207[43] and was widely known for his skill in medicine.[44] That meant that he was qualified to vouch for any cures that appeared to be miraculous and that could be attributed to Wulfsige. Since Wulfsige's miracles were almost the only ones recorded at Evesham after 1104, it would seem that his cult was created especially in order to stimulate popular interest in new cures at Evesham and to produce fresh income. His feast was celebrated annually on 24 February[45] and donations made by visitors to Wulfsige's tomb were probably among the sources of revenue used by Master Thomas of Norwich to pay for completion of the church's central tower, which rose above it under his supervision.[46]

[39] Bodleian Library, MS Rawlinson A.287, fols 116v–119v, from which the translation and miracles are printed in *Evesham Chron.* pp. 313–20.

[40] Cox 2010a, p. 60.

[41] *Evesham Chron.* p. 322; J. Worc. II, pp. 590–91.

[42] *Peterborough Chron.* p. 72.

[43] He died within a year of Adam Sortes's departure from Evesham, which was in 1206 (before 26 November): T. Marlb. pp. 416–17 n. 6.

[44] T. Marlb. pp. 198–9.

[45] Licence 2011, p. 177.

[46] T. Marlb. pp. 198–201, 270–71.

CHAPTER 19

Learning and writing

The Gesta abbatum

EVER since the early eleventh century Evesham abbey had attached importance to keeping up a narrative of its history, not just for the pleasure of contemplating the past but also as a useful collection of warnings and examples for the guidance of future policy. The *Gesta abbatum* retold the deeds of the abbots up to 1078, when Æthelwig died, and they were revised in the early twelfth century by a writer who also added his own continuation of the narrative, taking it up to the end of Walter's abbacy in 1104. The continuation was presumably written after Walter's death because it says that Walter did not complete the abbey church's central tower;[1] the statement could not have been made so confidently by someone writing before Walter's abbacy was over. The work of the reviser and continuator is recognizable by his habit of opening a clause with the phrase *qua de re* ('wherefore'). Seven clauses begin with those words in the *Gesta* text between c.970 and 1078 and one between 1078 and 1104,[2] but the subsequent narrative does not have the phrase; it was therefore not the mark of any other contributor to the *Gesta*. The author of the 1078–1104 continuation was evidently at work between 1104 and c.1121 because he did not go on to record the deeds of Walter's successor Maurice, who died c.1121. We are unable to put a name to the 1078–1104 continuator but Dom David Knowles did suggest that he might have been the contemporary hagiographer Dominic,[3] the only Evesham writer of the time who is known by name. It must be said, however, that there seems to be no resemblance of style or content between the plain continuation of 1078–1104 and Dominic's writings, all of which are hagiographical in purpose and rich in literary and religious colour.

The abbey seems to have lost interest in maintaining the *Gesta abbatum* by 1130 and no-one at Evesham troubled to bring them up to date again until the beginning of the next century.[4] Written archives were becoming more useful than a subjective

1 *Evesham Chron.* p. 97.
2 T. Marlb. pp. 142–5, 148–9, 160–61, 164–67, 172–3, 176–7.
3 Knowles 1963a, p. 705.
4 T. Marlb. pp. xxiii–xxv, xxxii.

chronicle. Moreover, a pious narrative, especially a truthful one, could cause the abbey some unforeseen trouble in the course of time, for it might preserve ancient details that would prove prejudicial to Evesham's current interests if the information were to fall into the hands of an adversary. By the early thirteenth century the abbey was aware that its pre-1104 *Gesta abbatum* contained unwelcome historical evidence of the bishop of Worcester's former powers over its affairs, and Evesham then felt obliged to cut or adjust the embarrassing material.[5] By then the *Gesta* were also of interest to a rival monastery, Crowland abbey, which had been in active contention with Evesham until c.1142 over an estate at Badby.[6]

The first evidence of Crowland's acquaintance with the Evesham *Gesta* lies in an obvious parallel between the pre-1104 *Gesta* and an alleged 'Testament of St Wulfsige' cited by the *Historia Croylandensis* (the Crowland chronicle). The *Historia* describes Wulfsige's 'Testament' as a 'collection of discourses (*schedula sermonum*) of the holy man, which was formed for the instruction of posterity' and which contained Wulfsige's account of

> the many ancient immunities and possessions of the monastery of Evesham, ... the many expulsions of the monks from Evesham by the tyrants of the province of the Hwicce and their restoration again by the most pious princes and prelates of the land, the many acquisitions of vills and estates throughout the whole of the Vale and the frequent alienations of the same.[7]

That is, in fact, a fair summary of the Evesham *Gesta* up to 1104. In its present form the *Historia Croylandensis* is a late medieval compilation containing much forged and invented material and designed to reinforce Crowland's title to its estates and privileges.[8] There may therefore have been no 'Testament of St Wulfsige' as alleged. Nevertheless, the above description of the 'Testament' appears in the so-called 'first continuation' (1090–1148) of the *Historia Croylandensis* and the author of that 'continuation' was evidently aware of the contents of the Evesham *Gesta*, some of which he used to justify Crowland's stance over Badby. The Crowland 'continuator' almost certainly invented the attribution of the pre-1104 Evesham material to the Evesham solitary Wulfsige (d.1104×1105), and he freely amplified

5 Cox 2002.

6 Clarke 1977, pp. 499–507a; S. Raban, *The Estates of Thorney and Crowland: A Study in Medieval Monastic Land Tenure*, University of Cambridge Department of Land Economy Occasional Papers 7 (Cambridge, 1977), pp. 28–9, citing Clarke 1977.

7 *Crowland Continuatio*, p. 123; translation based on H. T. Riley, trans., *Chronicle of the Abbey of Croyland with the Continuations by Peter of Blois and Anonymous Writers* (London, 1854), pp. 255–6.

8 A. Gransden, *Historical Writing in England*, II (London, 1982), pp. 400, 490–91.

and redacted all the Evesham content of his 'continuation', to Crowland's advantage. He used other information from the Evesham *Gesta* in dealing with the period from 1104 to 1148 and also inserted a few Evesham details into the pre-1090 part of the *Historia*.[9] Crowland's direct derivation of the post-1104 Evesham material from the post-1104 *Gesta* is clear because the Crowland author reproduces a mistake of the *Gesta* in placing the Evesham abbots Maurice and Robert (c.1104–c.1130) in reverse order. Since the post–1104 part of the Evesham *Gesta* was not written up until the early thirteenth century,[10] the Crowland 'first continuation' (1090–1148) could not have made use of it before then. One therefore infers that the Crowland 'first continuation' was written in or after the early thirteenth century. It is easy to imagine how Crowland may have contrived to gain access to the Evesham *Gesta* at that time, because the Crowland 'first continuation' was said to have been commissioned by Henry de Longchamp, who was abbot of Crowland 1190–1236;[11] we know from other sources that Henry had previously been a monk of Evesham[12] and that since 1190 he had maintained contact with Evesham in literary matters.[13]

Adam and his circle

Evesham's bid to celebrate and write about its local saints had begun in the later years of Abbot Adam, in a house that was already congenial to monastic literature thanks to Adam himself. He had studied at Paris and, as abbot 1161–89, he belonged to a circle that included such writers as Baldwin of Forde (archbishop of Canterbury from 1184), Peter of Blois, Serlo of Wilton, Gerald of Wales, and Stephen of Fougères (a scribe in Henry II's chancery, and bishop of Rennes from 1168). Their shared literary interests transcended their different religious affiliations: Baldwin was a Cistercian; Serlo was a Cluniac turned Cistercian; Peter, Gerald, and Stephen were seculars. For his part Adam wrote stylish letters and several elegantly composed sermon-like works for religious friends and acquaintances, including Gervase abbot of Winchcombe, Roger bishop of Worcester, Stephen of Fougères, the nuns of Godstow, and probably the monks of Abingdon. Adam would have written more than he did but for the demands on his time as abbot.[14] As a young man he had decided to abandon the life of a secular scholar and to become a monk, and he was not alone. In the twelfth century the emerg-

9 *Crowland Descriptio*, p. 54; *Crowland Continuatio*, pp. 123–4. Cf. T. Marlb. pp. 140–83.

10 T. Marlb. p. xxxii.

11 *Crowland Continuatio*, pp. 108–9.

12 Knowles et al. 2001, p. 42.

13 Below, this chapter.

14 Cox 2010b.

ing schools, the forerunners of the universities, were fostering an intellectual approach to religious understanding while the monasteries were maintaining the contemplative tradition. But some scholars, having distinguished themselves in the schools and having thus been prepared for good positions in the Church and in secular society, had failed ultimately to find spiritual satisfaction in the contemporary learned world and had turned instead to the cloister. In Adam's words:

> Let scholars study the constituents of the liberal arts; for us, however, let it be enough to study the lives of the Fathers, to consider the passions of the martyrs, to revere the deeds of the confessors, and to contemplate the miracles of the Apostles.[15]

In the late twelfth century at Evesham the former scholars included, apart from Abbot Adam, Master Adam Sortes (fl.1205–18), a student of literature who had taught liberal arts in the schools,[16] Thomas of Marlborough who had taught law at Exeter and Oxford,[17] and probably Master Thomas of Norwich (d.1206×1207), well known for his skill in medicine.[18] It may even be suggested that Evesham under Abbot Adam had become a refuge for disillusioned academics.

Books

The abbey's book collection may not have been kept in a single library but it had developed some coherence, having been built from the products of its own scribes and from gifts and purchases that had been made with Evesham's requirements in mind. By 1200, however, the collection also included books that had been recently given by mature scholars on entering religion at Evesham; they were books that they happened to have collected during their secular careers and thus were not necessarily of immediate interest at the abbey. The best documented example of such a gift before the later Middle Ages is the large accumulation of learned works that Thomas of Marlborough brought to Evesham in 1199 or 1200. It covered an impressively broad range. There was canon and Roman law (probably including Gratian's *Decretum* and the *Liber pauperum* of Vacarius),[19] medicine (with works attributed to Democritus, Galen, and Constantine the African), theology,

15 Ibid. pp. 158–9.
16 T. Marlb. pp. 274–5, 468–9.
17 Below, ch. 21.
18 T. Marlb. pp. 198–9.
19 Boyle 1983, pp. 113–14.

grammar, and ancient philosophy and literature (including books by Cicero, Lucan, and Juvenal).[20] The collection reflected Thomas's advanced education and personal interests, which are unlikely to have mirrored those of the Evesham monks in general. At any one time a few of the community would have been intellectually capable of studying or consulting Thomas's books and may have needed to do so, but only the works of classical literature and grammar would have lent themselves to everyday use, as textbooks for teaching Latin to the abbey's boys and young monks.

Among the scholarly books that were at Evesham in the twelfth century a few may survive today but one cannot be certain of that. All that can be asserted is that there exist some twelfth-century books of that kind, which seem to have been kept at Evesham in the later Middle Ages and for which no evidence has been found of previous and different ownership.[21] Among those are three earlier twelfth-century manuscripts that have similar handwriting and initials; they would therefore seem to have been made in one place:[22]

Oxford, Jesus College, MS 51, fols 2–105. Contains two works attributed to Bede (d.735): *De tabernaculo* (an allegorical commentary on the tabernacle of Moses, which is represented as prefiguring the Church); and *De ponderibus et mensuris* (on weights and measures), actually written by Isidore of Seville (d.636).[23]

Oxford, Jesus College, MS 54. Has Bede's commentary on the 'Song of Songs'; and the *Sigillum sanctae Mariae* by Honorius 'of Autun' (fl. early twelfth century), which consists of lessons on the Assumption of the Blessed Virgin and a commentary on the 'Song of Songs'.[24]

Oxford, Jesus College, MS 69. Consists mainly of Bede's commentary on the 'Catholic Epistles' (the New Testament letters of James, Peter, John, and Jude).[25]

Another manuscript, without established provenance, resembles them sufficiently to be of the same origin:

[20] R. Sharpe, J. P. Carley, R. M. Thomson, and A. G. Watson, eds, *English Benedictine Libraries: The Shorter Catalogues*, Corpus of British Medieval Library Catalogues 4 (London, 1996), pp. 134–7 no. B29.

[21] Ker 1964, p. 81.

[22] Gullick 1998, p. 18 n. 32.

[23] Coxe 1852, Jesus, p. 19. See Ker 1985, pp. 484, 489–90.

[24] Coxe 1852, Jesus, p. 20. See Ker 1985, pp. 484, 489–90.

[25] Coxe 1852, Jesus, p. 23. See also Gameson 1999, p. 143 no. 781.

London, British Library, Cotton MS Faustina C.I, fols 94–123. The 'Rule of St Benedict'.[26]

In the later Middle Ages Evesham seems also to have had the four later twelfth-century manuscripts below; they too call for closer examination than I can offer here:

London, British Library, Royal MS 6 C.IX. Bernard of Clairvaux (d.1153), sermons on the 'Song of Songs'.[27]

Oxford, Jesus College, MS 11. A miscellany culled from Christian writers of all periods, mostly treatises or sermons. It was probably compiled for Abbot Adam (1161–89) and copies of some of his letters of the 1160s were added in blank spaces.[28]

Oxford, Jesus College, MS 93. Contains Augustine of Hippo (d.430), commentaries on Psalms 51–100.[29]

Oxford, Magdalen College, MS Lat. 22. Consists mainly of Seneca (d.65), 'Moral Epistles to Lucilius', which is a collection of letters from the standpoint of a Stoic. Some short items attributed to Seneca are also included.[30]

Comparison of those eight manuscripts with others of the period may eventually help us to extend the list and to learn a little more about book production at Evesham.

Care of all the abbey's books, and their safe keeping, was placed in the hands of the precentor if he was deemed to be learned enough,[31] as no doubt he usually was. In 1206, if not before, he was also made responsible for the purchase of ink for all the abbey's own scribes, parchment for letters, pigments for illuminating manuscripts, and the materials for bookbinding.[32] It was the prior, however, who had to pay professional scribes for making books and to supply them with parchment. By then one cannot be sure that any members of the abbey community were involved in the making of high-quality books. As for service books, however,

[26] British Library, 'Search our Catalogue, Archives and Manuscripts' (online). See Gullick 1998, p. 18 n. 32; Gameson 1999, p. 100 no. 387.

[27] British Library, 'Catalogue of Illuminated Manuscripts' (online). See Ker 1964, pp. 194, 313; but cf. ibid. p. 81.

[28] Coxe 1852, Jesus, pp. 4–5. See Cox 2010b, pp. 118–20.

[29] Coxe 1852, Jesus, p. 33. See Ker 1985, pp. 484, 489–90.

[30] Coxe 1852, Magdalen, p. 16. See also Ker 1964, p. 81.

[31] Lanfranc, *Const.* pp. 122–3; *Penwortham Docs*, pp. 105–6.

[32] T. Marlb. pp. 522–3.

some were were still being copied by the Evesham monks.[33] Such manuscripts were in daily use and so would have had to be replaced more often than literary texts, and in a style that could be plainer; it was therefore a sensible economy to leave their production to capable monks.

Literary commissions

Under Abbot Adam Evesham's literary reputation rose as high as it would ever go, and it was helped on its way by Evesham monks who had moved forward to other places. One of them was Walkelin, who was the son of William Launceleve and his wife Edith ('Ediva').[34] In widowhood Edith became the first abbess of Godstow, a nunnery near Oxford,[35] and Reynold abbot of Evesham was present at the dedication of Godstow's abbey church in 1139.[36] His interest in a nunnery that was many miles from Evesham can be understood if one assumes that Edith's son Walkelin was already one of Reynold's monks. In 1159 Walkelin left Evesham abbey to become abbot of Abingdon and he died there in 1164, but he may have maintained contact with Evesham after 1159; that would explain why Abbot Adam wrote a sermon addressed to the nuns of Godstow, the house founded by Walkelin's mother, and a sermon on the passion of St Vincent that may have been intended for Walkelin's Abingdon, where there were substantial relics of the saint.[37]

Evesham's literary reputation travelled to the Fens with Henry de Longchamp, who was abbot of Crowland from 1190 to 1236. As abbot there, he invited an Evesham monk, known to us only as 'E', to compile a composite *vita* of St Thomas of Canterbury. Since Abbot Henry had been a monk of Evesham under Abbot Adam[38] he probably knew already that 'E', his contemporary there, would have the literary skill to carry out the commission. With Abbot Henry's support 'E' put the *vita* together from the works of St Thomas's earlier biographers and it became known as the *Quadrilogus* ('fourfold narrative').[39] 'E' completed the *Quadrilogus*

[33] T. Marlb. pp. 492–3, 522–3. See Gullick 1998, pp. 5–6; T. Webber, 'The Making of the Manuscript', T. Marlb. pp. lxvi–lxxii (at pp. lxxi–lxxii).

[34] A. Clark, ed., *The Life and Times of Anthony Wood, Antiquary, of Oxford, 1632–1695, described by Himself*, I, Oxford Historical Soc. 19 (Oxford, 1891), p. 339; Cox 2010b, pp. 149–50.

[35] E. Amt, ed., *The Latin Cartulary of Godstow Abbey* (Oxford, 2014), pp. xix–xxii.

[36] *Lincoln Acta 1067–1185*, pp. 22–3 no. 34.

[37] Cox 2010b, pp. 149, 163.

[38] Knowles et al. 2001, pp. 42, 247.

[39] J. C. Robertson, ed., *Materials for the History of Thomas Becket, Archbishop of Canterbury*, IV, Rolls Series (London, 1879), pp. 425–6. The *Quadrilogus* text is ibid. pp. 266–424.

at Crowland some time between September 1198 and April 1199[40] and the work went on to enjoy success in other places, for it passed into several new versions and translations.[41] According to John Leland (d.1552) the Evesham author of the *Quadrilogus* was called Elias,[42] but there is no earlier testimony of that. Of the monks of Evesham that were alive when the *Quadrilogus* was written only a minority are named in contemporary sources and of those the only one with a name beginning with *E* was called Ermefredus in Latin and Armfrei or Ermefrei in Anglo-Norman or English.[43] Ermefrei seems to have been at Evesham by 1189, when someone of that name witnessed one of Abbot Adam's deeds, and Henry de Longchamp witnessed it with him.[44] There may have been other Evesham monks with the same initial but Ermefrei has a special claim to our attention because he was just the kind of scholar that might have produced the *Quadrilogus*. Like other learned monks of Evesham in the late twelfth century, he was a *conversus*, an adult recruit.[45] He was described by a colleague as 'a man of good sense, well educated (*bene litteratus*) and an excellent notary'; in other words, he was suitably qualified to carry out the abbot of Crowland's commission. So capable was he generally that the monks of Evesham sent him to Rome in 1203 to pursue their case for exemption from the bishop of Worcester. While there Ermefrei had the misfortune in 1205 to be imprisoned by Abbot Norreis's creditors, though he was quite innocent, and he died in custody before the end of the year.[46] The *Quadrilogus* was only one of Henry de Longchamp's literary debts to Evesham after he moved to Crowland, for as abbot he was also patron of the 'first continuation' of the *Historia Croylandensis*, in which the continuator draws upon Evesham sources.

40 According to Roger monk of Crowland, writing in 1213: 'Sancti Thomae Cantuariensis archiepiscopi et martyris vita octava', *PL* 190, cols 257–64 (at col. 260C–D).

41 A. J. Duggan, 'The Lyell Version of the *Quadrilogus* Life of St Thomas of Canterbury', *AB* 112 (1994), 105–38; M. Staunton, *Thomas Becket and his Biographers* (Woodbridge, 2006), p. 7.

42 T. Hearne, ed., *Joannis Lelandi antiquarii de rebus Britannicis collectanea* (Oxford, 1715), IV, p. 39 (recording a manuscript at Whitby abbey); John Leland, *De uiris illustribus: Of Famous Men*, ed. J. P. Carley and C. Brett (Toronto, 2010), p. 372. Two secular priests called Elias of Evesham are known: the chaplain of Lower Gravenhurst (Beds.) 1209×1219 (J. Godber, ed., *The Cartulary of Newnham Priory*, I, Beds. Historical Record Soc. 43, pt 1 (Bedford, 1963), p. 62); and a canon of Hereford cathedral 1217×1227 (Le Neve 2002, p. 66).

43 *Worc. Acta 1186–1218*, p. 50; Harley 3763, fol. 87r. See C. T. Martin, *The Record Interpreter*, 2nd edn (London, 1910), p. 452 ('Amfridus').

44 Harley 3763, fol. 93v.

45 British Library, Lansdowne MS 427, fol. 10v, copied from British Library, Cotton MS Vitellius E.XII, fol. 78v, before its destruction by fire.

46 T. Marlb. pp. 228–9, 246–7, 344–5.

CHAPTER 20

Religious buildings

THE abbey's most expensive single commitment in the twelfth century was the probably the provision of new monastic buildings. They demanded great sums to construct, decorate, and furnish, because only the best masons and craftsmen were to be engaged and the best materials used to make the work a glory to behold. There was no absolute necessity to replace the pre-Conquest buildings — even in the 1150s parts of them were only 100 years old — but the impulse to do so was irresistible. Whatever the expense, God and the Virgin were to be glorified; and there might be selfish considerations too, such as the urge to emulate or surpass another great church or, for an abbot, to create a lasting memorial of his abbacy. In 1104 Abbot Walter had left his church incomplete, without a nave or a central tower of full height, but it already enclosed proper spaces for the essentials of monastic worship, the daily offices and the Mass, and for the cult of saints. Nevertheless, it wanted a nave to give it all the dignity of the Anglo-Norman grand manner and to allow impressive religious processions to take place. Because sufficient money was not continuously available several separate campaigns were needed in the course of the twelfth century to finish every stage of the new church and of the cloister attached to it. In the mean time, some part of the Anglo-Saxon church complex had to remain standing until the detached chapels of St Lawrence and All Saints were built in the later twelfth century, because until then the people of Evesham had no other place of worship.

When Abbot Walter died in 1104 the monks were using the pre-Conquest cloister and domestic buildings, which included an infirmary, a cellar, a kitchen, a bakehouse, and a bath-house[1] as well as a chapter house adorned with hangings (*dorselli*),[2] a dormitory, and a refectory. Presumably the main components were already arranged about a square cloister according to the usual Benedictine pattern, which the abbey had probably adopted at the tenth-century reform if not before. Walter's new church, though unfinished in 1104, was already adequate for daily use by the monks and so they decided to turn their limited funds towards something less expensive and more useful than a new nave. Walter's successor

[1] T. Marlb. pp. 570–71.
[2] Ibid. pp. 166–7.

Maurice (d. c.1121) built a new east cloister range to abut Walter's south transept. It included a chapter house and, at first-floor level, a dormitory. Maurice's chapter house was used not only for formal assemblies but also, until the nave was finished, for burying the abbots;[3] in death they would still be present when the chapter met. In part of the same range was a parlour (with a chapel of St Mary Magdalene)[4] in which monks were allowed to converse with each other at certain specified times. All the ground-floor components of the range were accessible from the east cloister walk that ran along its length.

Some years later, and at right angles to the east range of the cloister, Abbot Reynold (1130–49) built the south range, which contained a new refectory. He also built a parlour (with its own chapel) where monks could speak to visitors from the outside world, a guest hall (with a chamber), and a conventual or 'great' kitchen.[5] The great kitchen was presumably close to the refectory but it is not clear where the kitchen, the parlour, and the guest hall stood in relation to the cloister. Reynold was also able to build a large part of the nave. Its length and breadth were to remain as Abbot Walter had planned them, but architectural fashion had moved on and Reynold used columnar (cylindrical) piers for the main arcades (Fig. 8) instead of the compound piers that Walter had intended. Reynold's arcade piers were not of the 'colossal' type — exceptionally tall cylindrical columns — that had enjoyed a brief vogue in Worcester diocese at the abbeys of Gloucester, Tewkesbury, and Pershore, but were of a more traditional height. Because Reynold's piers were more slender than those intended by Walter, Reynold decided to have arcades of nine bays instead of eight, in order to keep the spacing between the piers suitably proportioned in relation to the length of nave that Walter had specified. At Reynold's death in 1149 the nave was still unfinished; whether or not the civil war had hindered progress, a shortage of money was probably what had caused the interruption, because work could not be resumed until the time of Abbot Adam (1161–89).

Adam completed the nave according to Reynold's intentions and had many 'glass windows' inserted;[6] they were presumably of stained glass because plain glass would not have called for special mention. Finishing the nave enabled him also to finish the west range of the cloister, which abutted the nave's south wall, and to build the north cloister walk, which flanked that wall. The west range of the cloister seems to have included the monastic school, which was situated near the

3 Cox 2010a, p. 61.
4 T. Marlb. pp. 180–81.
5 Ibid. pp. 182–3.
6 Cox 2010a.

Fig. 14. Stone lectern from the abbey. In the parish church at Norton by Evesham. Photo by B. G. Cox c.1970.

guest hall;[7] since Abbot Reynold's guest hall may have been near the south range, the school was probably at the south end of the west cloister walk. The abbey had taught children before the Conquest and was evidently still doing so. He finished off the cloister with a laver (*lavatorium*) for the monks to wash their hands in before entering clean areas such as the refectory.[8] It was fed, then or later, by a system of underground lead pipes that was laid from a source in the town's market place through the graveyard gateway, and thence across the graveyard, under the east end of the nave, and into the east walk of the cloister.[9] A short length of the pipe (though perhaps a later medieval replacement) is preserved at Evesham in the Almonry Heritage Centre. Outside the cloister Adam built a bakehouse, a brewhouse, a granary, an infirmary, and a private dormitory, and Dean Richard (of Wells) built a new hall for the abbots.[10]

Adam provided a lectern for the chapter house,[11] probably the elaborately carved stone one that was dug up at the abbey site in 1813 and is now preserved in the parish church at Norton by Evesham (Fig. 14). The central figure on the front is believed to be that of an abbot, and he is surrounded by deeply carved vines,

[7] *Evesham Officium*, col. 71 (composed in the early thirteenth century: ibid. pp. x–xiii).

[8] T. Marlb. pp. 184–7.

[9] E. J. Rudge, *Memoir, on the Antiquities discovered by Edward Rudge, Esq. F.S.A., F.R.S., F.L.S., in excavating the Ruins of the Abbey Church of Evesham*, Vetusta Monumenta 5 [pt 12] (London, 1835), pp. 3–4.

[10] T. Marlb. pp. 186–9. On Dean Richard see below, this section.

[11] T. Marlb. pp. 186–7.

which also cover the sides. The figure could be St Ecgwine or even St Benedict; in the chapter house a chapter from the 'Rule of St Benedict' was read daily. A very similar lectern survives in the parish church of Crowle, a village fourteen miles from Evesham, and there is some evidence that it may have been brought there from Worcester cathedral priory at the Dissolution. Both lecterns seem to have been carved at a workshop in or near Much Wenlock in Shropshire;[12] it is therefore possible that Worcester and Evesham conferred about the commissions. The lectern stands out as the only piece of fine Romanesque sculpture recorded at the abbey site. Not a single other fragment is known, even from the extensive excavations of the nineteenth century, and that raises the question whether there ever was any more.

The full cost of Abbot Adam's building works was not to be met from the abbey's ordinary income. At least some of the money had to come from private donors and through special fund-raising measures. The 'help of many good men' is acknowledged in the *Gesta abbatum*, and other help came from Richard dean of Wells (c.1164–c.1187).[13] He may have become involved through a colleague, Richard archdeacon of Bath (fl. c.1174–c.1182).[14] Abbot Adam described Archdeacon Richard as 'our brother and clerk',[15] which suggests that the archdeacon had formerly been one of his household clerks at Evesham. Dean Richard was able to raise money for building works at Evesham by negotiating an annual payment of fifteen marks from the rectory of Ombersley, an arrangement that the pope confirmed in or before 1176. In 1175 the pope also confirmed Evesham's appropriation of Stow on the Wold rectory, the income from which was designated to be used for building works at the abbey;[16] as patron of Stow church the abbey could nominate itself as rector and so receive the rectorial income and have a vicar to perform the pastoral duties. The abbot and convent assigned the Stow revenues to Archdeacon Richard.[17] It therefore seems that the archdeacon, probably a former clerk at Evesham abbey, had agreed to act as a treasurer for the Evesham building works and to manage the money raised by Dean Richard and others.

The final stage of the central tower seems to have been begun towards the end of Abbot Adam's time and it was completed by c.1201 with the help of the

12 G. L. Pearson, J. E. Prentice, and A. W. Pearson, 'Three English Romanesque Lecterns', *Ant. Jnl* 82 (2002), 328–39.

13 T. Marlb. pp. 186–9. For Dean Richard see Le Neve 2001, pp. 8–9.

14 Le Neve 2001, p. 36.

15 Harley 3763, fol. 88r.

16 T. Marlb. pp. 188–9; W. Holtzmann, ed., *Papsturkunden in England*, I, pt 2 (Berlin, 1931), pp. 393, 397.

17 Harley 3763, fol. 88r.

Evesham monk, Master Thomas of Norwich. With no financial support from Abbot Norreis, the monks paid for the work by diverting funds whenever possible from the pittancery and by drawing upon 'every other source of revenue which we could secure for that work',[18] which may have included donations made at the tomb of St Wulfsige.

Art for the abbey church

Some of the twelfth-century abbots were remembered as having provided *ornamenta* for the abbey church; the term could include plate, vestments, service books, hangings, and bells. They were the necessary equipment for a suitably splendid performance of the church services. Among Abbot Reynold's acquisitions were mentioned a valuable cross, gilded censers and candlesticks, a black cope, a large gospel book, hangings for the liturgical choir (depicting St Ecgwine), and bells. In the same spirit Abbot Adam provided a golden chalice, vestments that included a red cope decorated with golden birds, and two more bells; even Roger Norreis gave a mass-ring, a mitre, two albs woven with gold, and a cope of red samite decorated with gold. Together such items composed a rich treasury of liturgical art. Some of the works of fine craftsmanship had been newly commissioned for the abbey church, while others had been received ready-made. In the *Gesta abbatum* Abbot Reynold is said to have 'made' the gospel book, the plate, and two of the bells, and to have 'ordered to be made' the hangings, but he is said to have 'acquired' the vestments and two smaller bells. Adam is said to have 'made' the bells and to have 'ordered to be made' the chalice, but to have 'bought' vestments and to have instructed obedientiaries to 'buy' others, presumably out of their departmental funds. As for Adam's stained glass, he 'inserted' some of it himself and some he 'caused to be inserted', probably also through obedientiaries. The *Gesta* contributor seems careful to distinguish between plate, bells, hangings, and stained glass that were made to order, and vestments and bells that could be bought ready-made or acquired second-hand.[19] By the twelfth century books were probably the only works of art that the monks or the abbot's clerks had any personal part in making.

Chapels for the Vale

It seems to have been in the twelfth century that the abbey decided that it would build subordinate local chapels within the deanery of the Vale of Evesham, its

[18] T. Marlb. pp. 198–201.

[19] T. Marlb. pp. 180–83, 186–7.

single great parish. Only at Church Honeybourne is it clear that the deanery had any subordinate church before the twelfth century. Of the Vale chapels, the parish churches of today, none has architectural detail that can be dated earlier than 1100, while most of them have some 'Norman' fabric. There may have been at least two considerations that led to their construction. First, population growth was probably bringing an inconvenient number of lay people from the Vale to the abbey church; many of them could be kept away if they had the use of local churches instead. Secondly, the abbey might hope to consolidate its pastoral control of the deanery of the Vale by filling the area with subordinate chapels; that would make it harder for the bishops to claim that they should have the authority there. The original ground plans of the new chapels were of modest size and were without aisles, and there is no fine Romanesque carving to suggest that unnecessary expense was incurred in them.[20] Of the remaining twelfth-century fonts, that at Middle Littleton has some simple incised geometric decoration and those at Bretforton and Hampton have no decoration at all. Of the contemporary doorways, those at Evesham All Saints and South Littleton are plain and the north doorway at Badsey has only simple mouldings; none has a carved tympanum. It is likely that the modesty of the surviving early fabrics was intentional and is not a sign that impressive features have been removed; had there been rich Norman doorways or fonts in the first place, they would probably have been preserved by later builders. The chapels were therefore utilitarian structures, not expensive works of art. Their value was in enabling removal of the laity from the abbey church and in symbolizing the abbey's pastoral authority; their presence was important but their architectural appearance was not.

Provision of the chapels progressed slowly through the century. Some may have been standing before 1139, when the pope approved Evesham abbey's customary practice of distributing chrism 'around your churches';[21] chrism was a consecrated mixture of olive oil and balsam, for use in some of the sacraments. There is reason to think that Bretforton church may have been built in the earlier twelfth century, because by c.1200 the nave was being enlarged with aisles; that would probably not have happened if the original aisleless nave had then been of recent construction.[22] The churches at Hampton and Offenham may have been built in the time of Abbot Adam (1161–89) because they are dedicated to saints with whom he had a link. Hampton is dedicated to St Andrew, and that was also the dedication of Northampton priory, founded c.1095 by Simon de St Liz earl of Northampton as a daughter-house of the Cluniac priory of La Charité; Adam had

[20] Brooks and Pevsner 2007, pp. 119, 169–70, 291, 294, 494, 596, 662.

[21] T. Marlb. pp. 322–3.

[22] Brooks and Pevsner 2007, p. 169.

once been a monk at La Charité and Simon de St Liz, one of its benefactors, was probably a relative. Offenham church has a rare dedication to St Mildburg the patron of Wenlock priory, and that was another daughter-house of La Charité.[23] At South Littleton, however, the chapel and its graveyard were not dedicated or endowed until 1204.[24] The design of its font — often a feature preserved from a church's earliest phase — suggests that there had been no earlier chapel at South Littleton; the simple decoration of the bowl is presumably of 1204 because it resembles that found on other fonts of the period in south-east Worcestershire, at Bishampton and Bricklehampton.[25] South Littleton chapel thus seems to have been one of the last to be built in the Vale, others being mentioned before 1200 at Badsey, Bretforton, Evesham St Lawrence, Church Honeybourne (probably built before the Conquest), Middle Littleton, Norton, Offenham, and Wickhamford; the chapels of Lenchwick and Evesham All Saints should probably be added to the list, though they are not mentioned before 1206.[26] The chapelry boundaries followed township boundaries, not (where they differed) manorial ones; thus Bretforton (consisting of two townships), South Littleton, and Norton were not manors but each had its own chapel. Evesham, which was both a township and a manor, had two chapelries and the boundary between them was drawn down the middle of the High Street to meet the abbey precinct at the graveyard gateway.[27]

Although the abbey built subordinate chapels in the Vale, it continued to preserve the deanery as a single parish just as the churches of Worcester and Pershore had been doing within their Worcestershire hundreds in 1086.[28] The chapels of the Vale deanery usually had no graveyards in the twelfth century and the deceased of the Vale continued to be buried at Evesham; Christian burial did not require use of the abbey church and, as it was not a sacrament, it attracted a payment that the abbey may have wished to keep for itself. But the chapels were provided with fonts so that the sacrament of baptism could be offered outside Evesham. When fonts became available in local chapels the use of a font at the abbey became unnecessary, and it was discontinued before the late 1160s.[29] All the

[23] A. Binns, *Dedications of Monastic Houses in England and Wales 1066–1216* (Woodbridge, 1989), pp. 115–16; Cox 2010b, p. 115.

[24] D. C. Cox, 'Two South Littleton Documents from a Missal of Evesham Abbey', *VEHS Res. Pap.* 1 (1967), 27–34 (at 31).

[25] Brooks and Pevsner 2007, pp. 152, 172, 596. For dating see also *VCH Worcs.* III, p. 264 (Bishampton); *Worc. Acta 1186–1218*, p. 19 (Bricklehampton).

[26] Vesp. B.XXIV, fols 49v, 50r, 52r, 54r, 55r (Tindal 1794, pp. 52n, 54n, 56n, 57n); Harley 3763, fol. 75r; T. Marlb. pp. 196–7, 448–9, 522–3.

[27] Izod, 'Plan'.

[28] W. Page, 'Some Remarks on the Churches of the Domesday Survey', *Archaeologia* 66 (1915), 61–102 (at 62–3).

[29] T. Marlb. pp. 346–7.

time, the dependent status of the Vale chapels was carefully preserved. By the end of the century each of them sent a procession to the abbey at Whitsun, and from later evidence one may assume that the processions took place on Whit-Tuesday and that every household contributed one representative, whose duty was to pay the household's 'Whitsun farthing' to the mother church. In the deanery of the Vale the Whitsun farthings made everyone acknowledge the abbot's exclusive authority; in other parts of the diocese the payment was usually made to the bishop. It was also customary for the Vale chapels to receive from the abbey their supplies of chrism and holy oil, and this they probably did before the people returned home from the Whitsun procession;[30] again, churches elsewhere would normally have received their oils from the bishop.

By the 1190s each chapel was served by a resident priest whose livelihood was equivalent to that of a small peasant farmer. The abbey provided him with a house and enough agricultural land on which to support himself, and usually expected him to pay rent for them.[31] The arrangements were capable of variation in detail, however, which seems to be another sign that the local churches in Evesham deanery were not all founded at the same time. Thus at Norton the priest had to perform labour services[32] while the priests at Badsey and Wickhamford were entitled to receive substantial annual renders of wheat from the other manorial tenants.[33] The abbey seems always to have kept the local tithes[34] and probably the churchscot, both of which it had enjoyed for centuries. The abbey and its dean appointed and regulated the priests[35] but seem not to have insisted that their conduct met the highest standards of the day. The priest of 'Wichewen' (probably Wickhamford) was married; his widow was living at Evesham c.1190.[36] If the chaplains of the Vale were allowed to marry, their sons might hope to succeed them in office just as the sons of other manorial tenants might claim their fathers' holdings. In the twelfth century clerical marriage and hereditary benefices were denounced

30 T. Marlb. pp. 346–7, 350–51. See Brett 1975, pp. 162–6; C. N. L. Brooke, *The Normans as Cathedral Builders* (Winchester, 1980), p. 91.

31 Vesp. B.XXIV, fols 34v, 49v, 50r–50v, 52r, 54r, 55r (Tindal 1794, pp. 52n, 54n, 56n, 57n); Harley 3763, fol. 75r. Badsey, Hampton, and Offenham each had a small tenant with the by-name *clericus*, probably the local priest: Vesp. B.XXIV, fols 31v, 50r, 52r (Tindal 1794, pp. 54n, 57n, 61n). The status of tenants at Evesham called *capellanus* and *clericus* (Vesp. B.XXIV, fols 42v, 43v, 45v) seems less clear.

32 Vesp. B.XXIV, fol. 54r (Tindal 1794, p. 52n).

33 Vesp. B.XXIV, fols 49v, 50r (Tindal 1794, pp. 55n, 57n).

34 Vesp. B.XXIV, fols 49v, 50r, 51r, 52r, 53r, 54r (Tindal 1794, pp. 51n, 52n, 54n, 55n, 56n, 57n); Harley 3763, fol. 75r.

35 T. Marlb. pp. 350–51.

36 Vesp. B.XXIV, fol. 45v. *Childs*wickham was not an Evesham abbey estate.

by the higher clergy, including Abbot Adam,[37] but they remained common; reform was not consistently pursued and enforcement was hardly worth the trouble in cases where a priest was competent and of good character.

In the twelfth century the abbey was being forced to uphold by all possible means the *de facto* exemption of itself and its deanery from episcopal authority, because some of the contemporary bishops of Worcester were intent on having the exemption removed. The architectural simplicity of the new Vale chapels and the lowly status and remuneration of their clergy suggest that the abbey had provided the chapels for its own practical convenience and to demonstrate urgently and publicly its exclusive freedom of action within the deanery; those considerations probably weighed at least as much as any desire to enhance the religious life or personal convenience of the people.

[37] Cox 2010b, p. 139.

CHAPTER 21

Collapse and renewal

IN 1190 the disgraced former prior of Christ Church Canterbury, Roger Norreis, had been foisted upon Evesham abbey in succession to Abbot Adam. It turned out to be an even greater misfortune than the monks might have imagined, and one that would be compounded during Roger's long abbacy by a frustrating three-way struggle between Norreis, who was a charming but dangerous libertine, the Evesham monk Thomas of Marlborough, a vigorous, tenacious, and eloquent lawyer, and Master Mauger, their conscientious and respected bishop.

Norreis's family background is unknown except that he had a nephew (*nepos*) called Roger and a kinsman called Matthew Dolfin;[1] Dolfin and Norreis are surnames that indicate northern ancestry.[2] In his first few years at Evesham the abbot's conduct seemed acceptable but as he became accustomed to the privileges of office the flaws in his character began to assert themselves, and privilege then turned to licence and licence to utter wantonness.[3] All the while he was able to cloak his weaknesses in a seductive bonhomie that was hard to resist. Fluent and impressive in speech, he had the air of being both learned and courtly, and in his quarters he kept a convivial table at which good food and drink were freely enjoyed by his household, his guests, and himself. Norreis allowed himself the luxuries, unusual for a monk, of sleeping in linen sheets, of wearing comfortable shirts and linen garments, of sporting smart boots like a knight's, and of going about the abbey in a cape instead of in the customary monastic dress. Such were the attributes of a secular baron, not an abbot, and he made no attempt to conceal

1 T. Marlb. pp. 230–31, 236–7.

2 P. H. Reaney and R. M. Wilson, *A Dictionary of English Surnames*, 4th edn (Oxford, 1997), pp. 138, 324.

3 Thomas of Marlborough gives a detailed and unforgiving account of Abbot Roger and the period of his abbacy (1190–1213) in T. Marlb. pp. 189–467; another Evesham writer covered the same ground more briefly (ibid. pp. 484–7). The editors' introduction and notes to T. Marlb. add much important detail and discussion. Thomas's narrative forms the basis of G. G. Coulton, *Five Centuries of Religion*, II (Cambridge, 1927), pp. 347–78. The main events and issues of Roger's abbacy are summarized in Knowles 1963a, pp. 331–45, and are discussed at greater length in A. Boureau, 'How Law came to the Monks: The Use of Law in English Society at the Beginning of the Thirteenth Century', *Past & Present*, no. 167 (2000), 29–74.

them from the convent. Still less appropriate to a monk was Roger's enjoyment of carnal relations with women, with some of whom he was reputed to have fathered children.[4] Needless to say, he disappointed early expectations that he might sometimes attend the church, consult the monks in chapter, dine with them, or sit with them in the cloister. Although the abbots of Evesham had begun to live apart from the monks long before Abbot Roger's time, with him the separation was taken beyond acceptable limits. In order to indulge his appetites without distraction or inhibition Norreis would stay for weeks on end at remote manors, particularly at Broadwell and Bourton on the Water, both in the Cotswolds, some twenty miles from Evesham, and at Badby, over fifty miles away. In those conveniently distant places he rebuilt the manor houses on a noble scale befitting his baronial tastes. His excesses, however, were hardly less restrained when he was at Evesham. He openly entertained women in his chamber, and once a year he would stay at Bretforton near Evesham, where he would spend his time with like-minded companions, squandering the funds of the sacristy in feasting and drinking.[5]

The abbot's ordinary revenues did not suffice to pay for his luxurious way of life, and so he helped himself to money from the various obediences at the abbey; in doing so he could take advantage of the lack of any written agreement as to what were their proper revenues. Abbot Roger's irresponsible spending led to the monks being deprived of their proper food, drink, and clothing and to the buildings being allowed to fall into disrepair. Monks without decent clothing were unable to attend services, and a leaking roof prevented their use of the choir and presbytery in wet weather. Those without enough to eat were forced to roam in direct contravention of the 'Rule', seeking food at neighbouring abbeys or the homes of their relatives and friends. Corporate charity for the poor, which was a requirement of the 'Rule', had to be abandoned altogether. The monastic life at Evesham thus began to disintegrate in the 1190s, materially and spiritually. Monks who complained to the abbot were sometimes abused verbally or assaulted, or were expelled from the house. Despite a general breakdown of morale, however, some of the brethren managed to preserve their integrity; adversity may even have stiffened their resolve to be good monks. None of them, however, could match the efforts of John Denis, who went to extremes of fasting, prayer, weeping, mortifying the flesh, keeping vigils, enduring the cold through coarse and ragged clothing, and doing without anything that could be given to the poor.[6] Other brethren decided that their best interests lay in submitting to the abbot's charm.

[4] This accusation is also made by Gerald of Wales: 'Speculum ecclesiae', *Giraldi Cambrensis opera*, ed. J. S. Brewer, IV, Rolls Series (London, 1873), pp. 3–354 (at p. 91).

[5] *Evesham Chron.* pp. 260–61.

[6] T. Marlb. pp. 496–7.

They became his cronies and were allowed to share in the delights of his table. Like his relatives and friends they even received gifts from the money and property that he had misappropriated. Within the monastic community an unseemly rift had opened thus between the abbot's friends and his critics.

All this became well known in the diocese and beyond, and in normal circumstances it could have been corrected by the bishop. At Evesham, however, the scandal was allowed to continue because the abbey would not accept the bishop's authority over its internal affairs. Moreover, in the 1190s there were few opportunities for a bishop of Worcester to intervene at Evesham, even had he been allowed to, for there were four successive holders of the see in that decade; all of them died in office, which created a series of episcopal vacancies totalling nearly four years out of the ten.[7] There were also periods during the 1190s when the bishop, though living, was absent from the diocese.[8] One bishop, John of Coutances (1196–98), did come to Evesham to investigate the abbot's conduct but Norreis bought off the immediate threat of disciplinary action by agreeing to observe Bishop John's written statutes and decrees and by renouncing for John's lifetime some of the *insignia pontificalia*; Roger clinched the accord with a gift of sixty marks, equivalent to thousands of pounds in today's money. The abbot's undertakings, whether or not he meant to honour them, lapsed when Bishop John died in September 1198; John had never returned to Evesham and no bishop was consecrated to succeed him until June 1200.

Meanwhile, probably in 1197, the monks took their complaints about the abbot to Hubert Walter, the archbishop of Canterbury and papal legate (the pope's representative in England), as they were encouraged to do by Pope Constantine's supposed privilege of 709.[9] Norreis, however, eluded their accusations by bribing some of the monks to drop them, and he satisfied the archbishop by renouncing his current claim to certain of the convent's revenues and by making other minor concessions. The legateship ended in January 1198 and later the same year Hubert Walter went overseas. Once the bishop was dead and the archbishop out of the country, Norreis was able to revert to his old ways. The monks complained again to Archbishop Hubert and he eventually came to Evesham to investigate, probably in the spring of 1200. As before, however, Norreis evaded justice by bribing his accusers and granting concessions. The archbishop was soon too busy elsewhere to concern himself with Evesham's affairs and Abbot Roger then resumed his usual conduct.

The financial reforms conceded from time to time by Abbot Norreis were

7 Le Neve 1971, p. 100.

8 *Worc. Acta 1186–1218*, pp. 127–8.

9 Dominic, *V. Ecgwini*, p. 89.

short-lived but they did enable the monks to fund a completion of the central tower of the abbey church, which had been left unfinished at the death of Abbot Adam. The project was not overseen by the abbot, of course, but by one of the most cultured men at Evesham, the physician and hagiographer Master Thomas of Norwich.

Thomas of Marlborough and the bishop

It was in the tense period 1199–1200 that Thomas of Marlborough, then aged thirty or more, decided to enter the monastic life and come to Evesham, where he had been known for at least ten years. As usual a family background is not plainly recorded — a monk severed any formal family connection when he entered religion — but there are hints that Thomas of Marlborough may have been a grandson of John Marshal (d.1165), the king's hereditary marshal, who was sometimes known as John of Marlborough.[10] The surname is not the only clue. One of Thomas's uncles had a daughter called Muriel of Striguil (fl.1218×1230).[11] Since John Marshal's son the celebrated William Marshal (d.1219) had acquired the lordship of Striguil (Chepstow) in 1189 on marrying its heir the countess of Pembroke, it is possible that Muriel of Striguil's father, Thomas's uncle, was William Marshal. It is probably not a coincidence that another of John Marshal's sons, Henry, was bishop of Exeter 1194–1206 just at the time when Thomas of Marlborough is said to have taught law in the cathedral school there.[12] Thomas had a half-brother in London in 1213, their mother having been married more than once, but his name is not recorded.[13] Before Thomas came to Evesham he had acquired considerable learning and experience. He had studied at Paris under Stephen Langton, a future archbishop of Canterbury, and afterwards had studied and taught canon and Roman law not only at Exeter but also at Oxford.[14]

Abbot Norreis, whose standing with the church authorities was becoming insecure, would presumably have considered himself fortunate when a lawyer of Thomas's stature and connections became one of his monks. Thomas, for his part, as a mature convert to the monastic life, was full of the idealism that such

[10] D. Crouch, *William Marshal: Knighthood, War and Chivalry, 1147–1219*, 2nd edn (London, 2002), p. 18n.

[11] T. Marlb. pp. 494–5, 546–7.

[12] Ibid. pp. 490–91. For Exeter cathedral school at that time see K. Edwards, *The English Secular Cathedrals in the Middle Ages: A Constitutional Study with Special Reference to the Fourteenth Century*, 2nd edn (Manchester, 1967), pp. 186–7.

[13] T. Marlb. pp. 432–3.

[14] On Thomas's academic career see Boyle 1983, pp. 111, 113–14; T. Marlb. pp. xvii–xviii.

recruits typically brought to their calling,[15] and this was his moment. Until the 1160s the bishops had made intermittent attempts to assert their presumed rights at Evesham, while the abbots, with papal support, had responded by successfully extending their own rights at the bishop's expense. Neither side, however, had maintained its position consistently, preferring for much of the time to avoid confrontation and to abide by precedent. To Thomas's orderly legal mind the matter could no longer be allowed to rest unresolved. He had been a friend of Evesham abbey since the golden days of Abbot Adam and it soon became his obsession to eliminate further uncertainty by securing for ever the abbey's full exemption from the bishops of Worcester and by establishing beyond question the house's sole obedience to the pope and his legates.

Thus far Norreis had experienced little difficulty in sidestepping the attentions of the bishop and the archbishop and he was thought to have powerful friends, including Archbishop Hubert and the justiciar of England Geoffrey fitz Peter. He therefore had little reason to suspect that his flair for appeasing his critics and the authorities would ever fail him. The abbot's priority was to prolong his pleasurable career by avoiding disciplinary action; Thomas's was to make Evesham securely exempt from the bishop's jurisdiction. To that extent they had a common aim, and soon they had a common adversary in the person of Bishop Mauger. He was probably another former student at Paris and, as Master Mauger, had held the important office of treasurer of Normandy under Richard I.[16] Soon after King Richard's death Mauger had been elected bishop of Worcester, and he was consecrated in 1200. He was active in his new role and Thomas of Marlborough acknowledged that he was just, godly, and a 'child of truth' animated by goodwill and zeal. Mauger, unlike his immediate predecessors, was just as reluctant as Thomas to let matters slide at Evesham, and an early trial of strength between bishop and abbey became inevitable.

The exemption crisis

Relations between Roger, Thomas, and Mauger were naturally complex. Abbot Norreis wanted to be left alone to pursue a career of unbridled luxury. He and Thomas of Marlborough came to detest one another, but Thomas was determined to prevent the bishop from removing Norreis, because canon law would then deem it an irreversible admission of the bishop's jurisdiction over the abbey. Norreis and Marlborough thus chose to form an unnatural alliance against Bishop Mauger. Meanwhile, Mauger believed that it was his duty to intervene at Evesham,

[15] Cox 2010b, p. 142.
[16] *Worc. Acta 1186–1218*, pp. xxxiv–xxxvii.

both to end the immediate scandal and to establish permanently the right of future bishops to step in whenever they needed to. The conflicting agendas of the three principal actors made a tangle that eventually only the pope could straighten out.

In 1202 Mauger sent word to the abbot that he was coming to Evesham to perform a visitation (a disciplinary inspection). Norreis was confident that he could reassure or buy off Mauger, just as he had done with Bishop John and others, and he was therefore prepared to entertain the bishop lavishly and send him away satisfied. Thomas, however, knew Mauger to be incorruptible, and foresaw momentous consequences if he were to carry out a visitation; so clear a precedent would secure for ever the right of Mauger and his successors to subject Evesham to their jurisdiction. A disinterested observer might have argued that the other great abbeys of the diocese, Gloucester, Pershore, and Tewkesbury, had not suffered unduly by being under the bishop's authority and that an early dismissal of Abbot Norreis at the bishop's hands was eminently desirable. Thomas, however, from his long association with Evesham and his familiarity with its history and muniments, could not abide the thought. He failed to persuade the abbot to refuse the bishop's visit, but among the brethren Thomas did muster a majority of supporters for offering Mauger a courteous rebuff. The minority of monks that objected to Thomas's policy of resistance included the abbot's cronies (who thought that the bishop could be appeased), others who believed that it was more urgent to have the abbot dismissed by Bishop Mauger than to assert the principle of exemption, some who feared the expense of a legal challenge to the bishop, and some who were old or infirm and just wanted peace in their time. When it became clear, however, that most of the monks were prepared to defy the bishop, Abbot Roger retreated to Broadwell manor to avoid being implicated in their protest. Mauger did arrive at Evesham in August 1202 and the monks under Thomas's leadership told him courteously but firmly to abandon his plans for a visitation; they made it plain that they were not prepared to give the testimony upon which such a hearing would have to depend. The bishop had been thwarted, at least for the time being, and he withdrew angrily, having suspended the whole convent except the abbot.

Mauger was not going to let the matter rest there; nor were the monks, and they entered into a pact with a reluctant Abbot Norreis: he would allow them to pursue a case for exemption through the papal courts and they would continue to refrain from denouncing him before the authorities. Thus began an arduous sequence of hearings, which culminated three years later in Rome, where Thomas of Marlborough, on behalf of the abbot, and Master Robert of Clipston, representing the bishop, set out their arguments before Pope Innocent III in person.[17]

[17] On the practicalities and costs of Thomas's journey to Rome and of Evesham's appear-

Thomas was armed only with shaky precedents and suspect documents (some of them forged)[18] but he performed brilliantly, and on 24 December 1205 the pope pronounced in favour of the abbey's exemption from the bishop's jurisdiction. A few weeks later he also gave interim judgment in Evesham's favour in the related matter of the abbey's jurisdiction over the deanery of the Vale; the difficult point that remained to be decided was whether the now undoubted exemption of the abbey implied that the ancient *de facto* exemption of its deanery was also lawful. The abbey would not receive confirmation of that until 1248.

The fall of Abbot Norreis

In 1203, while the exemption proceedings of 1202–6 were going on, Archbishop Hubert again visited Evesham with a view to settling the differences between the abbot and the monks. As a friend of Roger Norreis, the archbishop was never going to act impartially, however, and Abbot Roger made sure of that by promising him a palfrey and a silver cup. On arrival at Evesham Hubert listened to the monks' evidence but decided not to use his authority to pronounce upon the matters in contention. Instead he deferred them for the decision of arbitrators. Meanwhile Norreis conceded some reforms and the archbishop ordered the abbey's administrative and financial customs to be put down in writing for the first time, as a precaution against future abuses. There is no record that the arbitrators ever met or that the customs, if written down, were put into practice; Norreis had once more evaded punishment.[19]

The pope's judgment in Evesham's favour at the end of 1205 meant that Norreis could be disciplined only by the pope's representative, the legate. Some months later, then, in 1206, the legate Cardinal John of Ferentino did visit Evesham. He took evidence from both sides but again nothing was achieved before he left the country later that year, other than a written agreement as to the cellarer's obligations and the correct revenues due to each obedientiary. It seems also to have been about that time that a new cartulary was begun, setting out the abbey's deeds and estate documents in a freshly organized way.[20] The legate's reluctance to take immediate disciplinary action at Evesham was fortified just before he left England when Norreis met him at Reading, won him over, and gave his nephew an annual

ance before the papal court see J. Sayers, 'English Benedictine Monks at the Papal Court in the Thirteenth Century: The Experience of Thomas of Marlborough in a Wider Context', *Jnl of Medieval Monastic Studies* 2 (2013), 109–29.

18 Sayers 1988, pp. 374–81.

19 T. Marlb. pp. 230–41.

20 Clarke 2012a, pp. 124–5. On the structure and evolution of the manuscript (Harley 3763, fos 58r–94v) see Clarke 1977, pp. 26–9.

rent of ten marks. Norreis's frequent use of bribery may have been consistent with his lack of moral scruple. On the other hand, even men of honour understood that those in the highest authority would accept sweeteners and would even expect them, and that having received them they would pay due attention to the donors' requests; in 1204 Thomas of Marlborough himself had presented the pope with a silver cup worth six marks.

After the legate's inconclusive visit of 1206 life at Evesham became intolerable for any monk who had tried to maintain his own morale. It was soon after 1206 that Master Adam Sortes, one of the most persecuted of Abbot Norreis's opponents among the monks, decided to leave the monastery and was allowed to become prior of the abbey's remote cell at Penwortham.[21] There he would be too far away to cause the abbot any trouble or to suffer further unpleasantness. On 23 March 1208, and before progress could be made towards having Abbot Roger removed by another legate, Innocent III placed England under an interdict (a form of excommunication) because of King John's refusal to approve Stephen Langton's election as archbishop of Canterbury. The interdict lasted until the king relented in 1213; Langton remained overseas the whole time and Bishop Mauger, exiled in 1208, died abroad in 1212. Thus for more than seven years Abbot Norreis had nothing to fear from the bishop, the archbishop, or a papal legate and he took advantage of the respite to continue in his familiar ways. King John did not seek to intervene. In 1209 he was on his way from Tewkesbury to Kenilworth and stayed 17–18 July at Evesham abbey, where he dined twice; during the visit he gave 'Brother Thomas' (probably Thomas of Marlborough) enough money to provide 100 poor people with a penny each.[22] It is not known whether the abbot was present at the time but the king may have been aware that he should place the money directly into Thomas's hands instead of the abbot's, though there is no evidence that Thomas was then the almoner; Norreis usually bestowed hospitality on the rich while giving nothing to the poor.[23] On this occasion the king seems to have been content to accept Evesham's hospitality without calling the abbot to order; and in any case John by himself had no authority to impose ecclesiastical discipline. A particularly low point of the interdict years was reached in 1210, when part of the central tower collapsed in a storm[24] and caused great damage to the eastern arm of the church, and within it to the high altar and the reliquary

21 T. Marlb. pp. 416–17.

22 T. D. Hardy, ed., *Rotuli litterarum patentium in turri Londinensi servati*, Record Commission (London, 1835), 'Itinerary of King John &c.' (unpaginated) following p. xlviii; T. D. Hardy, ed., *Rotuli de liberate ac de misis et praestitis, regnante Johanne*, Record Commission (London, 1844), p. 122.

23 T. Marlb. pp. 444–5.

24 'Annales prioratus de Dunstaplia', *Ann. mon.* III, pp. 3–408 (at p. 32).

of St Wigstan. The monks alleged that the tower had been in disrepair because the abbot had depleted the fabric fund. Within two years, however, Thomas of Marlborough was able to raise enough money to repair the tower and to rebuild the eastern arm on a new plan, this time with an ambulatory. Evesham enjoyed one great advantage from the interdict, which was the freezing of the abbey's huge debt to the Roman businessmen from whom it had borrowed money to pursue the exemption case. After the hearings in Rome they had followed Thomas of Marlborough back to England and were claiming 400 marks and an even greater amount in costs, altogether well over £100,000 at today's values. In retaliation to the interdict, however, the king had banished all Romans from the country, and that included Evesham's creditors. They left empty-handed.

It was November 1213 before a new papal legate could come to Evesham. He was Nicholas bishop of Tusculum and he was determined to remove Abbot Norreis at last; he summoned the whole convent to appear before himself and his colleagues in the chapter house at Evesham on Thursday 21 November. Seated with him that day were Robert abbot of York, Richard abbot of Selby, and John abbot of San Martino al Cimino in Tuscany; also in his entourage was Pandulf the papal envoy. At first Thomas maintained a pose of loyalty to the abbot. Thomas had entered into a pact with him years earlier, and the 'Rule' required a monk to obey his superior. Thomas also feared Norreis's personal retribution if the legate should fail, like all previous inquisitors, to depose him. At the legate's stern insistence, however, Thomas stood up and began a well-prepared and detailed exposition of the misdeeds that Abbot Roger had allegedly committed over a period of some twenty years. Norreis offered no defence to the accusations other than to claim that he had acted within his authority as head of the house, that his alleged negligence had been due to a shortage of money, and that he was the victim of a conspiracy by the monks. The hearing lasted two days, at the end of which the legate told Norreis to rise from his seat, resign the abbacy, and ask forgiveness and mercy for his numerous crimes. At first the abbot would not rise, but being commanded a second time he got up, prostrated himself at the legate's feet, and repeated after him the necessary words. Finally he surrendered the matrix of his personal seal (which was then broken to prevent its reuse) and his key to the conventual seal matrix, and gave up all the vestments, plate, and documents that were in his possession. He was then escorted from the chapter house and the monks followed, 'rejoicing that God had destroyed a wicked man and freed us from the hand of Pharoah'.[25]

[25] T. Marlb. pp. 192–9, 438–67.

Epilogue: A fresh start

Bishop Nicholas then ordered the monks to choose a new abbot from among their own brethren. On 25 November the legate personally questioned each monk and wrote down the replies, but after considering those he angrily announced that 'although he had been involved in many elections he had never found as much dissent or antagonism in any other community'.[26] Most of the wiser monks were said to have favoured Randal ('Randulphus'), the prior of Worcester, a native of Evesham, but there had been much controversy. The legate's colleagues warned the monks that, if they could not agree among themselves, Bishop Nicholas might impose a complete stranger on them or, even worse, a foreigner. With that in mind the monks told the legate that they would elect Randal. A week later, however, and before Nicholas could announce his decision about the abbacy, the monks of Worcester elected Randal to be their bishop. Fortunately for Evesham the legate quashed the Worcester election in order to allow the king's chancellor Walter de Gray to be made bishop there, and on 20 January Bishop Nicholas advised the Evesham monks to elect Prior Randal to the abbacy, which they did. The legate and the king then confirmed the election.[27] Roger Norreis was made prior of Penwortham, Evesham's remote cell on the bank of the Ribble, but he was removed within a year for misconduct. After further years as a monastic outcast he was allowed to return to Penwortham as prior but, still unrepentant and at a safe distance from the mother house, he resumed his usual habits and for the rest of his days refused to be reconciled with Evesham. His bitterness could not be assuaged by the monks' expressions of forgiveness or their pleas that he would return to them as one of their own.[28]

The removal of Abbot Norreis and the election of a reforming abbot, with Thomas of Marlborough as his adviser,[29] were generally welcomed but offered no guarantee against an unforeseen return to scandal, because for the time being Evesham abbey was subject to no external control other than that of a distant pope. In 1215, however, Abbot Randal and Thomas (by then the abbey's dean of the Vale) attended the Fourth Lateran Council in Rome.[30] There Pope Innocent III decreed that the heads of the black-monk houses in each province should assemble in a provincial general chapter every three years. The provincial chapter was to make and enforce rules governing the conduct of the constituent houses, and to appoint

26 T. Marlb. pp. 488–9.

27 T. Marlb. pp. 468–73; Smith and London 2001, p. 41.

28 T. Marlb. pp. 466–9.

29 On the abbacy of Randal (1214–29) and on the work of Thomas of Marlborough under him and as his successor (1230–36) see T. Marlb. pp. 480–511.

30 Ibid. pp. 488–9.

visitors in each diocese to carry out inspections and to correct shortcomings. Memories of the tortuous procedures that had been necessary to remove Abbot Norreis had probably been in Pope Innocent's mind when he introduced the new scheme.[31] It required Evesham to give up a little of the independence that it had so long fought to preserve, but supervision by a provincial chapter did not nullify Evesham's prized exemption from the bishop of Worcester. Abbot Randal was himself one of the earliest visitors appointed for the black monks in Worcester diocese and he was a president of the general chapter of Canterbury province in 1219 and 1225.[32] Another outcome of the Lateran Council was that the pope confirmed the abbey's administrative and financial customs in 1216.[33] They had first been ordered to be put in writing in 1203, but the papal legate had not confirmed them. They had been written down again in 1206 and confirmed by the legate, but could not be enforced during the interdict (1208–13). Only after the dismissal of Abbot Norreis had it become possible to draw up a document that would in future be used and respected by abbot and convent alike.

Meanwhile, on 21 November 1214 King John had granted that religious houses should thenceforward be free of royal interference of any kind in their elections; all that would be required would be the royal licence to elect and the royal assent to the result, neither of which would be unreasonably withheld.[34] The pope still had to confirm the appointment,[35] but after 1214 he usually never refused. The only instances of outside interference in an abbatial election at Evesham after that date seem to have occurred in 1236, when a prominent royal adviser, Richard le Gras prior of Hurley in Berkshire, was appointed abbot,[36] and in 1266, when the papal legate overturned the election of an Evesham monk William of Marlborough, a sympathizer of the late rebel and excommunicate Simon de Montfort. In that instance the legate appointed William of Whitchurch, the abbot of Alcester, to be the new abbot of Evesham.[37] For the next 300 years the monks of Evesham normally chose one of their own number, often the current prior or

31 Knowles 1963a, p. 345.

32 W. A. Pantin, ed., *Documents Illustrating the Activities of the General and Provincial Chapters of the English Black Monks 1215–1540*, I, Royal Historical Soc. Camden Third Series 45 (London, 1931), pp. 7–21.

33 T. Marlb. pp. 384–7, 412–13.

34 W. Stubbs, ed., *Select Charters and Other Illustrations of English Constitutional History from the Earliest Times to the Reign of Edward I*, 9th edn, reprint (Oxford, 1921), pp. 282–4.

35 e.g. T. Marlb. pp. 498–501.

36 *Evesham Chron.* pp. 278–9; D. A. Carpenter, 'King Henry III and Saint Edward the Confessor: The Origins of the Cult', *EHR* 122 (2007), 865–91 (at 875–6).

37 Cox 1988, p. 20.

cellarer, and their choice was never overruled.[38] In fact the king had shown no interest in the election of abbots of Evesham since the early twelfth century, and from the thirteenth century onwards neither did the archbishop of Canterbury or the pope. By 1215 the conduct and continuity of Evesham abbey, and of others like it, had ceased to engage the active concern of the nation's leaders; the abbey would be upheld in future by a framework of laws, within which during three more centuries it would offer to its local people the blessings of stability, employment, education, and charity, and the consolations of religion.

[38] Smith and London 2001, pp. 41–3; D. M. Smith, *The Heads of Religious Houses: England and Wales*, III (Cambridge, 2008), pp. 41–2.

Afterword

FROM the thirteenth century onwards Evesham abbey's rich estates and its security in law enabled it to meet every challenge and opportunity. As a perpetual corporation the abbot and convent could recover from setbacks that would have defeated an ordinary person, and could always raise large loans. In 1316 the abbot's annual net income, separate from that of the convent, was estimated at 640 marks (£426 13s 4d); and in 1379, after decades of economic adversity and the ravages of the Black Death, the estimate was the same.[1] It is striking that the abbot's actual receipts in the accounting year 1456–7, at £418 13s,[2] were similar to the estimate of 1316. Such figures are mere snapshots, and there are none for the abbey as a whole before 1535, when its net income was £1,183 a year.[3] Even those few details, however, imply that Evesham abbey's capital was such that it could cope with any temporary loss of revenue.

The outlook was different for individuals, and many of them suffered or died as a result of economic adversity or sudden calamity. For instance, in 1265 the town and the monastery were pillaged after the battle of Evesham[4] and in the fourteenth century the Black Death killed several of the monks;[5] it was one of the reasons why there were only twenty-eight of them c.1380.[6] The peasants of the Vale had less protection than the monks and the plague must have taken many lives. Nevertheless, for the survivors in the abbey, the town, and the Vale, the outcome could be positive. At the abbey the continuations of the domestic chronicle before and after the Black Death offer an unbroken recital of estates acquired and improved, lawsuits won and lost, great architectural schemes accomplished, and lavish purchases of

1 Harley 3763, fols 136r–v, 146r–147v.

2 Worcester, Worcestershire Archives, ref. 705:56, BA 3910/33(iv).

3 [J. Caley, ed.] *Valor ecclesiasticus temp. Henr. VIII auctoritate regia institutus*, III, Record Commission (London, 1817), p. 254.

4 D. C. Cox, 'The Battle of Evesham in the Evesham Chronicle', *Historical Research* 62 (1989), 337–45 (at 343).

5 Tindal 1794, pp. 192–4.

6 TNA, PRO E179/58/11, m. 1d.

plate and vestments lovingly described.[7] The battle and the plague are not mentioned and it is recorded that even in difficult times Abbot John of Ombersley (1367–79) left the monastery 'full of all good things'.[8]

The emphasis of the chronicle is on expressions of religion that were visible, tangible, and frankly expensive. They could be seen as aids to private contemplation; but the keenest monastic minds were more interested in scholastic learning. Abbot John of Brookhampton (1282–1316) built private studies above the east walk of the cloister[9] and in 1288 he and the abbot of Westminster pressed the Canterbury provincial chapter to set up an Oxford college for black monks; in 1298 the chapter appointed Walter, a monk of Evesham (probably Walter of Oddington), to a small committee charged with the arrangements.[10] The most able Evesham monks went to Oxford for long periods of study and it was there that some would achieve eminence; such were Walter of Oddington (fl.1301), who wrote on astronomy, mathematics, music, and alchemy, and John Feckenham (d.1584), the Catholic controversialist, who became abbot of Westminster under Mary I. At Evesham learned monks were allowed to build personal book collections, and Nicholas Hereford, the prior, left ninety-one separate items to the abbey in 1392.[11] Nevertheless, wide reading does not imply creative scholarship; in the sixteenth century Evesham and the Vale were home to several men of refined intellect and culture, but in comparison with Oxford the abbey was seen as an academic backwater.[12]

The high mortality of the fourteenth century presumably explains why the town did not grow outwards until well after the Dissolution. A smaller population, however, did not imply a poorer community, and by 1400 Evesham was one of Worcestershire's principal cloth-making towns.[13] Vacant urban plots could

7 *Evesham Chron.* pp. 260–310, 338–40. See also Bond 1973, pp. 1–61; Bond 1975, pp. 51–9; Cox 1990, pp. 128–34.

8 *Evesham Chron.* p. 303.

9 T. Hearne, ed., *Joannis Lelandi antiquarii de rebus Britannicis collectanea* (Oxford, 1715), I, p. 249.

10 W. A. Pantin, ed., *Documents illustrating the Activities of the General and Provincial Chapters of the English Black Monks 1215–1540*, I, Royal Historical Soc. Camden Third Series 45 (London, 1931), pp. 126–7, 138.

11 R. Sharpe, J. P. Carley, R. M. Thomson, and A. G. Watson, eds, *English Benedictine Libraries: The Shorter Catalogues*, Corpus of British Medieval Library Catalogues 4 (London, 1996), pp. 133, 138–50.

12 D. Knowles, *The Religious Orders in England*, III (Cambridge, 1959), pp. 100–107; H. Aveling and W. A. Pantin, eds, *The Letter Book of Robert Joseph, Monk-Scholar of Evesham and Gloucester College, Oxford 1530–3*, Oxford Historical Soc. new series 19 (Oxford, 1967).

13 Hilton 1982, pp. 5–6.

be merged and larger houses then built on them; and, when traders were fewer, encroachments could be made on the ancient market place. One such was the great timber-framed Round House, perhaps built as an inn. The population of the town is unlikely to have increased much after the mid-fourteenth century and it may even have declined, but individuals seem to have prospered.[14] The inhabitants never had independence from monastic control but they were electing two bailiffs by the early fourteenth century. The abbey gradually delegated responsibilities and some powers to them,[15] and a bellman and serjeants at mace affirmed their dignity.[16]

The abbey fostered spectacular growth in the religious aspirations of the townspeople. About 1380 St Lawrence's church had no less than nine priests and fourteen 'clerks' (or lesser clergy), while All Saints had six priests and six clerks and Bengeworth three priests and two clerks.[17] Moreover, in the fourteenth and fifteenth centuries St Lawrence's was wholly rebuilt and All Saints greatly enlarged.[18] Public benefactions of all kinds were thought to earn remission from purgatory. Thus in the later fourteenth century the monastery provided a grammar school for local boys, apparently in the chapel of the recently built charnel house near St Lawrence's church; Abbot Clement Lichfield (1514–38) moved the school to a new building in the Merstow, and its porch still has an inscription requesting prayers for his soul.[19]

In the surrounding countryside, meanwhile, survivors of the fourteenth-century plagues could create larger farms and probably hold them on more favourable terms than before.[20] In the Vale, as in the town, public religion flourished. The abbey rebuilt the chancels of several chapels in the late thirteenth century;[21] and visible improvements and additions to the naves[22] show that in the fourteenth and fifteenth centuries the worshippers themselves wanted to enhance their churches and could afford to do so. By c.1380 each of the parochial chapels of the Vale had its own priest as before, but there were assistant priests too, and most chapels also had one or two other clergy,[23] probably chantry priests paid for

14 C. Dyer and T. R. Slater, 'The Midlands', Palliser 2000, pp. 609–38 (at pp. 636–8).

15 *VCH Worcs.* II, p. 373.

16 Tindal 1794, p. 93n.

17 TNA, PRO E179/58/11, m. 1d.

18 Brooks and Pevsner 2007, pp. 291–3.

19 *VCH Worcs.* IV, p. 498; N. I. Orme, 'Evesham School before the Reformation', *VEHS Res. Pap.* 6 (1977), 95–100; Cox 1990, pp. 132, 135–6.

20 R. H. Hilton, 'A Rare Evesham Abbey Estate Document', *VEHS Res. Pap.* 2 (1969), 5–10.

21 Dugdale, *Mon.* II, p. 34; *Evesham Chron.* p. 287.

22 Brooks and Pevsner 2007, pp. 119, 169, 294, 307, 382–3, 494, 501–2, 506, 596.

23 TNA, PRO E179/58/11, m. 1d.

by parishioners. Eventually at least two successful men, Robert Hunkes (d.1523) at St Lawrence's Evesham[24] and Thomas Smith (d.1532) at Middle Littleton,[25] were allowed to build private chantry chapels attached to their churches. In such ways Bishop Ecgwine's original desire to take Christianity to the people seemed amply fulfilled.

The monastery might thus have supported itself and the Vale indefinitely, and in the early 1530s no-one at Evesham imagined otherwise.[26] But when papal protection was taken away by the legislation of 1532–4 and when the smaller monasteries were dissolved under the Act of 1536 some of the convent came to accept the reality of Henry VIII's intentions, though some would not.[27] Whatever their differences, however, the monks wanted to hold on and they did so until the evening of 30 January 1540. Then, as they neared the conclusion of vespers, the authorities interrupted their singing and, to quote an eyewitness, 'would not suffer them to make an end'.[28] They went their ways and soon their ancient and glorious church had been reduced to 'nothing but a huge deal of rubbish overgrown with grass'.[29]

24 D. C. Cox, *Evesham Abbey and the Parish Churches: A Guide* (Evesham, 1980), p. 15.

25 *VCH Worcs.* II, p. 411.

26 D. Knowles, *The Religious Orders in England*, III (Cambridge, 1959), p. 106.

27 C. W. Clarke, 'Evesham Abbey: The Final Disunity', *VEHS Res. Pap.* 1 (1967), 35–46.

28 M. D. Knowles and T. Dart, 'Notes on a Bible of Evesham Abbey', *EHR* 79 (1964), 775–8 (at 776).

29 [J. Gairdner and R. H. Brodie, eds] *Letters and Papers, Foreign and Domestic, of the Reign of Henry VIII, preserved in the Public Record Office, the British Museum, and elsewhere in England*, XVI (London, 1898), p. 93; T. Habington, *A Survey of Worcestershire*, ed. J. Amphlett, II, WHS (Oxford, 1899), p. 91.

APPENDIX

The abbots of Evesham to 1215

Æthelwald fl.713–25
Ealdberht
Ealdberht (another?)
Ealdferth
Tilberht fl.759
Cuthwulf
Ealdmund
Credan fl.777
Thingcferth fl.803
Ealdbald
Ecgberht fl.824
Ealhferth fl.855×?
Wulfheard
Wulfsige fl.897
Cynehelm fl.899–904
Cynath fl.916–29
Eaba fl.929?
Cynath (again) fl.930
Eadwine fl.931–9
Osweard fl.970–74
Freothegar fl.?×983
Ælfric fl.997
Ælfgar fl.1002
Brihtmær
Æthelwine ?–1013
Ælfweard c.1014–1044
Manni (Wulfmær) 1044–58
Æthelwig 1058–78
Walter 1078–1104
Maurice c.1104–c.1121
Robert c.1121–c.1130
Reynold 1130–49
William de Andeville 1149–59
Roger 1159–60
Adam 1161–89
Roger Norreis 1190–1213
Randal 1214–29

Select bibliography

Atkins, I. (1940), 'The Church of Worcester from the Eighth to the Twelfth Centuries', pt 2, *Ant. Jnl* 20, pp. 203–29

Barrow, J. (2008), 'The Chronology of the Benedictine "Reform"', *Edgar, King of the English, 959–975: New Interpretations*, ed. D. Scragg (Woodbridge), pp. 211–23

Baylis, T. J. S. (2008), *Evesham Inns and Signs: Collected Articles*, ed. S. B. Brotherton (Evesham)

Blair, J. (2005), *The Church in Anglo-Saxon Society* (Oxford)

Bond, C. J. (1973), 'The Estates of Evesham Abbey: A Preliminary Survey of their Medieval Topography', *VEHS Res. Pap.* 4, pp. 1–61

——(1975), 'The Medieval Topography of the Evesham Abbey Estates: A Supplement', *VEHS Res. Pap.* 5, pp. 50–59

Boyle, L. E. (1983), 'The Beginnings of Legal Studies at Oxford', *Viator* 14, pp. 107–31

Brand, P. (1992), 'The Rise and Fall of the Hereditary Steward in English Ecclesiastical Institutions, 1066–1300', *Warriors and Churchmen in the High Middle Ages: Essays Presented to Karl Leyser*, ed. T. Reuter (London), pp. 145–62

Brett, M. (1975), *The English Church under Henry I* (London)

Brooks, A., and N. Pevsner (2007), *Worcestershire*, The Buildings of England (New Haven and London)

Brooks, N., and C. Cubitt (1996), eds, *St Oswald of Worcester: Life and Infuence* (London)

Bryant, R. (2012), *The Western Midlands*, Corpus of Anglo-Saxon Stone Sculpture 10 (Oxford)

Clarke, H. B. (1977), 'The Early Surveys of Evesham Abbey: An Investigation into the Problem of Continuity in Anglo-Norman England', unpublished Ph.D. thesis, University of Birmingham

——(2007), 'Evesham J and Evesham L: Two Early Twelfth-Century Manorial Surveys', *Anglo-Norman Studies* 30, pp. 62–84

——(2012a), 'Uses and Abuses of Foundation Legends: The Case of Evesham Abbey', *The Medieval Imagination* mirabile dictu*: Essays in Honour of Yolande de Pontfarcy Sexton*, ed. P. Gaffney and J.-M. Picard (Dublin), pp. 123–45

——(2012b), '"Those five knights which you owe me in respect of your abbacy": Organizing Military Service after the Norman Conquest: Evesham and Beyond', *Haskins Soc. Jnl* 24, pp. 1–39

Coates, R. (2013), 'The Name of the Hwicce: A Discussion', *ASE* 42, pp. 51–61
Cox, B. G. (1967), 'Romano-British Occupation Sites in the Vale of Evesham, *VEHS Res. Pap.* 1, pp. 11–16
Cox, B[arrie] (1976), 'The Place-Names of the Earliest English Records', *EPNS Jnl* 8, pp. 12–66
Cox, D. C. (1975), 'The Vale Estates of the Church of Evesham, c.700–1086', *VEHS Res. Pap.* 5, pp. 25–50
——(1988), *The Battle of Evesham: A New Account* (Evesham)
——(1990), 'The Building, Destruction, and Excavation of Evesham Abbey: A Documentary History', *TWAS* 3rd series 12, pp. 123–46
——(2002), 'St Oswald of Worcester at Evesham Abbey: Cult and Concealment', *Jnl of Ecclesiastical History* 53, pp. 269–85
——(2006), 'Blackminster and the Hundred of Blackenhurst', *TWAS* 3rd series 20, pp. 77–86
——(2010a), 'Evesham Abbey: The Romanesque Church', *JBAA* 163, pp. 24–70
——(2010b), 'The Literary Remains of Adam, Abbot of Evesham (1161–1189)', *Jnl of Medieval Latin* 20, pp. 113–66
Coxe, H. O. (1852), *Catalogus Codicum MSS, qui in Collegiis Aulisque Oxoniensibus hodie adservantur* (Oxford), pt 2 [cited by college and page]
Cracknell, S. (1996), ed., *Roman Alcester: Defences and Defended Area*, CBA Research Report 106 (London)
Dalwood, H., and S. Ratkai (1998), 'Salvage Recording at Bennett's Hill Anglo-Saxon Cemetery, Offenham: Interim Report', Hereford and Worcester County Council Archaeological Service internal report no. 539 (Worcester), in the 'Online Archaeology Library' of Worcestershire Archive and Archaeology Service
Darlington, R. R. (1933), 'Æthelwig, Abbot of Evesham', *EHR* 48, pp. 1–22, 177–98
Edwards, R., and D. Hurst (2000), 'Iron Age Settlement, and a Medieval and Later Farmstead: Excavation at 93–97 High Street, Evesham', *TWAS* 3rd series 17, pp. 73–110
Farmer, D. H. (2011), *The Oxford Dictionary of Saints*, 5th edn revised (Oxford)
Finberg, H. P. R. (1972), *The Early Charters of the West Midlands*, 2nd edn (Leicester)
Foot, S. (2006), *Monastic Life in Anglo-Saxon England, c.600–900* (Cambridge)
Gameson, R. (1999), *The Manuscripts of Early Norman England (c.1066–1130)* (London)
Gelling, M. (1974), 'Some Notes on Warwickshire Place-Names', *Birmingham and Warwickshire Archaeological Soc. Transactions* 86, pp. 59–79
——(1997), *Signposts to the Past: Place-Names and the History of England*, 3rd edn (Chichester)
Gullick, M. (1998), 'Professional Scribes in Eleventh- and Twelfth-Century England', *English Manuscript Studies 1100–1700* 7, pp. 1–24
Hallam, H. E. (1988a), ed., *The Agrarian History of England and Wales*, II (Cambridge)
——(1988b), 'Population Movements in England, 1086–1350', Hallam 1988a, pp. 508–93

Hart, C. R. (1975), *The Early Charters of Northern England and the North Midlands* (Leicester)
Hayward, P. A. (1993), 'The Idea of Innocent Martyrdom in Late Tenth- and Eleventh-Century English Hagiology', *Martyrs and Martyrologies: Papers read at the 1992 Summer Meeting and the 1993 Winter Meeting of the Ecclesiastical History Society*, ed. D. Wood, Studies in Church History 30 (Oxford), pp. 81–92
Higham, N. J. (2013), ed., *Wilfrid: Abbot, Bishop, Saint: Papers from the 1300th Anniversary Conferences* (Donington)
Higham, N. [J.], and M. J. Ryan (2013), *The Anglo-Saxon World* (New Haven and London)
Hilton, R. H. (1982), 'The Small Town and Urbanisation—Evesham in the Middle Ages', *Midland History* 7, pp. 1–8
Hooke, D. (1985), *The Anglo-Saxon Landscape: The Kingdom of the Hwicce* (Manchester)
——(1990), *Worcestershire Anglo-Saxon Charter Bounds* (Woodbridge)
Hughes, J. (1990), 'Survey and Excavation at Evesham Abbey', *TWAS* 3rd series 12, pp. 147–99
Hurst, D., and C. Patrick (2012), 'Childswickham Roman Villa', *TWAS* 3rd series 23, pp. 39–48
Ker, N. R. (1964), *Medieval Libraries of Great Britain: A List of Surviving Books*, Royal Historical Soc. Guides and Handbooks 3, 2nd edn (London)
——(1985), 'Sir John Prise', *Books, Collectors, and Libraries: Studies in the Medieval Heritage*, ed. A. G. Watson (London), pp. 471–96
Knowles, D. (1963a), *The Monastic Order in England: A History of its Development from the Times of St Dunstan to the Fourth Lateran Council 940–1216*, 2nd edn (Cambridge)
——(1963b), 'Cistercians and Cluniacs: The Controversy between St Bernard and Peter the Venerable', *The Historian and Character and Other Essays*, ed. C. Brooke and G. Constable (Cambridge), pp. 50–75
——, C. N. L. Brooke, and V. C. M. London (2001), *The Heads of Religious Houses: England and Wales*, I, 2nd edn (Cambridge)
Lapidge, M. (1977), 'The Medieval Hagiography of St Ecgwine', *VEHS Res. Pap.* 6, pp. 77–93
Le Neve, J. (1971), *Monastic Cathedrals*, ed. D. E. Greenway, Fasti Ecclesiae Anglicanae 1066–1300 2 (London)
——(2001), *Bath and Wells*, ed. D. E. Greenway, Fasti Ecclesiae Anglicanae 1066–1300 7 (London)
——(2002), *Hereford*, ed. J. S. Barrow, Fasti Ecclesiae Anglicanae 1066–1300 8 (London)
Licence, T. (2011), *Hermits and Recluses in English Society 950–1200* (Oxford)
Locket, N., and L. Griffin (2006), 'Roman and Medieval Evesham: Excavation at 13 Vine Street', *TWAS* 3rd series 20, pp. 65–74
Mawer, A., and F. M. Stenton (1927), *The Place-Names of Worcestershire*, EPNS 4 (Cambridge)
May, G. (1845), *A Descriptive History of the Town of Evesham, from the*

Foundation of its Saxon Monastery: With Notices Respecting the Ancient Deanery of its Vale (Evesham)

Monkhouse, F. J. (1971), 'Worcestershire', *The Domesday Geography of Midland England*, ed. H. C. Darby and I. B. Terrett, The Domesday Geography of England, 2nd edn (Cambridge), pp. 217–72

Ogilby, J. (1675), *Britannia*, I (London) [no more published]

Palliser, D. M. (2000), ed., *The Cambridge Urban History of Britain*, I (Cambridge)

Reynolds, P. J. (1971), 'Exploratory Examination of a Romano-British Site at Wickhamford, Worcs.', *VEHS Res. Pap.* 3, pp. 11–18

Rollason, D. (1981), *The Search for St Wigstan, Prince-Martyr of the Kingdom of Mercia*, Vaughan Papers in Adult Education 27 (Leicester)

Rudge, E. J. (1820), *A Short Account of the History and Antiquities of Evesham* (Evesham)

Sayers, J. (1988), '"Original", Cartulary and Chronicle: The Case of the Abbey of Evesham', *Fälschungen im Mittelalter*, Monumenta Germaniae Historica: Schriften 33, pt 4 (Hanover), pp. 371–95

Scharer, A. (1982), *Die angelsächsische Königsurkunde im 7. und 8. Jahrhundert* (Vienna)

Sims-Williams, P. (1990), *Religion and Literature in Western England, 600–800* (Cambridge)

Slater, T. R. (1996), 'Medieval Town-Founding on the Estates of the Benedictine Order in England', *Power, Profit and Urban Land: Landownership in Medieval and Early Modern Northern European Towns*, ed. F.-E. Eliassen and G. A. Ersland (Aldershot), pp. 70–92

Smith, A. H. (1956), *English Place-Name Elements*, 2 vols, EPNS 25–6 (Cambridge)

Smith, D. M., and V. C. M. London (2001), *The Heads of Religious Houses: England and Wales*, II (Cambridge)

Southern, R. W. (1958), 'The English Origins of the "Miracles of the Virgin"', *Mediaeval and Renaissance Studies* 4, pp. 176–216

Stenton, F. M. (1970), *Preparatory to Anglo-Saxon England: Being the Collected Papers of Frank Merry Stenton*, ed. D. M. Stenton (Oxford)

Tindal, W. (1794), *The History and Antiquities of the Abbey and Borough of Evesham* (Evesham)

Tinti, F. (2010), *Sustaining Belief: The Church of Worcester from* c.*870 to* c.*1100* (Farnham)

Williams, A. (1982), '*Princeps Merciorum gentis*: The Family, Career and Connections of Ælfhere, Ealdorman of Mercia, 956–83', *ASE* 10, pp. 143–72

Wrottesley, G. (1903), *A History of the Family of Wrottesley of Wrottesley, Co. Stafford*, William Salt Archaeological Soc. *Collections for a History of Staffordshire* new series 6, pt 2 (London)

Zarnecki, G., J. Holt, and T. Holland (1984), eds, *English Romanesque Art 1066–1200: Hayward Gallery, London 5 April–8 July 1984* (London)

Index

Abbetot
  Urse d', sheriff of Worcestershire 80, 110, 111, 139
  family 111, 165
Abingdon
  abbey 53, 114, 178
  abbot of *see* Walkelin
Acton Beauchamp 80, 94
Adam (Evesham monks so named c.1104) 91
Adam, reeve 147
Adam de St Liz, abbot of Evesham *see* St Liz, Adam de
Adlestrop 148
Æfic, monk of Evesham 59, 63–4, 84
Ælfflæd, sister of Queen Osthryth 5
Ælfgar, abbot of Evesham 54, 55–6
Ælfgar (fl.1002), an abbot (? the same) 55
Ælfgar, son of Earl Leofric 58
Ælfgeat, monk of Evesham 68
Ælfgifu (Emma), queen 59, 62
Ælfgifu of Northampton 58–9
Ælfgifu, 'Lady' (fl.1023) (? the same) 58–9
Ælfgifu, half-sister of King Æthelstan 40
Ælfheah, St, archbishop of Canterbury 67
Ælfhere, ealdorman of Mercia (formerly ealdorman of the Hwicce) 47, 48, 52–3
Ælfric, abbot of Evesham 54–5
Ælfric, monk of Evesham 78, 82, 83
Ælfsige, monk of Evesham 85
Ælfstan, bishop of London 53, 54
Ælfthryth, queen 52
Ælfweard, abbot of Evesham and bishop of London 56–67, 69, 104, 169, 170
Ælfwig, monk of Evesham 86, 125
Ælfwine, recluse 84–5
Ærngrim (fl.1066) 80, 111
Æthelbald, king of the Mercians 31, 35
Æthelflæd, lady of the Mercians 38, 39
Æthelheard, under-king of the Hwicce 21, 31–2
Æthelhun, bishop of the Hwicce 39
Æthelmær (fl.1023) 60
Æthelred (?d.716), king of the Mercians 3–7, 10, 13, 20, 30, 31
Æthelred (d.911), lord of the Mercians 38
Æthelred (d.1016), king of the English 52, 53, 54, 56, 58
Æthelric, under-king of the Hwicce 35, 43
Æthelric, archdeacon of Worcester 108
Æthelsige, bishop of Sherborne 53
Æthelstan, king of the English (formerly king of the Anglo-Saxons) 39–41, 44
'Æthelstan' (?Ælfstan), bishop 53, 54
Æthelwald, abbot of Evesham 33, 35
Æthelwald (fl.713), monk of Evesham (? the same) 33–4
Æthelwald, (fl.725×737), an abbot (? the same) 35
Æthelwig, abbot of Evesham
  family and early career 68, 78, 80
  appointed 78
  and bishopric of Worcester 78
  in public life 78, 79–81, 83
  estates 79–80, 94, 109-11, 114, 115, 116
  building works 71, 81, 99, 101
  charitable works 81–3
  internal administration under 78–9, 90, 91, 94, 124, 125
  seal 96–8
  ascetics under 84–6, 125
  sickness and death 89, 92, 109, 165, 176
  posthumous biography 9, 176
Æthelwine (fl.1013), abbot of Evesham (later bishop of Wells) 56
Æthelwine (fl.1077), monk of Evesham 78, 79
Æthelwold, bishop of Winchester 48
Agatho, pope 33
agriculture 14, 23, 42, 74, 112–13, 158–9, 207; *see also* arable; barns; cereals; dovecotes; field systems; horses; labour services; labourers; livestock; markets; meadow; mills; orchards; oxen; park; pasture; timber; vineyard; woodland
Alban, St 91

Alban, monk of Evesham 90
Albreda (Aubrey), sister of Abbot Walter 110
Alcester 10, 12–13
abbot of *see* Whitchurch, William of
Aldington (Worcs.) 96
Aldwin (Ealdwine), monk of Winchcombe (later prior of Durham) 86, 106
Alexander II, pope 78
Alexander III, pope 134, 187
Alfred, bishop of Worcester 134
Alhhun (Ealhhun), bishop of the Hwicce 37–8
Alnoth, priest 138
Ambrose, monk of Evesham 90–91
Ameline, recluse 85
ampulla (for holy water) 173–4
Andeville, William de, abbot of Evesham (formerly prior of Dover) 130–31, 166
Andoversford 36
Andrew, St 189
Andrew, monk of Evesham 90
'Anglo-Saxon Chronicle' 66
Anselm, archbishop of Canterbury 129, 133
Anthony, monk of Evesham 90
Aquitaine (France) 82
arable 76–7, 112–13, 158; *see also* cereals
Arden, the 42
Armfrei (Ermefrei), monk of Evesham 183
Arosætna, the 10–12
Arrow, river 10–12
art and architecture 71, 149–50, 162, 164, 188–90, 194, 207–8; *see also under* Evesham, church of; Worcester cathedral priory
Ashingdon, battle of 58
Asser, bishop of Sherborne 45
Aston Somerville 40
Atsere (fl.1066) 80
Aubrey (Albreda), sister of Abbot Walter 110
Augustine, St, bishop of Hippo 181
Augustine, St, archbishop of Canterbury 3
Augustine, monk of Evesham 90
Augustinians 136
Avon, river 3, 7–8, 17, 166
as boundary 30
crossings 19, 21, 75, 162, 163, 165
navigation 18, 165
tributaries 12, 22

Badby 59, 110, 145, 152, 177, 194
Badsey 147, 148, 189, 190, 191
Badsey (Blackminster, Broadway) brook 22, 25
Baldwin, archbishop of Canterbury (formerly bishop of Worcester, formerly abbot of Forde) 131–2, 173, 174, 178
baptism 190
Bardney minster 7
barns 159
barrows (mounds) 24, 110, 138
Basing, recluse 84
Bath
abbey 83
abbot of *see* Wulfwold
archdeacon of *see* Richard
Bayeux (France), bishops of *see* Odo; Vigor
Beauchamp
Richard, earl of Warwick 18
William de, sheriff of Worcestershire 165, 166
family 164, 166
Becket, St Thomas, archbishop of Canterbury 172, 174, 175
vita 182–3
Bede 47, 50, 84, 180
'Ecclesiastical History' 4, 13, 86, 118
Bedford, Ralph of, prior of Worcester 172
Belgium *see* Flanders
Benedict, 'Rule' of St 47–8, 63, 84, 95, 136, 171
MSS at Evesham 36–7, 65, 181
observed at Evesham 48, 64, 99, 105, 140–41, 187
breached at Evesham 85, 194, 201
Benedict, monk of Evesham 90
Benedict Biscop 33, 34
Bengeworth 28, 162–4
castle 164, 165, 166
clergy 207
estates 59–60, 80, 111, 114, 121, 164
Port Street 75, 163–4
tenants 80, 147, 163
tithes 94
Berhtwald, archbishop of Canterbury 119–20, 123
Berkeley (Glos.) minster 37
Berkeley, William of 136
Bermondsey
minster and priory 33, 130, 131
prior of *see* St Liz, Adam de
Bernard, abbot of Clairvaux 181
Bewdley 160
Binton 53
Birlingham 8
Bishampton 190
Black Death, the 205–7
Blackenhurst hundred 138–9; *see also* 'Fissesberg' hundred

Blackminster 24, 138
Blackminster (Badsey, Broadway)
brook 22, 25
Blois, Peter of 171–2, 178
Bodleian Library, Oxford, MS Hatton
48 36–7, 65
Boniface, St 31
Bordesley abbey 136
Bourton on the Water 46–7, 143, 194
Bow brook 12
Bransford 94
Breteuil, Roger de, earl of Hereford 81
Bretforton, 42–3, 76, 96, 110, 149–50, 189, 190, 194
Brian fitz Count and his wife 137
Bricklehampton 190
Brihtmær, abbot of Evesham 56
Bristol 18
British Library, London
Cotton MS Faustina C.I 181
Cotton MS Vespasian B.XXIV 156–7
Cotton MS Vitellius E.XII 54 n.20
Cotton MS Vitellius E.XVII 55 n.21
Harley MS 3763 199
Lansdowne MS 427 54 n.20, 55 n.21
Royal MS 6 C.IX 181
Britons 3, 14, 21, 25–6, 28–30
Broadway (Badsey, Blackminster)
brook 22, 25
Broadwell (Glos.) 194, 198
burgages 159, 163–4
Burgred, king of the Mercians 38
burial
Christian 36, 55, 64, 69, 83, 85, 114, 131, 175, 190, 207
pagan 22, 24, 29
Bury St Edmunds abbey 104
Bussel
Maud 113
Warin and his son 113, 136
family 137
Byrhtferth of Ramsey 6, 9–10, 61, 62–3, 103, 118–19

Caen (France)
abbey of St Étienne 89, 99
abbot of *see* Lanfranc
Camden, William 112
Canterbury 71, 131
archbishops of 37, 120, 122–4, 129, 130, 204; *see also* Ælfheah; Anselm; Augustine; Becket, St Thomas; Berhtwald; Dunstan; Lanfranc; Langton, Stephen; Theobald; Walter, Hubert
Christ Church cathedral priory 89–90, 91, 99, 123, 130, 131, 132, 145
prior of Christ Church *see* Norreis, Roger
St Augustine's abbey (formerly minster of St Peter and St Paul) 33–4, 99, 131
Canterbury, province of 132, 203, 206; *see also* Canterbury: archbishops of
Carbonel, Thomas, abbot of Gloucester 172
carrying services 18, 101, 148, 151
cartularies 116, 155–7, 199
Ceadwealla (unidentified) 21
Cecily, recluse 85
Celestine III, pope 135
Cenwald (Koenwald), bishop of the Hwicce 39–41, 46, 47
Ceolred, king of the Mercians 31, 32
cereals 60, 64, 112–13, 158–9; *see also* arable
Cerisy-la-Forêt (France) abbey 89, 170
Chadbury 21, 32, 42
chantries 207–8
Chepstow (Striguil), lordship of 196
Chertsey
abbey 83
abbot of *see* Wulfwold
Cheshire 82
Chester
bishop of *see* Peter
constable of *see* Niel
Chich (St Osyth) minster 67
Childswickham 25, 42, 43, 44, 191 n.36; *see also* 'Wycweon'
churchscot 64, 191
Cicero 180
Cirencester abbey 136
Cistercians 84, 136, 171, 172, 178
Clare
Avice de, ? wife of Robert of Stafford 114
Isabel de, countess of Pembroke and 'countess of Striguil' 196
Cleeve hill (nr Evesham) 18, 101
Clement III, pope 135
Clement, monk of Evesham 90–91
Clipston, Robert of 135, 198
'Clofesho' (unlocated), councils at 34, 37
Cluniacs 131, 171–2, 178, 189
Cluny (France)
abbey 92, 171
abbot of *see* Peter 'the Venerable'
Cnut (d.1035), king of Denmark and of the English 57, 58–9, 60–64, 66–7
Cnut (d.1086), king of Denmark 105
Coenred, king of the Mercians 13, 20, 21, 32, 62, 118–22
'Coleham'
Henry of, monk of Evesham 145
Hugh of (? Hugh, abbot's chaplain) 145

Colnbrook 114
Comberton 26
Constantine I, pope 33–4, 118–24, 129, 132–3, 135, 195
Constantine, abbot's chamberlain 144 n.24
Constantine the African 179
Copenhagen (Denmark) *see* Kongelige Bibliotek
Corbucion, Piers 136
Cotswolds, the 22, 42, 75, 101, 164
councils, church
  English 3, 10, 12–13, 34, 37, 119–20, 131
  general 133, 134, 202–3
councils, royal 40, 68, 119
courts
  church 123, 130, 153, 154, 198–9
  secular 24–5, 49, 52, 56, 60, 79–80, 96, 110–11, 114–16
  see also law
Coutances (France), bishop of *see* Geoffrey
Coutances, John of, bishop of Worcester 195, 198
Coventry
  abbey 71, 112
  abbot of *see* Leofwine
Craycombe (nr Fladbury) 21
Credan, St, abbot of Evesham 36, 69, 102, 104, 170
Credan, St (another) 69
Crispin, Miles and his wife or daughter 114, 137
Cropthorne 59, 111
Crowland 84
  minster and abbey 38, 104, 177–8, 182–3
  abbot of *see* Longchamp, Henry de
Crowle 187
customary payments 151; *see also* renders in kind; rents in cash
'Cuthburgehlaw' hundred 59
Cutsdean 38
Cynath (Kenod, Kinath), abbot of Evesham 39–40, 46, 47
Cynath (fl.899–904), a deacon (? the same) 39
Cynehelm (Kenelm), St, chapel of 71, 84
Cynehelm (Kinelm), abbot of Evesham 38–9
Cynehelm (fl.899–904), an abbot and deacon (? the same) 38–9

Danes, the 56–7, 59, 62, 68, 86; *see also* Vikings, the
Daylesford 47
Deerhurst minster 52
Deira, king of *see* Eadwine
demesnes 113, 148, 149, 150–52, 157, 158–9, 160
Democritus 179
Deneberht, bishop of the Hwicce 37
Denis, John, monk of Evesham 194
Denmark 59, 105–6; *see also* Danes, the; Kongelige Bibliotek; Odense
Denmark, kings of *see* Cnut (d.1035); Cnut (d.1086); Erik I; Swegn 'Forkbeard'
Deormann (Evesham monks so named c.1104) 91
Derbyshire 39, 82
diseases 67, 78, 89, 92, 109, 205, 206
Dispenser, Robert 110
Dolfin, Matthew 193
Domesday inquest 111, 113, 115, 117, 150
Dominic, monk of Evesham 9, 15, 90–91, 103, 119–24, 167–8, 174
Dorchester, bishop of *see* Wulfwig
Dorsington 94
dovecotes 159
Dover
  priory 130
  prior of *see* Andeville, William de
Drayton, Michael 112–13
Droitwich 21; *see also* Witton
Dublin 45
Dumbleton 40, 47
Dunstan, archbishop of Canterbury (formerly bishop of the Hwicce, formerly abbot of Glastonbury) 48
Durham
  cathedral priory 86, 105–6
  prior of *see* Ealdwine

'E', monk of Evesham 182–3
Eaba (Ebba), abbot of Evesham 40
Eadgyth (Edith), queen of the English 70
Eadgyth, queen of Germany 40
Eadred, king of the English 46–7
Eadwine, St, king of Deira 173–4
Eadwine, abbot of Evesham 40–41, 44, 45, 46, 56
Ealdgyth (fl.1044×1058) 70
Ealdred, bishop of Worcester 68, 70, 78
Ealdred, ealdorman of the Hwicce 36
Ealdwine (Aldwin), monk of Winchcombe (later prior of Durham) 86, 106
Ealdwulf, bishop of Worcester 54, 55, 56
Ealhferth (Elferd), abbot of Evesham 37–8
Ealhferth (Eueferth) (fl.855), a deacon (? the same) 37–8
Ealhhelm, ealdorman (? of the Hwicce) 45, 46, 47, 48, 52
Ealhhun (Alhhun), bishop of the Hwicce 37–8
East Anglia, earl of *see* Gael, Ralph de

East Saxons, rulers of the *see* Offa (fl.709); Sighere
Ebba (Eaba), abbot of Evesham 40
Ecgberht (Ecbrith), abbot of Evesham 37
Ecgberht (fl.824), an abbot (? the same) 37
Ecgwine, St, bishop of the Hwicce
birth and family 4
appointed bishop 4, 5, 10
mission 4–6, 30, 32, 208
and Virgin Mary 61, 154, 167, 169
founds minster 7, 13, 17–18, 30, 61, 132
builds church 10, 13, 50
as abbot 32, 34, 35, 37, 108, 123
and 'Rule of St Benedict'36
estates 6–7, 13, 31–2, 107, 114, 120
at Rome 118–22
at 'Clofesho' 34
'Testament' 6, 9–10, 13, 118–20
death and burial 34, 50, 104
vita 6, 9–10, 15, 61, 62–3, 103, 118–24, 169–70, 172–3, 174
miracles 51, 62, 102, 103, 172, 174
images 154, 173, 187, 188
as patron saint and dedicatee 56, 71, 91, 103, 154, 169
feasts 63, 71, 104, 168
shrines made and repaired 56, 62, 69, 70, 104, 169, 172
shrines and relics preserved 50, 67, 99, 169
shrines and relics venerated 51, 55, 61, 64, 101–2, 173–4
shrines and relics sworn upon 111, 114
shrines and relics harmed 50, 56–7, 62, 70, 152, 169
holy well 174
pilgrim's ampulla 173–4
Ecgwine (fl.c.1104), monk of Evesham 90
Edgar, king of the English 47, 48–9, 51–2, 54, 59
Edith (Eadgyth), queen of the English 70
Edmund (d.946), king of the English 44–5, 47
Edmund (d.1016), king of the English 58
Edric, carpenter 162
education 65, 178–81, 185–6, 196, 197, 207
Edward (d.924), king of the Anglo-Saxons 38
Edward (d.978), king of the English 51–2
Edward (d.1066), king of the English 66, 68, 70, 74, 78, 79, 84
'egsan mor, (on)' (nr Murcot) 25
Elferd, abbot of Evesham *see* Ealhferth
'Elias', monk of Evesham 183
Emma (Ælfgifu), queen 59, 62
English language 3, 26, 83, 91, 121
Eof (Eoves) 16–17, 167
Eofor (name) 16
Erik I, king of Denmark 105
Ermefrei (Armfrei), monk of Evesham 183
Ernald, chamberlain 147
Essex (the East Saxons), rulers of *see* Offa (fl.709); Sighere
Essex, earl of *see* Geoffrey fitz Peter
Eueferth, deacon *see* Ealhferth
Eugenius III, pope 130
Evenlode *see* 'gild beorh', the
Evesham 6–7, 12, 13, 19–20, 32, 52, 120
Almonry Heritage Centre (formerly Almonry Museum) 55, 186
Barton, the 160
battle (1265) 205, 206
borough status 74, 112 n.26, 159, 207
boundary 43, 44
bridge 19, 75, 162, 163, 165
Bronze Age occupation 14
burgages, house plots, and houses 113, 137, 146, 147, 159, 206–7
charnel house 207
Cheltenham Road (at Little Hampton) 19
churches (parochial) 63–4, 71, 148, 184, 189, 190, 207–8
clergy 147–8, 191 n.31, 207
conduit 162
Cross Churchyard (later Upper Abbey Park) 72
demesne 113, 160
Domesday valuation 113, 159
'Eibbesford' 19, 75
ferry 75
fords 19, 21
graveyard 73, 82, 165–6, 186, 190
householders and tenants 113, 144–8, 159–60, 162, 191, 207
Iron Age occupation 14, 19
Little Abbey Lane 72
market places 19 n.23, 74–5, 160, 162, 165, 186, 207
market 74–5, 77, 151, 164, 207
meadow 19
Merstow, the 19 n.23, 75 n.31, 160, 207
name 7–9, 16
New Borough, the 160
occupations 72, 74, 113, 146–7, 159, 162, 206
physical features 7–9, 14–18, 72–3
Pig Market (Vine Street) 19, 72, 160, 165–6
population 149, 159, 206, 207
rents 113, 159
river navigation 18, 165

Evesham (*cont.*)
road connections 18–19, 21–2, 60, 75, 114, 163–4
Romano-British occupation 14–15
Round House 207
rural worshippers at 64, 74, 189
Rynal, the 15–16, 162
St Ecgwine's well 174
school 207
streets (named) 15, 18–19, 75, 159–60, 162, 190
town origin and plan 74–5, 159–62, 206
Vine Street (Pig Market) 19, 72, 160, 165–6
vineyard (at Great Hampton) 95, 112, 142
washing-place 162
water defences 166
see also Bengeworth; Evesham, church of
Evesham
Elias of, priests called 183 n.42
Payn of (fl.1178), abbot's clerk 145
Ralph of 145–6
Evesham, church of
art and architecture 10, 63–4, 69–71, 99–102, 184–8, 196, 200–201, 205–6
asceticism and private prayer 64, 84–6, 90
Benedictine revival 47–9, 54–7
charity and hospitality 63, 64–5, 70, 81–3, 142, 185, 194
education at 65, 180, 185–6, 207
endowments 19–23, 30–32, 42–4, 59–60, 79–80, 113–14, 136–8
estate management 76-7, 109–17, 142, 149–64
financial management 94–5, 96, 143–4, 194–6
foundation and setting 6–19, 24–30
graveyard 73, 82, 165–6, 186, 190
hagiographic writing 9–10, 61, 103, 104, 172–3, 174, 182–3
historical writing 51, 54–5, 65–6, 92, 116, 176–8, 205–6
homiletic writing 178, 182
internal organization 63, 78–9, 83, 90–92, 96–8, 129–32, 140–42, 144–8, 171–2, 194–5, 202–3; *see also* Evesham, abbots of: household
manuscripts 36–7, 65, 81, 92–4, 106, 142, 179–82
pastoral care 30, 37, 45–6, 64, 187; *see also* Evesham, deanery of the Vale of
precinct boundary and gates 72–4, 160, 164–6
relations with bishop 35–41, 48, 54–6, 83, 120, 132–6, 154, 195–9
relations with pope 33–4, 118–24, 198–9, 203–4
saints and relics 50–51, 60–62, 67, 69–70, 102–5, 167–70, 172-5
seal, conventual 153–4, 155, 168, 201
secularization 44–7, 51–4
vineyard (at Great Hampton) 95, 112, 142
water supply 162, 186
worship, conventual 62–5, 92–4, 103–5, 142, 171–2
see also Evesham, abbots of
Evesham, abbots of
appointment 37–41, 54, 129–32
household 95–8, 114, 138, 144–7
income 143, 149, 205
insignia pontificalia 133, 135, 195
current list (to 1215) 209
pre-Conquest list 35, 51
seals, personal 153–4, 201
see also named abbots
Evesham, deanery of the Vale of 107–8, 119, 124, 188–92, 199, 207–8
Exeter
cathedral school 179, 196
bishop of *see* Marshal, Henry

Farnborough (Warws.) 39
Feckenham, John, abbot of Westminster 206
Ferentino, John of 199, 203
his nephew 199–200
field systems 43, 76–7
fish 95, 113, 151, 159, 174
'Fissesberg' hundred 48–9, 52, 60, 80, 96, 107, 138–9
meeting place 24–5, 138
see also Blackenhurst hundred
Fladbury 21, 31–2
minster 5–6, 31, 36
see also Craycombe
Flæde (fl.?×697) 5
Flanders (Belgium, France, and Netherlands) 62
Flaxley abbey 136
Foliot, Gilbert, bishop of Hereford (formerly abbot of Gloucester) 130–31, 133–4
Forde, abbot of *see* Baldwin
Foss Way 164
Fossard
Alexander 137
Robert 137
— (fl.c.1190) 137

Fougères, Stephen of, bishop of Rennes 178
France *see* Aquitaine; Bayeux; Caen; Cerisy-la-Forêt; Cluny; Coutances; Flanders; Jumièges; La Charité-sur-Loire; Normandy; Paris; Rennes; Senlis; Tours
Franceis, Richard 148
Freothegar, abbot of Evesham 53, 56
Freothegar (fl.c.960), a monk (? the same) 53
fruit *see* orchards

Gael, Ralph de, earl of East Anglia 81
Galen 179
game 42, 158
Geoffrey, bishop of Coutances 111
Geoffrey, brother of Abbot Walter 110
Geoffrey, marshal 147
Geoffrey fitz Peter, earl of Essex 197
Gerald of Wales 178
Gerard, abbot's chamberlain 145
Germany 39–40, 47, 70, 78
  kings of *see* Henry I; Otto I
  queen of *see* Eadgyth
  see also Magdeburg
Gervase, abbot of Winchcombe 171, 178
Giffard, clerk 147–8
Gilbert, abbot's clerk 145
Gilbert, fuller 162
Gilbert fitz Thorold 79–80
'gild beorh', the (nr Evenlode) 110–11
Glastonbury
  abbey 48, 51, 169
  abbot of *see* Dunstan
Gloucester 59, 70, 78
  abbey 185, 198
  abbots of *see* Carbonel, Thomas; Foliot, Gilbert; Serlo
  St Oswald's priory 136
Gloucester
  Miles of, earl of Hereford 130, 136, 165, 166
  Roger of, earl of Hereford 136, 166
Gloucestershire 33, 43, 44, 55, 79, 80, 110, 117
Glover, Robert 20
Godfrey, abbot's *serviens* 146
Godgifu ('Lady Godiva'), wife of Earl Leofric 60, 63, 64, 68, 71, 84
Godric, abbot of Winchcombe 86
Godric, goldsmith 69, 91
Godstow
  abbey 178, 182
  abbess of *see* Launceleve, Edith
Godwine, ealdorman of Lindsey 53, 56, 58, 60
Goldor 112 n.19, 113
Gras, Richard le, abbot of Evesham (formerly prior of Hurley) 203
Gratian 179
Gravenhurst, Lower 183 n.42
Gray, Walter de, bishop of Worcester (formerly chancellor of England) 202
Greek language 92
Gundulf, bishop of Rochester 89

Habington, Thomas 18, 208
Hackington college 132
Hákon Eiriksson, earl of Worcester 57, 60
Halton (Ches.) 113
Hamelin, carpenter 162
Hampton (nr Evesham) 42, 59–60, 111, 114, 116
  church 189
  clergy 191 n.31
  tenants 110, 146, 147, 148, 152, 191 n.31
Hampton, Great 24, 42, 96, 142; *see also* Evesham, church of: vineyard
Hampton, Little 24 n.5, 42; *see also* Evesham: Cheltenham Road
Harold (d.1040), king of the English 62
Harold (d.1066), king of the English 79
Harrow hill (nr Middle Littelton) 29
Harthacnut, king of the English 62, 66
Heahberht, bishop of the Hwicce 37
Heahstan, bishop of London 38
Henry I, king of England 136, 138, 153
Henry II, king of England 131, 153, 178
  as duke of Normandy 153
Henry VIII, king of England 208
Henry I, king of Germany 40
Henry, abbey gatekeeper 146
Hereford
  cathedral 183 n.42
  bishop of *see* Foliot, Gilbert
Hereford, earls of *see* Breteuil, Roger de; Gloucester, Miles of; Gloucester, Roger of; William fitz Osbern
Hereford, Nicholas, monk of Evesham 206
Herefordshire 79, 80, 81
Heremann, monk of Evesham 102
Herluin, monk of Bath 83
Hexham minster 34
Hilary, monk of Evesham 90
Hild (Hilda), abbess of Whitby 4, 85
Hillingdon 114, 137
Honeybourne 42, 44, 107
Honeybourne, Church 42–4, 106–7, 145, 189, 190; *see also* Poden
Honeybourne, Cow 42–4, 107
Honorius 'of Autun' 180
horses 57, 147, 148

houses and house plots
  rural 44, 76, 114, 137, 158, 191
  urban 59, 113, 137, 138, 146–7, 159, 163–4, 206–7
Howick 113
Hubald, bishop of Odense 105
Hugh, abbot's chaplain (? Hugh of 'Coleham') 145
Hugh, nephew of Abbot Walter 110
Hugh, gatekeeper 146–7
Hugh fitz Roger and his wife 137
Hunkes, Robert 208
Huntingdon, earl of *see* St Liz, Simon de (d.1184)
Huntington (Yorks.) 137
Hurley, prior of *see* Gras, Richard le
Hwicce, the, 3, 10, 20, 21, 30, 35, 38, 42, 45, 52
  rulers of 3, 4, 21, 36; *see also* Æthelheard; Æthelric; Oshere
  ealdormen of *see* Ælfhere; Ealdred; Ealhhelm
Hwicce, diocese of the (to 961) 4–5, 7, 33, 35–8, 45–6, 48; *see also* Hwicce, bishops of the; Worcester, diocese of
Hwicce, bishops of the (to 961) 4, 5, 7, 32, 35, 37
  familia 37–9, 41, 45
  relations with Evesham 7, 37, 42, 45, 47, 132, 177
  see also Æthelhun; Deneberht; Dunstan; Ealhhun; Ecgwine; Heahberht; Koenwald; Oftfor; Wærferth; Wilfrith (d.743×745); Wilfrith (d.928×929); Worcester, bishops of

Innocent II, pope 131, 133, 189
Innocent III, pope 135, 198–9, 200, 202–3
Ireland 82; *see also* Dublin
Iron Age 14, 19, 25, 28, 29
Isidore, bishop of Seville 180
Italy *see* Rome; San Martino al Cimino; Tusculum
Itchington, Long 65

Jarrow minster 33
Jesus College, Oxford
  MS 11 181
  MS 51 92–3, 180
  MS 54 180
  MS 69 180
  MS 93 181
John, king of England 200, 201, 202, 203
John, abbot of San Martino al Cimino 201
John, gatekeeper 147
John Denis, monk of Evesham 194
Jumièges (France) abbey 130
Juvenal 180

Kenelm (Cynehelm), St, chapel of 71, 84
Kenod (Kinath), abbot of Evesham *see* Cynath
Kent
  Richard of, abbot's chamberlain 145, 147
  Richard of (fl.c.1229) (? the same) 147
Kidderminster *see* 'Sture'
'Kikeswic', Robert of 137
Kinath (Kenod), abbot of Evesham *see* Cynath
Kinelm, abbot of Evesham *see* Cynehelm
Kingswood abbey 136
Kinwarton 109
knight service 81, 110, 151–2, 157, 165
Koenwald (Cenwald), bishop of the Hwicce 39–41, 46, 47
Kongelige Bibliotek, Copenhagen (Denmark), Gl. Kgl. Sam., MS 1595 106

La Charité-sur-Loire (France) priory 131, 171, 189–90
labour services 150–51, 158, 191
labourers 150, 151
Lacy, Walter de 81
Lanfranc, archbishop of Canterbury (formerly abbot of Caen) 83, 89–90, 96, 99, 132
  'Monastic Constitutions' 83, 91–2, 103, 124, 142
  relations with Evesham 79, 83, 102, 103, 129
Langton, Stephen, archbishop of Canterbury 196, 200
Lateran Council
  Second (1139) 133
  Fourth (1215) 202–3
Launceleve
  Edith (Ediva), abbess of Godstow 182
  William 182
law 141, 179, 204, 205
  ecclesiastical 124, 138, 179, 196, 197
  secular 78, 114, 124, 138, 147, 152, 179, 186
  see also courts
Leicester, earl of *see* Montfort, Simon de
Leland, John 112, 183
Lench, Church 106–7, 165
Lench, Sheriffs 79–80, 94
Lenches, the ('lencdune') 21
Lenchwick 16, 21, 42–3, 96, 110, 158, 190; *see also* 'wænnacumbe, (æt)'

Leofric, earl of Mercia (formery sheriff of Worcestershire) 58–60, 63–4, 66, 68, 71, 84, 116
Leofwine, bishop of Lichfield (formerly abbot of Coventry) 70–71
Lewes priory 102
Lichfield, bishop of *see* Leofwine
Lichfield, Clement, abbot of Evesham 207
Lindsey 3, 7
  ealdorman of *see* Godwine
Littleton (Worcs.) 42–3, 96, 109; *see also* Pickersom
Littleton, Middle 42, 189, 190, 208; *see also* Harrow hill
Littleton, North 42
Littleton, South (Worcs.) 42, 96, 189, 190
livestock 15, 16–17, 42, 60, 148, 151; *see also* fish; horses; oxen
Llanthony priory 136
London 62, 68, 102, 114, 149, 169, 196
  bishops of *see* Ælfstan; Ælfweard; Heahstan; Wulfsige
  Evesham abbey's assets 138
  roads from Evesham 75, 114
  St Paul's cathedral 67
  see also British Library
Longchamp
  Henry de, abbot of Crowland 178, 182–3
  Robert de, abbot of St Mary's York 201
Loynton 114
Lucan 180
Lyfing, bishop of Worcester 68

Macarius, monk of Evesham 90
Magdalen College, Oxford, MS Lat. 22 181
Magdeburg (Germany) cathedral 40
Malmesbury abbey 83
Malmesbury, William of 14–15
Manni (Wulfmær), abbot of Evesham 62, 68–71, 78, 81, 92, 107
manors 96, 117, 149, 159, 164, 190, 194
  officers of 82, 147–8
manuscripts 67; *see also under* Bodleian Library; British Library; Evesham, church of; Jesus College, Oxford; Kongelige Bibliotek; Magdalen College; Worcester cathedral priory
Mappleborough 53
Margaret, wife of Hugh fitz Roger 137
markets 74–5, 77, 151, 159, 164, 207
Marlborough
  John of (John Marshal) 196
  Thomas of, monk of Evesham 193, 196–7, 201
    family and early career 179–80, 196
    writings 6, 20, 66, 104, 172–3, 174
    and exemption proceedings 123, 135, 153, 197–9, 200, 201
    building works 201
    as dean of the Vale 202
    see also Thomas
  William of, abbot-elect of Evesham 203
marriage, clerical 191–2
Marshal
  Henry, bishop of Exeter 196
  John (John of Marlborough) 196
  William, earl of Pembroke 196
Martin, monk of Evesham 90
Mary Magdalene, St, chapel of 185
Mary the Virgin, St
  and St Ecgwine 61, 154, 167, 169
  as patron and dedicatee 61, 71, 103, 154, 168
  cult 99, 167–8, 184
  image 154
Mary I, queen of England 206
Maud, empress 136, 153, 165, 166
Mauger, bishop of Worcester (formerly treasurer of Normandy) 135, 193, 197–8, 200
Maugersbury 47, 143
Maurice, abbot of Evesham 90, 141, 176, 178, 185
  appointed 129, 132
  estates 141, 145, 151–2
meadow 19
Melling, William of 152
  his brother *see* Simon
Mercia (the Mercians) 3, 5, 13, 47, 57, 61, 79
  rulers of 4, 21, 61–2; *see also* Æthelbald; Æthelflæd; Æthelred (?d.716); Æthelred (d.911); Burgred; Ceolred; Coenred; Offa (d.796); Penda
  ealdorman of *see* Ælfhere
  earls of 68; *see also* Leofric
Mildburg, St, abbess of Wenlock 9, 190
mills 18, 112, 147, 148, 159
Montfort, Simon de, earl of Leicester 203
Morton, Abbots 109, 120, 143
Moses, monk of Evesham 90
Murcot 25–6, 44
Murdac, Henry, archbishop of York 136

Netherlands *see* Flanders; Stavoren
Newnham (Nthants.) 59, 145
Nicholas, St, chapel of 71, 81
Nicholas, bishop of Tusculum 201–2
Nicholas (Evesham monks so named c.1104) 91
Niel, constable of Chester 113
  his son *see* William, son of Niel

Normandy (France) 56, 110
treasurer *see* Mauger
see also Normans, the
Normandy, duke of *see* Henry II
Normans, the 79, 80, 90
Norreis, Roger, abbot of Evesham (formerly prior of Christ Church Canterbury, later prior of Penwortham) 141, 142, 173, 183, 188, 196–202
surname and family 193
at Christ Church 132
appointed 131–2, 136, 193
household 135, 145, 193
misconduct 132, 141, 144, 153, 193–7, 200–201
seal 201
deposed 201, 203
his nephew *see* Roger
Northampton 59
priory 189
Northampton, earls of *see* St Liz, Simon de (d.c.1111); St Liz, Simon de (d.1184)
Northampton, Ælfgifu of 58–9
Northamptonshire 59, 117
Northolt, William of, bishop of Worcester 136
Northumbria 4, 10, 47, 86
Norton (nr. Evesham) 21, 42–3, 60, 61, 96, 110
church 186–7, 190
priest 191
tenants 60, 110, 148, 152, 190
Norway 59
Norwich, Thomas of, monk of Evesham 175, 179, 187–8, 196
Noyers, Pain (Payn) de 137

Oddington, Walter of, monk of Evesham 206; *see also* Walter (fl.1298)
Odense (Denmark)
bishop of *see* Hubald
cathedral priory 90, 105–6
prior of *see* William
Odo, bishop of Bayeux 110, 115, 117
Odulf, St 62, 69–70, 104–5, 168, 170, 174–5
Offa (fl.709), 'king' of the East Saxons 13, 20, 21, 22, 31, 67, 118–22
Offa (d.796), king of the Mercians 36
Offenham 8, 52, 96, 101, 158, 189, 190, 191 n.31
Oftfor, bishop of the Hwicce 5–6, 10, 30, 31
Ombersley 52, 115, 187
Ombersley, John of, abbot of Evesham 206
orchards 15 n.11, 22, 88, 95
Ordwig, thegn 78
Orgar 'the proud' 138
Osgyth (Osyth), St 21, 67
Oshere, 'king' of the Hwicce 35, 43
Osthryth, queen 5, 31
Oswald, St, bishop of Worcester 48–9, 52, 53, 56, 61, 104, 168, 169–70
Oswaldslow hundred 48–9, 52, 59, 80, 111
Osweard, abbot of Evesham 48, 49, 50, 51–2
Osweard, brother of Æthelheard 21, 31–2
Oswulf, bishop of Ramsbury 47, 48
Osyth (Osgyth), St 21, 67
Otto I, king of Germany 40
Ottobuono, papal legate 203
Oundle minster 72
oxen 18, 60, 101, 158
Oxford 102, 114, 179, 196, 206; *see also* Bodleian Library; Jesus College; Magdalen College
Oxfordshire 79, 80, 110

Pagham, John of, bishop of Worcester 134
Pandulf, papal envoy 201
parchment 162, 181
Paris, students at 178, 196, 197
park 158
pasture 158; *see also* livestock
Paul, monk of Evesham 90
Payn (fl.?×c.1121), abbot's clerk 145–6
Pembroke
countess of *see* Clare, Isabel de
earl of *see* Marshal, William
Penda, king of the Mercians 3
Pensham 8
Penwortham 113, 136
priory 136–7, 173, 202
priors of 137, 142; *see also* Norreis, Roger; Sortes, Adam
Pershore
abbey 48, 52, 97, 185, 190, 198
see also Walcot
Peter, bishop of Chester 98
Peter (Evesham monks so named c.1104) 91
Peter 'the Venerable', abbot of Cluny 171
Peterborough abbey 169
Philip, abbey steward 146, 147, 154
Philip, monk of Evesham 90
Pickersom (nr Littleton, Worcs.) 8
Piddle brook 12
Pintelthein, William 148
Pixley 137
Poden (nr Church Honeybourne) 107 n.30
Poitevin, Roger the 113
poor, the 81–2, 83, 142, 143, 194, 200
popes 37, 119, 122, 124, 197, 203–4; *see also* Agatho; Alexander II; Alexander

III; Celestine III; Clement III; Constantine I; Innocent II; Innocent III; Rome
population 42, 149–51, 158, 159, 189, 206, 207
Porter, Nicholas 146 n.44
Protasius, monk of Evesham 90

Quadrilogus 182–3

Ralph, abbot of Winchcombe 83
Ralph (Evesham monks so named c.1104) 91
Ralph, catchpole 147
Ralph, clerk 147–8
Ralph, cook 144 n.24
Ralph, tithingman 147
Ramsbury, bishop of *see* Oswulf
Ramsey abbey 56, 61, 67, 169
Randal, abbot of Evesham (formerly prior of Worcester) 159, 202–3
Randal, brother of Abbot Walter 109–10, 114
  his descendants 164–5
Randal, chaplain 147
Randal, dyer 162
Reading 199
refugees 82–3
Regularis concordia 54, 62–3, 65, 81, 83, 91–2
Regulus (Rieul), St, bishop of Senlis 170
Reinfrid, monk of Evesham 85–6, 125
renders in kind 64, 94, 136, 137, 150–51
Rennes (France), bishop of *see* Fougères, Stephen of
rents in cash 113, 143, 146–7, 150–51, 159, 163, 164
Repton minster 61, 104, 170
Reynold, abbot of Evesham 131, 141, 153, 169, 182, 188
  family 130, 165
  estates 138, 152
  building works 165–6, 185, 186
  conflict with bishop 133–4, 135
  death 130, 166
Reynold, parchment maker 162
Ribble, river 113, 202
Richard I, king of England 131–2, 197
Richard, abbot of Selby 201
Richard, dean of Wells 186, 187
Richard, archdeacon of Bath 187
Richard (Evesham monks so named c.1104) 91
Richard (fl.1149), monk of Evesham 131
Richard, tithingman 147
Rieul (Regulus), St, bishop of Senlis 170
Ripon minster 34
Risborough, Monks 38
Robert, abbot of Evesham 130, 132, 141, 147, 151–2, 178
Robert, abbot of Tewkesbury 172
Robert (Evesham monks so named c.1104) 91
Robert, mason 162
Robert, mercer 162
Rochester (Kent) 102
  bishop of *see* Gundulf
Roger, abbot of Evesham (formerly monk of St Augustine's Canterbury) 131
Roger, bishop of Worcester 134–5, 178
Roger (Evesham monks so named c.1104) 91
Roger (fl.1149), monk of Evesham 130
Roger, nephew of Roger Norreis 193
Roger, miller 147
Roger, physician 162
Romano-British period 3, 10, 12, 14–15, 21–2, 23, 25–6, 28, 44
Rome
  Bishop Ecgwine at 118–22
  Bishop Wilfrid at 10
  Coenred and Offa at 13, 20, 21, 31, 118–22
  creditors at 183, 201
  Evesham represented at 33, 130–31
  exemption proceedings at 123, 133–5, 183, 198–9, 200, 201, 203
  Lateran Councils 133, 202–3
  see also popes

St Liz
  Adam de, abbot of Evesham (formerly prior of Bermondsey)
    family and earlier career 130, 131, 170, 171, 178, 189
    appointed 130, 131
    household personnel 144–5, 147, 187
    internal administration 143, 170, 171, 172, 173
    seal 154
    estate management 146, 147, 152, 154, 158, 162
    art and architecture under 143, 162, 185–7, 188, 189, 196
    literary interests 172–3, 174, 178–9, 181, 182
    relations with bishop 134–5
    as judge-delegate 154
    opinions 171, 178–9, 192
    writings 134, 171, 178, 181, 182
    death 131–2, 135
  Simon de (d.c.1111), earl of Northampton 189

St Liz (*cont.*)
Simon de (d.1184), earl of Huntingdon and Northampton 130, 190
family 170
St Osyth (Chich) minster 67
Salford, Abbots 147
Salisbury cathedral 104
Sambourne 143
Samson, monk of Evesham 131
Samuel, monk of Evesham 90
San Martino al Cimino (Italy), abbot of *see* John
Sankt-Gallen (Switzerland), abbey of St Gall 40, 47
schools
cathedral 178–9, 196, 197
see also education
seals 96–8, 153–4, 155, 168, 201
Sedgeberrow 36
Selby, abbot of *see* Richard
Seneca 181
Senlis (France) 170
bishop of *see* Rieul
Serlo, abbot of Gloucester 83
sermons 106, 178, 181, 182
'Serpham' (nr Stanford on Teme) 137–8
settlement patterns 23, 76–7
Severn, river 3, 18, 81
Sherborne, bishops of *see* Æthelsige; Asser
Shropshire 79, 82
Sighere, king of the East Saxons 21
Simon, bishop of Worcester 133–4
Simon, brother of William of Melling 152
Smith, Thomas 208
soldiers 80–81, 165–6; *see also* knight service
Sortes, Adam, monk of Evesham (later prior of Penwortham) 175 n.43, 179, 200
Southstone Rock (nr Stanford on Teme) 137
'Sperckulf' (?Sþertwulf), monk of Coventry 71
Sperling, priest 138
Stafford, Robert of 113–14
his wife and son 114
Staffordshire 79, 82
Stanford on Teme *see* 'Serpham'; Southstone Rock
Stavoren (Netherlands) church 62
Stephen, St, feast of 92
Stephen, king of England 130, 131, 152, 153, 165, 166
Stoke, Lark 109
stone, building in 10, 18, 50, 99, 101, 137, 165
stone, carving in 55, 96, 186–7
Stow (Lincs.) minster 68
Stow on the Wold 164, 187
Stratford (Warws) 20, 31–2
minster 21
Striguil (Chepstow), lordship of 196
Striguil, 'countess' of *see* Clare, Isabel de
Striguil, Muriel of, and her father 196
Studley priory 136
'Sture' (?Kidderminster) 38
Sutton Hoo ship 18
Swegn 'Forkbeard', king of Denmark 56, 57
Swell 70, 143
Switzerland *see* Sankt-Gallen

Taunton minster 83
taxes 115, 138, 147, 151
Teme, river 138
tenants
rural 60, 64, 76, 80, 109–11, 145–8, 150–52, 157, 165, 191
urban 113, 137, 138, 145–8, 159–60, 162–5
Tewkesbury
abbey 185, 198
abbot of *see* Robert
thegns 45, 47, 53, 60, 78
Thelwall 112 n.19, 113
Theobald, archbishop of Canterbury 130–31
Thingcferth, abbot of Evesham 37
Thingcferth (fl.803), an abbot (? the same) 37
Thomas, monk of Evesham (? Thomas of Marlborough) 200
Tilberht (Tildbrith), abbot of Evesham 35
Tilberht (fl.759), an abbot (? the same) 35–6
timber 42, 99, 101, 158, 207
tithes 64, 94, 136, 137, 191
Tours (France), Council of 134
Towcester 53
Trent, river 102
Tusculum (Italy), bishop of *see* Nicholas
Twyford (nr Evesham) 21–2, 31–2, 42, 43, 44

Vacarius 179
Vale of Evesham, deanery of the *see* Evesham, deanery of the Vale of
Vigor, St, bishop of Bayeux 170
Vikings, the 45, 46, 54, 62; *see also* Danes, the
Vincent, St, cult of 182
Vincent, monk of Evesham 90
vineyard 95, 112, 142

'wænnacumbe, (æt)' (nr Lenchwick) 21
Wærferth, bishop of the Hwicce 38–9
Walcot (nr Pershore) 26
Wales, Gerald of 178
Walkelin, abbot of Abingdon 182
Wallingford 114
Walter, abbot of Evesham
  family and early career 89–90, 96, 109, 146, 151, 170
  appointed 89, 129, 132
  internal administration 103, 141
  documents fabricated under 114–25
  seal 96–8
  building works 99, 101–2, 105, 124, 167, 184–5
  cultural interests 92, 94, 124
  estates 94, 96, 109–14, 120–21, 124, 136, 141, 151
  sends monks to Odense 105–6
  and deanery of the Vale 106–8, 124
  relations with bishop 108, 119–20, 124, 132–3
  cult of saints under 91, 99, 102–5, 174, 184
  liturgical practices under 92, 94, 99, 101–5, 184
  death 129, 174, 176
  his relatives *see* Aubrey; Geoffrey; Hugh; Randal
Walter (fl.1298), monk of Evesham (? Walter of Oddington) 206
Walter, fuller 162
Walter, Hubert, archbishop of Canterbury 195, 197, 199, 203
Wantage 54
Warin, son of Warin Bussel 136
Warwick 18
Warwick, earl of *see* Beauchamp, Richard
Warwick
  Nicholas of 135
  Thomas of 135, 145, 154
Warwickshire 33, 57, 79, 80, 110
water, holy 29, 174
water supply 162, 186
Waterville, William de 152
'Weardburh' (unlocated) 39
Wearmouth minster 33, 34
Weethley 109
Wells
  bishop of *see* Æthelwine
  dean of *see* Richard
Wenlock, Much 187
  minster and priory 9, 190
  abbess of *see* Mildburg
Wenlock, Walter of, abbot of Westminster 206
Weogoran, the 12
Wessex 40, 45
Westbury on Trym 37
Westminster
  abbey 84
  abbots of *see* Feckenham, John; Wenlock, Walter of
Whitby (Yorks.)
  minster and abbey 4, 85–6, 173–4
  abbess of *see* Hild
  Synod of 3
Whitchurch, William of, abbot of Evesham (formerly abbot of Alcester) 203
'Wichewen' (?Wickhamford), priest and his wife 191
Wickhamford 25, 42–4, 96, 148, 190, 191; *see also* 'Wichewen'; 'Wycweon'
Wickhamford, John of 148
Wigod (Evesham monks so named c.1104) 91
Wigred, monk of Evesham 63, 64
Wigstan, St 61–2, 102–3, 104, 168, 170, 174, 200–201
Wilfrid, St 5, 10, 12–13, 31, 34, 36, 72, 119–20
Wilfrith (Wilfrid) (d.743×745), bishop of the Hwicce 34
Wilfrith (Wilferth) (d.928×929), bishop of the Hwicce 39
Willersey 96
William I, king of England 79, 82, 83, 85, 110, 111
William II, king of England 105, 129, 133
William, prior of Odense 106
William (fl.c.1130), abbey steward 147
William (fl.c.1191–1206), abbey steward 146, 147, 154
William, abbot's chaplain 145
William, baker 147
William, chamberlain 147
William, gatekeeper 147
William, son of Niel 113 n.28
William fitz Osbern, earl of Hereford 80
Wilton, Serlo of 178
Winchcombe 19, 59
  abbey 52, 86, 171
  abbots of *see* Gervase; Godric; Ralph
Winchester 102
  bishop of *see* Æthelwold
Wither, Ralph 148
Witton (nr Droitwich) 68
Wixford 53
Wlfard, abbot of Evesham *see* Wulfheard
Woking minster 33
Wolvey, Robert of 145, 154
women in religion 4, 5, 9, 85, 90, 178, 182
woodland 15–16, 29, 42, 77, 151, 158
Wootton Wawen 35

Worcester 12, 75, 111, 113
Worcester, diocese of (from 961)
  boundary 83
  religious houses 52, 83, 85, 112, 136, 203
  English traditions 90
  vicars general 78, 131
  archdeacons 108, 124
  see also Hwicce, diocese of the; Worcester, bishops of
Worcester, bishops of (from 961)
  pastoral care 108, 124, 134, 189, 191, 192, 199
  relations with Evesham 35–41, 48, 54–6, 83, 120, 132–6, 154, 195–9
  hundreds 48–9, 52, 59, 80, 111, 190
  see also Alfred; Baldwin; Coutances, John of; Ealdred; Ealdwulf; Gray, Walter de; Hwicce, bishops of the; Lyfing; Mauger; Northolt, William of; Oswald; Pagham, John of; Roger; Simon; Wulfstan (d.1023); Wulfstan (d.1095)
Worcester cathedral priory
  estates 48, 59–60, 80, 109, 111, 116
  cartularies 116
  dependent parishes 190
  cult of saints 56, 104, 169
  art and architecture 57, 101, 187
  manuscripts 36, 106
  plundered (1013) 57
  consecration of abbot of Evesham (1130) 133
  election of bishop (1213) 202
  priors of *see* Bedford, Ralph of; Randal
Worcester, earl of *see* Hákon Eiriksson
Worcester
  John of 120, 175
  Ralph of 166
Worcestershire 16, 43, 44, 110, 117
  shire court 60, 79
  sheriffs 138–9; *see also* Abbetot, Urse d'; Beauchamp, William de; Leofric
  hundreds 48–9, 80–81, 139, 190; *see also* Blackenhurst; 'Cuthburgehlaw'; 'Fissesberg'; Oswaldslow
  religious houses 48–9
  Danes in 57
Wrottesley 113
Wulfgeat (fl.1046×1047) 68–9
Wulfheard (Wlfard), abbot of Evesham 38
Wulfheard (fl.849–55), a priest (? the same) 38
Wulfmær, abbot of Evesham *see* Manni
Wulfric 'ripa' 47
Wulfsige, St 59, 63, 84–5, 90, 168, 175, 188
  'Testament' 177
Wulfsige, bishop of London 38
Wulfsige, abbot of Evesham (? the same) 38
Wulfstan (d.1023), bishop of Worcester 55, 56
Wulfstan (d.1095), bishop of Worcester 80, 83, 96, 101, 111
  family and early career 65, 78, 84
  appointed 78
  seal 97–8
  death 109
Wulfwig, bishop of Dorchester 68
Wulfwold, abbot of Bath and Chertsey 83
'Wycweon' 25–6, 42–4

York
  archbishop of *see* Murdac, Henry
  St Mary's abbey 86
  abbot of St Mary's *see* Longchamp, Robert de
Yorkshire 82

Other volumes in
Studies in the History of Medieval Religion

I: Dedications of Monastic Houses in England and Wales 1066–1216
Alison Binns

II: The Early Charters of the Augustinian Canons of
Waltham Abbey, Essex, 1062–1230
Edited by Rosalind Ransford

III: Religious Belief and Ecclesiastical Careers in Late Medieval England
Edited by Christopher Harper-Bill

IV: The Rule of the Templars:
The French text of the Rule of the Order of the Knights Templar
Translated and introduced by J. M. Upton-Ward

V: The Collegiate Church of Wimborne Minster
Patricia H. Coulstock

VI: William Waynflete: Bishop and Educationalist
Virginia Davis

VII: Medieval Ecclesiastical Studies in honour of Dorothy M. Owen
Edited by M. J. Franklin and Christopher Harper-Bill

VIII: A Brotherhood of Canons Serving God
English Secular Cathedrals in the Later Middle Ages
David Lepine

IX: Westminster Abbey and its People c.1050–c.1216
Emma Mason

X: Gilds in the Medieval Countryside
Social and Religious Change in Cambridgeshire c.1350–1558
Virginia R. Bainbridge

XI: Monastic Revival and Regional Identity in Early Normandy
Cassandra Potts

XII: The Convent and the Community in Late Medieval England:
Female Monasteries in the Diocese of Norwich 1350–1540
Marilyn Oliva

XIII: Pilgrimage to Rome in the Middle Ages: Continuity and Change
Debra J. Birch

XIV: St Cuthbert and the Normans: the Church of Durham 1071–1153
William M. Aird

XV: The Last Generation of English Catholic Clergy:
Parish Priests in the Diocese of Coventry and Lichfield in
the Early Sixteenth Century
Tim Cooper

XVI: The Premonstratensian Order in Late Medieval England
Joseph A. Gribbin

XVII: Inward Purity and Outward Splendour:
Death and Remembrance in the Deanery of Dunwich, Suffolk, 1370–1547
Judith Middleton-Stewart

XVIII: The Religious Orders in Pre-Reformation England
Edited by James G. Clark

XIX: The Catalan Rule of the Templars:
A Critical Edition and English Translation from Barcelona,
Archito de la Corona de Aragón, 'Cartes Reales', MS 3344
Edited and translated by Judi Upton-Ward

XX: Leper Knights:
The Order of St Lazarus of Jerusalem in England, c. 1150–1544
David Marcombe

XXI: The Secular Jurisdiction of Monasteries
in Anglo-Norman and Angevin England
Kevin L. Shirley

XXII: The Dependent Priories of Medieval English Monasteries
Martin Heale

XXIII: The Cartulary of St Mary's Collegiate Church, Warwick
Edited by Charles Fonge

XXIV: Leadership in Medieval English Nunneries
Valerie G. Spear

XXV: The Art and Architecture of English Benedictine Monasteries, 1300–1540:
A Patronage History
Julian M. Luxford

XXVI: Norwich Cathedral Close: The Evolution of the
English Cathedral Landscape
Roberta Gilchrist

XXVII: The Foundations of Medieval English Ecclesiastical History
Edited by Philippa Hoskin, Christopher Brooks and Barrie Dobson

XXVIII: Thomas Becket and his Biographers
Michael Staunton

XXIX: Late Medieval Monasteries and their Patrons:
England and Wales, c.1300–1540
Karen Stöber

XXX: The Culture of Medieval English Monasticism
Edited by James G. Clark

XXXI: A History of the Abbey of Bury St Edmunds, 1182–1256:
Samson of Tottington to Edmund of Walpole
Antonia Gransden

XXXII: Monastic Hospitality:
The Benedictines in England, c.1070–c.1250
Julie Kerr

XXXIII: Religious Life in Normandy, 1050–1300:
Space, Gender and Social Pressure
Leonie V. Hicks

XXXIV: The Medieval Chantry Chapel: An Archaeology
Simon Roffey

XXXV: Monasteries and Society in the British Isles
in the Later Middle Ages
Edited by Janet Burton and Karen Stöber

XXXVI: Jocelin of Wells: Bishop, Builder, Courtier
Edited by Robert Dunning

XXXVII: War and the Making of Medieval Monastic Culture
Katherine Allen Smith

XXXVIII: Cathedrals, Communities and Conflict in the Anglo-Norman World
Edited by Paul Dalton, Charles Insley and Louise J. Wilkinson

XXXIX: English Nuns and the Law in the Middle Ages:
Cloistered Nuns and Their Lawyers, 1293–1540
Elizabeth Makowski

XL: The Nobility and Ecclesiastical Patronage in Thirteenth-Century England
Elizabeth Gemmill

XLI: Pope Gregory X and the Crusades
Philip B. Baldwin

XLII: A History of the Abbey of Bury St Edmunds, 1257–1301:
Simon of Luton and John of Northwold
Antonia Gransden

XLIII: King John and Religion
Paul Webster